UNMET
EXPECTATIONS

——————— Lisa Hughes ———————

UNMET
EXPECTATIONS

Reshaping Our Thinking
in Disappointments, Trials, and Delays

Appreciations

• • • • • • • • • • •

Lisa Hughes, author of *God's Priorities for Today's Woman,* has done it again in writing an excellent resource for women. Not only does she challenge the reader regarding unbiblical responses to unmet expectations, but she also assists the reader in understanding the heart, and by offering practical, biblical help. Get it and be blessed by it!
SHELBI CULLEN, Professor at The Master's University, Santa Clarita, CA

Lisa has broached a subject that few authors have tackled: how to deal with our hearts when disappointments come and often linger. She boldly encourages the believer to know and be convinced that it is possible to be content, even when life is different than we expected. This is based not on our own ability, for we are weak and so often selfishly wanting our own way. It is based on knowing the lovingkindness of our God. Moses said it so well: "O satisfy us in the morning with Your lovingkindness, that we may sing for joy and be glad all our days" (Ps. 90:14). Read this book with the expectation that you will be challenged and find great help in your walk with Christ.
JANIE STREET, Wife of Dr. John Street and co-author of *The Biblical Counseling Guide for Women*

In *Unmet Expectations,* Lisa skillfully uses the Old and New Testaments and storytelling to reveal the depth of sin in our hearts when we place our hope in this life and our own expectations, instead of placing our hope in God and His Word.
JOSIE PADILLA, Head of women's counseling First Baptist Church of Jacksonville, Florida under Dr. Ernie Baker

Unmet Expectations—we all have them. But, sometimes, we don't realize how many we have and what to do with them. Lisa shows us how to identify them, discusses the main areas that are common to women, and presents us with a biblical solution to handle them in a manner that will glorify God and result in growth in us. The personal and relatable illustrations that bring application to her lessons make this book a must in discipling women as well as for personal growth.
BARBY WOODFIELD, Pastor's wife, discipler, Hickman Community Church

Lisa's engaging, conversationlike style complements the contents of this book's burden. It is all about biblically identifying, critiquing, and remedying unmet expectations. She rightly begins with the "bad news" of their presence in our hearts. Such unmet expectations lead to discontentment for which there is only one sure cure: the appropriation of biblically defined contentment. Such divinely delineated contentment is fittingly the focus of the remainder of the volume. This practical book's value reaches its apex with specific exhortations, bearing the heading of *Nine Sure-Fire Ways to Grow More Grateful No Matter What Your Circumstances*. Consequently, this short but practically powerful treatment dealing with unmet expectations should be put at the top of your list of required reading.

JUDY ZEMEK: Director of Women's Ministries, Grace Immanuel Bible Church Jupiter, Florida

Do you have dreams and desires? Have they always been fulfilled? How do you react when life does not go as planned? Lisa takes us on an adventure—exploring biblical text and examples so we can redeem life's disappointments, grow in our trust of God, and bring glory to Christ in our responses to life's difficulties. This is a rich resource to encourage and equip women in the church.

MISSY MEHRINGER, Wife of Pastor Ray Mehringer, Bible teacher, discipler, mother, grandmother

Lisa Hughes has written an important book for today's Christian women. Sometimes in our lives, we may not realize that some of our unwelcome feelings have come from unmet expectations. This book, which is enjoyable to read, gives us solutions. Lisa's biblical illustrations, personal examples, and thought gems from a variety of other authors' work together to make a significant contribution to this key issue. She has produced practical and relatable material in this volume. It's a book I'll be sharing with others. Grab your cup, your Bible, and settle in for a good time of mentoring from Lisa as she connects so many dots for our Christian lives today, and as we grow in grace and knowledge of our Lord Jesus Christ.

BARBARA BARRICK, Wife of Dr. William D. Barrick, professor at The Master's Seminary, seminary wives' leader, women's ministry director, mother, grandmother

Wonderfully convicting in all the best ways! With biblical accuracy, Lisa pulls back the curtain to let us take a long, hard look at the roots of our unmet expectations. She's helping me wean myself off my own desires by showing me God's trustworthy love and goodness! This will be a must read for the women in my ministry to help them break free from the darkness of unmet expectations!

KRIS GOERTZEN, Women's Ministry Director, international conference speaker and Bible teacher, www.KrisGoertzenministries.com

How should a Christian woman respond to life's inevitable difficulties and disappointments? Lisa Hughes candidly answers this question in a warm, transparent, and conversational style. This biblically based, God-honoring, down-to-earth, practical guide encourages those who aspire to consistently practice a godly contentment in an imperfect world.

"B" MAYHUE, Formerly, the Seminary Wives' Director at The Master's Seminary, pastor's wife, discipler, Bible teacher

If we're honest, we all have expectations on how we think our lives and relationships should go. Often, they are unspoken and not acknowledged until life doesn't work out the way in which we desired it to and we are left struggling, sometimes depressed, sometimes irritated or angry with others, and often wondering where God is in it all. With biblical accuracy and practical application, Lisa Hughes helps women expose the desires and expectations of their hearts and deal with them in ways that please God. For those desiring to change, this book will be life changing!

BETH MACK DE SWARDT, Pastor's wife and biblical counselor

Reading Lisa's book is like sitting down with your best friend and sharing your heart, your disappointments, your hurts, and your reactions when your expectations aren't met. If you do sit down with Lisa, you'll find she understands and offers you help from the Scripture. You will come away encouraged, knowing how to deal biblically with your unmet expectations in a way that will bring glory to God.

CAROL MACK, Wife of Dr. Wayne Mack, counselor, mother, and grandmother

Unmet Expectations
Reshaping Our Thinking in Disappointments, Trials, and Delays
Lisa Hughes

Copyright © 2022 Lisa Hughes

ISBNS:
978-1-63342-243-8   paper
978-1-63342-244-5   epub
978-1-63342-245-2   mobi

Unless noted otherwise, Scripture quotations are taken from the New American Standard Bible® (NASB), Copyright © 1960, 1962, 1963, 1968, 1971, 1972, 1973, 1975, 1977, 1995 by The Lockman Foundation
Used by permission. www.Lockman.org

Cover design and typeset by www.greatwriting.org

Printed in Colombia

Shepherd Press
P.O. Box 24
Wapwallopen, PA 18660
www.shepherdpress.com

COUNSEL FOR THE HEART

A RESOURCE for WORD-BASED TRANSFORMATION and PRACTICAL DISCIPLESHIP

For our daughter, Leah, who, in the refining fires of unmet expectations, learned to rely on the grace, wisdom, and power of God.

First Thoughts: Unmet What?

And He has said to me, "My grace is sufficient for you, for power is perfected in weakness." Most gladly, therefore, I will rather boast about my weaknesses, so that the power of Christ may dwell in me. Therefore I am well content with weaknesses, with insults, with distresses, with persecutions, with difficulties, for Christ's sake; for when I am weak, then I am strong.
2 Corinthians 12:9–10

"Y-you want me to speak on what?"

I admit I was a bit lost at first when asked to teach on the subject of unmet expectations. But it wasn't long before the suggestion took on shades of pure genius. I have wrestled with a few unmet expectations myself and I figured other women must have had similar struggles. It seemed like the perfect topic to tackle!

I couldn't wait to dig into the Scriptures and see what God had to say about unmet expectations. As I thought, studied, and prayed, I made some encouraging and soul-searching discoveries. Before long, I felt as though I was an archeologist, unearthing expectations everywhere I dug. Some expectations were easy to find and identify, lying readily upon the surface of my heart, while others were buried deeper. My amateur digging soon exhumed different expectations I had about life, the Lord, my family, myself, the best route to the grocery store, and so on. Expectations were coming to light by the spadeful.

There's nothing wrong with expectations in and of themselves. And it's easy to see, when digging around in the soil of our hearts, that we have all kinds of thoughts and plans for our lives. All well and good. Expectations aren't the problem. But when we come face to face with thwarted plans, dismantled hopes, and unanswered prayers, what then? Will we respond with gentle faith and trusting submission to God's unfolding plans for our lives? Or will bitterness, anger, self-pity, fear, or depression emerge from the miry clay of unbelief?

We have so many thoughts about how things could be different, fine-tuned, tugged into place, fixed, or changed, that when things turn out differently than we anticipated, we may find our hearts waging quite a battle. It's possible that the cantankerous beginnings of the contentious woman mentioned in Proverbs were the result of her unmet expectations. In fact, it's more than possible that she grew into her peevish little self, when her life turned out differently than she thought it should. Before she even realized it, her husband preferred to live on their rooftop—in the desert—rather than stay in the same room with her continual nagging. If only she had sought counsel in God's Word. If she had, she would have been known as the "contented woman" rather than the contentious one.

I doubt that you want to be known as a contentious woman. I sure don't. And I'm not saying that experiencing unmet expectations automatically make us grumpy and difficult to live with, but the possibility is there. Thankfully, the key to responding well lies in the Word of God. And that's where we're headed, straight for the help that only God can provide for those times when we find it difficult to accept our circumstances as God-ordained and good.

When I was around eight or nine years old, I would walk to and from school. It probably wasn't very far, maybe a few blocks, but it felt like a long way, especially on cold, wintry days in Idaho, when the wind would sting my cheeks and rush right through my jacket. Yet my little journey became bearable when I would imagine I was a pioneer girl, trudging across the prairie, seeking help for Ma and Pa, who lay sick at home in our sod house. Then the walk home from school became an adventure, instead of something to dread.

So, here's my proposal. Will you go on a pioneer-girl journey with me? As we study God's Word together, we'll discover that, though life may turn out differently than we expected, God always intends our good. We'll look at unmet expectations from a biblical perspective, consider ways we've engaged in wrong thinking, repent of sinful responses, and look to the Scriptures to provide the sure footing we need to continue our trek. As we do so, we'll gain a deeper and better understanding of the Lord and His perfect ways. Just like the pioneers, who were forever changed by their expedition west, we too will be changed through the study of God's Word.

You may well be thinking, "Wait, wait. Hold it. I don't want to do the pioneer-girl thing! I don't have a problem with expectations. They're not something I struggle with." Don't worry. You don't have to put on a bonnet just yet, but I'd love to have you join me in the adventure, just the same. As we get underway, you may discover—as I did—areas of sinful struggle stemming from unmet expectations. It's my hope and prayer that, as we press on together, we'll gain encouragement and strength from the Lord Himself to respond with obedient faith and growing love for His faithful work in our lives.

Let's embark on a journey together, a journey of growth, discovery, and change. I can't guarantee it will be easy; real heart-growth rarely is. It is my hope that you're not the kind to give up easily and my prayer that your love for the Lord will drive you to discover how you can give Him the most honor and glory possible, no matter what your circumstances. Are you ready?

PART 1: PRAIRIE DOGS AND UNMET EXPECTATIONS

Prairie Dogs live in the grassy plains of the United States. Captivating to watch, these playful, little rodents pop up from their underground dens whenever the sun shines. Below ground their dens are interconnected, with some prairie-dog villages spanning an area of two to three miles. Like prairie-dog tunnels, unmet expectations can remain below the surface, until thwarted plans or trials bring them to our attention.

• •

I

"If Only"
and
Other Expectations

It is contrary to the nature of faith for a believer to seek peace in his earthly enjoyments. It is folly to expect any stable peace or solid joy that does not come from Christ as the fountain. O that Christians would learn to live with one eye on Christ crucified and the other on His coming in glory! No wonder you are comfortless when heaven is forgotten. When Christians let fall their heavenly expectations but heighten their earthly desires, they are preparing themselves for fear and trouble.

Richard Baxter[1]

1 Richard Baxter, *Practical Works*, 11:884-885 quoted in *Voices from the Past: Puritan Devotional Readings,* vol. 1, ed. Richard Rushing (Edinburgh: The Banner of Truth Trust, 2009), 138.

It's a no-brainer to say that when we expect things, we hope for and anticipate something. Without boasting even a bit, I think I can safely be dubbed the "Queen of Expectations." The expectation gremlins popped up early in my life. I remember having glorious ideas for my birthday party or a holiday, only to grow despondent when the day didn't match up to the rosy-hued picture I had developed in my mind.

Don't you think it's sad that you can't spontaneously break out into song, dance in the middle of the street, and have everyone else join you as if it were the most normal thing in the world? The flash-mob phenomenon certainly satisfies this desire, though no one's asked me to join in one. I have had some moments that were close, like caroling to the employees at Starbucks when our daughter worked on Christmas day, joining in with a worker at Costco who couldn't quit singing "What a Wonderful World," and waltzing along the Boise River Greenbelt while belting out songs from "The Sound of Music." These memories make me tingle all over, just thinking of them! Times like that peg out my expectation meter at Expectation #354, "This is How Life Should Be." Generally, our boys prefer *not* to be in the vicinity when Expectation #354 gets fulfilled, though my husband is always game.

More from the Queen of Expectations

While my husband, Jack, willingly does goofy stuff with me in public, there are times when meeting my expectations aren't as fun for him. When we're out running errands together is one such time: "Oh, you're going this way? But I thought you would go the other way. Don't you think it would be faster to take the other way that goes past the grocery store?" Now the problem isn't with my expectations or even with my husband choosing a different route, it's *my response* to it that's the problem—but more on that later.

Anytime I have our family gathered together, I battle the crowd of my expectations. Norman Rockwell couldn't paint a homier scene; Louisa May Alcott couldn't write a more tender tale; Frank Sinatra couldn't evoke a more heartwarming tune. Their skills all pale in comparison with the ideas I have for our family gatherings. Like heaven, but we're here on earth. *Sigh.*

When our kids were teenagers, I discovered I had expectations about their convictions, goals, even their likes and dislikes. After all those years of teaching them to do things the "right" way (you know, *my way*), it was a bit disconcerting to discover they had their own ideas about music or what to do with free time or even the kinds of clothes they liked. Amazing!

I often expect my poor husband to be perfect—after all, he is a pastor! Isn't he supposed to have an impeccable response, right away, every time? In my heart, I don't give him room to wrestle through issues. Of course, I would expect him to give me plenty of latitude to work through *my* issues. Ahem.

Oh, and I have expectations about my walk with the Lord. I expect to be way more godly, bold, and zealous for the Lord than I am. And then, when I come face to face with my weaknesses, I may get discouraged. Wait, *may get*? I *do get* discouraged.

When Expectations Trip Us Up

I confess these things for a couple of reasons. First, I want you to know that I haven't arrived when it comes to this whole "unmet expectations" thing. I've had a lot of practice working on it, though! And second, I've shared some of the lighter expectation scenarios to show you that even little things can trip us up at times. *Is it any wonder we struggle when we come face to face with a major this-isn't-what-I-signed-up-for expectation?*

Having expectations about things isn't all bad, though we might be tempted to think so. There's nothing more rewarding than anticipating something and then finding it's better than we even dreamed. When that happens, we respond with thanks and joy to the Lord. God's kindness humbles us; we delight in His wisdom. There's no problem with expectations then. When they are met, we truly rejoice and enjoy what the Lord has given.

No, we run into trouble with our expectations when God's plan for our lives unfolds differently than we thought it would. When that happens, it can be difficult to submit to and trust what the Lord has planned for us. It may be the car breaking down on a day set aside for running errands, the kids getting sick the first day of vacation, or discovering that we'll soon miscarry our baby. When the unexpected disrupts what we thought would happen, we may find ourselves anxious, fretful, discouraged, fearful, bitter, or angry. We may wonder:

- Why is it so difficult to get on board with God's plan, even if things aren't proceeding the way I thought they would?
- What is it that hinders me from experiencing joy and peace when circumstances are different than I thought they'd be?
- How can I give God glory when life turns out differently than I thought it would?
- How can I respond with joy and trust, even if my longings are never realized?

- Can I truly have peace and trust when my hopes for something different grow dim?

First, let me encourage you, *it is possible* to respond well no matter what our circumstances. And this is coming from no one other than the "Queen of Expectations"! Our God is the One who makes possible that which is impossible. There is hope! The Scriptures give us all we need to respond in a God-honoring way to the unmet expectations in our lives. Step one to giving God glory, no matter what happens, begins with understanding where the problem lies. Once we figure that out, we can apply the proper remedies for fixing it from God's Word. Without step one, we can end up exerting a lot of energy without seeing any lasting, life-changing growth.

Discovering our Heart Problem

The first part of step one includes some bad news. *The bad news is that we all have a heart problem.* Until we recognize that truth, we won't get much traction with those pesky expectations that can so easily get us bent out of shape. The problem starts when we become aware of some unmet expectations and then nurture the little seeds of discontentment in our hearts. While they germinate, other sins may sprout too. When it comes to unmet expectations, the weed of discontentment is the root of our troubles.

Discontentment is a "feeling of wanting something better or an improved situation."[2] It means to be dissatisfied with the current situation in some way. I don't know about you, but that just about always describes my response when it comes to unmet expectations. When I'm struggling, it's usually because I want to improve or change the situation. And, of course, I've got some great ideas on how to fix it.

Apparently, I'm not the only one to make these observations about discontentment. Thomas à Kempis, who lived from 1380 to 1471, said, "Why are you so easily troubled because things don't happen to you as you desire? Who is the man who has all things as he would have them? Neither you nor I nor any man living, for no one lives in this world without some trouble or anguish, be he king or pope."[3] I love the way Thomas à Kempis so rationally summarizes the problem. In effect, he says, "Why are you upset when things don't go your way? Does anyone ever get anything entirely his way? Of course not." But we want it to go *our way*, don't we? And that's when the temptation to become discontent can begin to take root.

2 http://dictionary.cambridge.org/dictionary/british/discontent
3 Thomas à Kempis, *The Imitation of Christ: A Modern Version of the Immortal Spiritual Classic*, ed. Harold G. Gardiner, S. J. (New York: Image Books, 1955), 60.

It's interesting to consider the different ways discontentment may manifest itself in our hearts. Here are some examples that other women have experienced. I've seen them in my life too.

- Discontentment with our situation or circumstances may tempt us to say, "This is what God gave me, but I don't like it. I want something different than what I have received."
- Discontentment with our situation may lead us to argue, "My way is better than God's. What He's given me just isn't good enough."
- Discontentment with what's happening in our lives may cause us to respond, "I don't have what I want. I want more. In fact, I want what they have."
- Discontentment with our situation, whatever it might be, may reveal itself in this way: "Oh, how I wish things were different. If only this or that would change, *then* I would be happy."
- In 1 Samuel 22:2 discontentment literally means being "bitter of soul." When left to fester, bitterness can show up in our lives as pure venom—"If I can't have it, then no one can!" Yikes!

Most of the time we don't verbalize our discontentment in such bold or openly selfish ways. But if we're honest, *those are the words of our hearts.* Whether we verbalize those thoughts or not, if they continue to consume our time and energy, they will eventually move from shadowy notions to the real world of words and deeds.

Our Discontented Forbearers

Time hasn't changed the human heart. We find many instances of discontentment in the Scriptures, beginning with Eve in the Garden of Eden in Genesis 3. While listening to Satan's evil whispers, Eve grew discontent. She thought she was missing out. She wanted more than what she'd been given. Now, if ever there was a woman who could have been completely satisfied, it was Eve. Yet her perfect home, her perfect husband, her perfect body, her perfect life, even her perfect relationship with God wasn't enough—she wanted more. That is the epitome of discontentment. *Eve lusted for something more, something new, improved, better.*

Abraham's wife, Sarah, grew impatient with God's timing in her life. God had promised He would make Abraham into a mighty nation and He had assured Abraham that Sarah would have a child. Splendid idea! Only she thought it would have happened much sooner, at the stage of life when she was still physically able to bear children.

Sarah was so discontent with God's timing that in Genesis 16:1–2 we are told that she gave her maid, Hagar, to Abraham to bear a child in her place. Sarah wanted to help God carry out his plans. But the result of her decision was disastrous, not only for Abraham and Sarah, but for Hagar and her son, Ishmael. All kinds of petty jealousies and conflicts occurred because of Sarah's unwillingness to be satisfied with the time *when* God would put His plan into effect. *Her discontentment made her impatient with God's timing.*

Just like Sarah, Jacob's wife, Rachel, suffered from barrenness. Rachel fully expected to bear Jacob children, just like her sister, Leah, had done. But God had other plans for her. Rachel's discontentment with her situation in life made her frantic and desperate. In Genesis 30:1 we read: "Now when Rachel saw that she bore Jacob no children, she became jealous of her sister; and she said to Jacob, 'Give me children, or else I die.'" She blamed Jacob for her barrenness and considered that her happiness was conditional upon bearing a child. *She believed she would find happiness in a changed situation.*

And if ever there was a woman who looked at her life and found it lacking in every area, it was Job's wife! In Job 1 and 2 we learn that Job and his wife had it all—a home, servants, grown children living close by, a place in society, financial stability, health. And then, suddenly, everything was gone! As Job's wife surveyed the growing pile of her previously successful life, she bitterly declared to her suffering husband: "Curse God and die!" (2:9). *Her discontentment turned to bitterness in her changed circumstances.*

Discontentment led the Israelites to complain that God's provision of daily manna wasn't enough. Numbers 11:1 records this sad story: "Now the people became like those who complain of adversity in the hearing of the LORD; and when the LORD heard it, His anger was kindled, and the fire of the LORD burned among them and consumed some of the outskirts of the camp." Their complaining was an affront to the Lord. The people completely discounted God's miraculous and faithful care for them.

Then a little further in Numbers 11:4–6 we read: "The rabble who were among them had greedy desires; and also the sons of Israel wept again and said, 'Who will give us meat to eat? We remember the fish which we used to eat free in Egypt, the cucumbers and the melons and the leeks and the onions and the garlic, but now our appetite is gone. There is nothing at all to look at except this manna.'" Their discontentment with God's provision moved them to murmur and grumble against Him. *God had provided for them. As it wasn't quite what they had in mind, they complained against Him.*

Desiring something different than what we've received, growing impatient with God's timing, trying to find happiness in changed circumstances, or complaining about what the Lord has given us are some of the ways we may struggle with discontentment in our lives. Discontentment is no respecter of persons and spans the gaps of gender, time, and culture. In fact, we've got the guarantee from the Scriptures that we'll all battle with this emotion at one time or another. Proverbs 27:20 sheds light into our hearts when it states: "Sheol and Abaddon are never satisfied, nor are the eyes of man ever satisfied." Or look at Ecclesiastes 6:7 which states: "All a man's labor is for his mouth and yet the appetite is not satisfied." The Scriptures show us the fallen state of our hearts that crave more than we have, desire something different, and long for things to change.

When Longing Becomes a Detriment

Have you ever found yourself thinking, "If only this hadn't happened" or "If only things had turned out differently?" *If only.* Two harmless-sounding words. At times, they are exactly that—harmless. But there are times when these two little words so grip the heart that nothing else in life matters except the fulfillment of that "if only" longing.

"If only" finds fertile soil in unmet expectations. When we struggle with discontentment in some area, it means our focus has locked onto the "if only" for satisfaction. The list is varied and endless when it comes to the "if only" longings of our hearts: If only I had more money; if only I was pretty; if only I was short; if only I was thin; if only I was married; if only I was single; if only I had children; if only I had many children; if only I had healthy children; if only I had a job; if only I had that house; if only I could buy whatever I wanted, whenever I wanted.

If only; if only; *if only*—its litany peals forth like the ringing of a great bell, persistently crying out in our hearts for fulfillment. What's astounding is that we're often fully convinced that if the longing were gratified, it would bring complete satisfaction. But I've discovered that my heart is fickle. My "if only" list changes all the time. It's different from day to day and from year to year.

The short shelf life of our "if only" desires is amazing, considering how much mental energy and emotional angst they produce. We long for something, put effort into procuring it, and then, when we get it, we move on to the next thing on our "This will satisfy my heart" list. Oh yes, our hearts are capricious and don't really know what they need to satisfy them. Much like a prairie dog that can dart below the surface, run through underground tunnels, and pop up in a new location, unmet expectations can emerge in places and at times we never considered possible.

Drains, Forks, and Constant Refrains

I don't think an occasional "if only" is going to run us aground spiritually. *"If only" desires become dangerous when they are the constant refrain of our hearts.* That's when they can tempt us to find our hope, joy, and satisfaction in things, in changed circumstances, and in other people, rather than in Jesus Christ.

Not too long ago, I was visiting my mother. As we did dishes and chatted away, we noticed that her kitchen sink wasn't draining as it should. She told me that she'd tried different things to unclog the drain, but the problem had persisted. Having been married to a fix-it guy for a long time, I've picked up a few things from him. So bravely, or maybe brashly, we decided to do some plumbing. Without flinching, we unscrewed the P-trap, preparing ourselves for the globby mess, only to find a fork in there instead! How it managed to get down the drain we couldn't imagine. But there it was wreaking all kinds of havoc, or at least blocking things a bit.

There are times when our unmet expectations become like that fork in my mom's kitchen drain. We can wash dish after dish and the fork doesn't seem to make any difference, but eventually, if it stays there, it's going to clog the drain. When we grow despondent, fearful, anxious, or angry when our expectations remain unmet, our negative response becomes like that fork. We might not notice its effects right away. But, eventually, we'll experience the results of its presence because it will block our spiritual growth.

You've heard the bad news. Now here's the good news—we're on our way to responding to unmet expectations, disappointments, and sorrows in a way that will glorify the Lord. But first we've got to get that fork out of there!

QUESTIONS for REFLECTION

Chapter 1: "If Only" and Other Expectations

1. Ecclesiastes 7:29 says, "Behold, I have found only this, that God made men upright, but they have sought out many devices." This verse gives us a few things to think about as we begin our study of unmet expectations. First, what two things do we learn about mankind from Ecclesiastes 7:29?

2. Let's dig a bit deeper into the phrase "God made men upright" by looking at the following verses: Deuteronomy 32:4; Job 1:1; Psalms 7:10; 11:7; Proverbs 16:17. What do you learn about the word "upright" from this small sampling of verses?

3. From John 17:3; 2 Corinthians 3:18; Ephesians 4:13; and Titus 2:11–14, what do we learn about God's plan for "uprightness" for man?

4. Instead, what happened to God's lovely intention for man? See the second part of Ecclesiastes 7:29.

5. Rather than seeking the Lord and His ways, man seeks out other things. The verse calls these things "devices." What are some examples of devices or schemes mankind searches for, rather than God? Why do you think that is?

6. What is man's intention in seeking out other things rather than God? What are some of the reasons that you find yourself doing the same thing?

7. What schemes or devices do you find yourself turning to when you're disappointed, fearful, hurt, or frustrated?

8. What is the answer for our hearts when we find ourselves living out the second half of Ecclesiastes 7:29? See Psalm 73:21–28; John 6:68; Acts 4:12.

None But Christ

O Christ, in Thee my soul hath found,
And found in Thee alone,
The peace, the joy I sought so long,
The bliss till now unknown.

I sighed for rest and happiness,
I yearned for them, not Thee;
But, while I passed my Savior by,
His love laid hold on me.

I tried the broken cisterns, Lord,
But ah, their waters failed,
E'en as I stooped to drink they fled,
And mocked me as I wailed.

The pleasures lost I sadly mourned,
But never wept for Thee,
Till grace my sightless eyes received,
Thy loveliness to see.

Now none but Christ can satisfy,
None other name for me,
There's love, and life, and rest, and joy,
Lord Jesus, found in Thee.

Unknown[4]

4 Unknown author quoted by H. A. Ironside, *Addresses on The First Epistle to the Corinthians* (Neptune, NJ: Loizeaux Brothers, 1973), 284.

2

Take Discontentment
Off the Menu

When I garden, I have to pull up a certain kind of weed called spurge. Spurge is tough, doesn't need much water to survive, and can even grow in the tiny cracks of a concrete sidewalk. It has a large tap root that digs itself deep into the ground. The tap root is what allows the weed to survive as it can access the moisture in the soil below the concrete. If you chop off the top of the spurge, but fail to get the tap root, it grows back. Well, this is how it is with certain besetting sins in our life. We may casually confess them, but confession is often like chopping off the top part of spurge. Unless we get to the root issue of the sin, that particular sin will often come back and sometimes come back stronger than before.

Dr. Jack Hughes[5]

5 Dr. Jack Hughes on Romans 8:12-13 in a sermon titled, "How to Kill Your Beloved Sin!" For more information on this or other sermons, contact www.drivennails.com.

Most of us know how a fruit tree grows, even if we were sleeping in seventh-grade biology. But just in case it's been a while, here's a mini review. A fruit tree grows when a seed is planted in the ground. That seed germinates and sprouts, sending its tendrils up toward the surface. Over time, it grows into a delicious, fruit-laden tree.

Sometimes, the fruit isn't quite what we expect, at least that's what happened to us. When we lived in Southern California, we planted some citrus trees in our backyard. I just couldn't wait to harvest those first oranges! My husband had spent his early years in Ventura and Ojai, California, and had recounted wonderful stories of eating fresh oranges from their orchard. I grew up in Idaho, land of crisp apples, sweet peaches, and juicy pears. I had never eaten lemons or oranges right off the tree.

So, you can imagine my eagerness when one of our young citrus trees produced a most glorious tangelo. Though it looked ready to pick, it still needed more time to ripen and sweeten. Almost daily I went outside to check on it. Finally, the day came when it was ready to be picked. I reached up cradling that hefty tangelo, plump with sweet juices, plucked it from the tree, only to discover that it must have gone on a diet or something. The heft was gone and all that remained was the rind! A fruit rat or a raccoon had expertly hollowed out my poor tangelo so that no fruit was left, and barely a drop of juice remained. It was so nice of the little pest to leave the rind still hanging from the tree as a sort of thank offering! Truly, it was the fruit of disappointment. Sometimes things just don't turn out the way we hope.

Discontentment Produces Some Nasty Fruit

I was sure disheartened about my poor, hollowed-out tangelo, but, at least, it wasn't like the nectarines we tried to grow. Lovely to look at, but the fruit just didn't cut it. The nectarines weren't sweet or juicy; they were just awful! Sometimes even the fruit rats disdained them, knocking them off the tree to rot on the ground while they crept by them on the fence. But really, if you think about it, the problem with those mealy nectarines could be traced back to their root stalk. And that is amazingly similar to our topic at hand. For discontentment, like our nectarines, yields some less than appealing fruit. And just like our nectarines, the fruit of discontentment is produced at the root of it all, our hearts. Often, we're not even aware that there's something wrong in our hearts until we see what kind of fruit grows in our lives.

For me it works this way: "I sure have been anxious lately, and for some reason it makes me really grumpy with my family. Why am I feeling so fearful? What's causing these sinful responses in my heart and life?" As I consider my ways and what's happening in my heart, I'm often surprised to discover what's really at the root of my ungodly responses.

We can tell that David understood this process well because he wrote about it in Psalm 139:23–24: "Search me, O God, and know my heart; try me and know my anxious thoughts; and see if there be any hurtful way in me, and lead me in the everlasting way." It's interesting that sometimes we're not even aware of what's lurking in our hearts until the Lord helps us see what's there. Asking the Lord for insight into what's going on in the murky depths of our souls is the first step to responding well to the unmet expectations in our lives.

When our daughter, Leah, was sixteen years old, she inexplicably developed a chronic headache that lasted for eight long years. During those eight years, she didn't experience one pain-free day. Up to that point in our child-rearing, we had never experienced anything major with our kids—no broken bones, no surgeries, no hospital stays. Band-Aids and kisses pretty much fixed what was wrong. I really had expected some stitches or a broken bone or two, but, for some reason, the possibility of a chronic or long-term illness hadn't entered into my thinking. When I was challenged with Leah's long-term headache and unrelieved pain, I came face to face with my expectation that moms are supposed to take care of their kids, fix their boo-boos, and bring comfort. I really struggled when I couldn't *fix* what was wrong.

As Leah's headache continued unabated for one month, two months, then three months and more, I grieved over how it might affect the rest of her life. At that point in her journey, Leah wasn't able to engage in "normal" everyday activities because she was still learning how to live with constant pain. It broke my heart to imagine what it must be like to hurt like that. Inevitably my mind jumped to the future: What would happen to her? How would she cope day after day? Would she be able to have a "normal" life? I grieved over her unrelieved pain. I grieved over the things she couldn't do. *Plain and simple, I struggled with God's plan for our lives at that time.*

When I traced my sorrow and despair back to their source, I discovered they were firmly rooted in my discontentment over God's plan for Leah and our family. In my heart, I struggled to accept these new circumstances as *good* from the Lord (Rom. 8:28). My wrestling revealed what lay buried in my heart. I was prepared for trials, *just not ones like this*. I had expected *something different* from God when it came to how He would sanctify Leah and our family.

As I sought the Lord, worked through the Scriptures, and struggled to overcome my sorrow and discontentment, the Lord gave me some insights I never would have gained without Leah's sickness. I learned that the fruits, the symptoms of the things we do and say, are the indicators of what we're really feeling and thinking. That's why the psalmist's admonition from Psalm 119:59 is so important for us to heed: "I considered my ways and turned my feet to Your testimonies." Taking stock of what's really behind our fear, anger, or bitterness helps us to "consider our ways" and turn toward the Lord in repentance and humility. In many ways, recognizing that noxious fruit in our lives is a well-timed, wake-up call from the Lord. The Lord uses trials and disappointments like a strong cup of coffee to open our eyes to the sinful responses that often lie unnoticed in the recesses of our hearts.

Becoming a Fruit Expert

In case you don't have any idea of what becoming a "fruit expert" might look like, I've come up with nine ways discontentment may manifest itself in our lives. Real healing and growth can only begin when we recognize the fruit of discontentment for what it really is—a sinful response. One of my good friends perceptively remarked, "Unmet Expectations seem to be one of the biggest hindrances to believers walking in a manner worthy of the high calling in Jesus Christ"[6] —all the more reason then for us to identify any fruit of discontentment in our lives.

Before you read the list of fruit given below, ask the Lord to help you see if any of these symptoms are showing up in your life. Then ask Him to help you begin to understand *why* they're showing up, for we aren't wise judges when it comes to assessing our own hearts. Jeremiah 17:9 reminds us: "The heart is more deceitful than all else and is desperately sick; who can understand it?" Indeed, who can understand our hearts? Jeremiah tells us in the next verse: "I, the LORD, search the heart, I test the mind, even to give to each man according to his ways, according to the results of his deeds."

I think that's why I always choke on my popcorn a bit whenever I watch *The Lord of the Rings: The Return of the King*. When Aragorn asks Gandalf, "What does your heart tell you?", I always want to cry out, "Dude, don't listen to your heart! It's not trustworthy!" So, while our hearts are fickle, the Lord isn't. He guides us by imparting understanding and wisdom to us as He uses His Word to shine the light on the dark places of our hearts. He'll give us insight into what's really going on so that true transforming change can begin.

---

6 From a personal email communication with me.

Would you join me in doing a bit of detective work to see how those unmet expectations affect us? Let's consider whether any of the following responses are loitering around the corners of our hearts:

1. *Bitterness.* Discontentment over our circumstances can turn into bitterness. Janie Street described it as "a perpetual animosity that leads to harsh, unreasonable choices."[7] That's what was happening to Job when he exclaimed in Job 7:11: "Therefore I will not restrain my mouth; I will speak in the anguish of my spirit, I will complain in the bitterness of my soul." Bitterness is discontentment that has grown sour and twisted. It's often accompanied by a complaining spirit, just as Job described it. Do you remember the story of the two women who came to King Solomon because they were arguing over a baby? They both claimed to be the child's mother, both saying the other woman's baby had died (1 Kings 3:16–28). And do you remember what wise King Solomon did to determine the identity of the real mother? He commanded that the child be cut in half. The women responded just as he expected. The genuine mother begged that the child's life be spared, even if it meant, in order to spare his life, that she had to give her child to the other woman. Yet the other woman seconded Solomon's judgment and applauded it as just. She was so bitter over the death of her own child that she desired to inflict suffering on the real mother and cause her to lose her son too. Discontentment left to rot turns to bitterness.

2. *Anger.* Discontentment over unmet expectations can manifest itself as anger, impatience, and irritability. If our hearts were able to express themselves, they might say, "I'm mad because you didn't meet my needs." Or it might explode, "That's it! I've had it. God didn't do what I wanted so I'm out of here."

3. *Depression.* We can become depressed when things turn out differently than we expected. In the end, our brooding and moping reveal an unwillingness to trust the Lord in our unmet expectations.

4. *Conflict.* Disunity or conflict can result from unmet expectations. It might happen when someone doesn't meet our expectations and we get annoyed or angry about it. It's all too easy to get mad

---

7 From Dr. John Street's lecture notes for the PM512 Pastoral Counseling class at The Master's University. Used with permission.

at others for something you think they should be doing or, worse still, get mad at them for something God isn't doing. Those tensions and hidden expectations can affect the harmony of our relationships.

5.   *Pouting.* It's amazing how discontentment can turn us into two-year-olds. Of course, we would never throw ourselves on the floor and scream when things don't go as we want them to. But it isn't that uncommon for us to resort to the grown-up form of pouting which slams doors, gives the silent treatment, and holds grudges. We're disappointed, so we pout.

6.   *Complaining.* This verbal fruit is an easy one to sink our teeth into. Things don't go the way we planned, and before we know it, grumbles and gripes dribble from our lips. Complaining is simply a verbal temper tantrum. It's just a more sophisticated expression of it.

7.   *Jealousy and coveting.* Jealousy and coveting are also fruits of discontentment. We can grow jealous, envious, or covetous of the blessings God has granted to others. We want what they have. We may even believe we deserve what they have.

8.   *Fear.* We grow fearful when things don't turn out the way we thought they would, so we try to take control or respond with, "You can never be too safe." We mentally begin to think, "What might happen? I don't know if I can trust them. What else will God bring my way?" Not trusting others or not trusting God stems from this fruit. It says, "You hurt me. I can't trust you or I don't want to trust you because I don't want to get hurt again."

9.   *Rebellion.* There's a temptation to declare, "This is not what I signed up for!" when life turns out differently than we planned. When we get to the rebellious stage, we're stubbornly clinging to our ways rather than submitting to the Lord's plan. When we rebel against the Lord and His revealed will for us, we're essentially saying, "Nope, it's my turn to be king. I'm not following You anymore."

Well, that's my little basket of nasty fruit. If we did some brainstorming, I'm sure we would find more to add to the basket. The purpose of this little exercise is to help us recognize the fruit of discontentment in our lives. Once we've identified it for what it is, we can begin the work of uprooting it.

Claiming the Nasty Fruit as Our Own

My husband's mom was an enthusiastic supporter of every one of her eight kids, and she showed her support for my Sweety by attending as many of his basketball games as she could when he was in high school. She always threw herself wholeheartedly into whatever she was doing. So, it wasn't a big surprise that, at one particular game, she screamed like crazy whenever *her* son did anything of note in the game. She even made herself heard above the din of the other mothers cheering for *their* sons. So much so, that one of the players on the team nudged Jack, asking, "Who is that lady screaming like crazy?" His answer was "I don't know." Later he admitted to his mom that he had denied her just like Peter denied Christ; but she didn't mind and laughed good-naturedly every time that tale was told. She was committed to encouraging her kids. This little story serves a good purpose in reminding us that there are times when we don't want to claim something as ours, when we really should— just like when we see ungodly responses in our lives.

The basket of bad fruit points to a problem in our hearts. *The fruit reveals what we're thinking or feeling about the circumstances in our lives.* If the Lord Jesus Christ has redeemed us from sin and death and is in the process of transforming our lives, then we should want to deal with anything that crops up that's dishonoring to Him. That is our purpose, isn't it? We are to live *every* moment, *every* day to please Him. Paul prayed that all believers would do just that in Colossians 1:10: ". . .that you will walk in a manner worthy of the Lord, to please Him in all respects, bearing fruit in every good work and increasing in the knowledge of God."

Giving God glory means uprooting sin in our lives, which can be a tricky business. Pastor Robert C. Chapman gives us some helpful counsel: "We may be dealing honestly with sin that is seen outwardly, and yet not skillfully and effectually, because of not striking at the deep roots of evil within."[8] Chapman put his finger on one of the problems we encounter when trying to overcome sin. We're trying to deal with it, but not in an effective and insightful way. We hack at the *branches* of sin rather than going after the *root* of the sin.

No Expectations Isn't the Answer

By this time, you may have determined that you're not going to have ex-

8 Robert C. Chapman, *Choice Sayings* (Glasgow: Gospel Tract Publications, 1988), 8.

pectations anymore, no more expectations of how things should turn out, no more expectations of how people should respond. That's it, *finis*. You're done with the whole business of expectations. You may have reasoned that if discontentment over unmet expectations produces that much sin, then you're just not going to have expectations anymore.

How'd I guess what you were thinking? Because I've thought the same thing! I figure if I were more godly, then I wouldn't get all bent out of shape when things don't go the way I think they should. But the truth is that I am a sinner with my sinful nature still residing in me. Though I am saved by grace through faith and am being transformed by the grace, mercy, and power of God, I will do battle against my sin until my salvation is completed and made perfect in heaven. This means that, as long as I walk this earth, there will be times when I will still struggle to respond rightly to those expectations the Lord has allowed to remain unmet.

I would just love it if I could respond perfectly and in a godly way to every situation, but I don't. I would rather not have to combat my sin or struggle to gain a good attitude toward my circumstances. Those things keep me feeling off balance. It's so much nicer to feel "together" and really "with-it" spiritually! I would like to experience heaven here on earth. But the truth is that I am going to continue to battle my own heart all my days, until the Lord calls me to be with Him in glory.

The good news is that we're not alone in this battle. The Lord is our Captain who has fitted us with all we need for going to war. However, it is important that we understand that the ongoing, relentless fight with our sinful nature doesn't mean that we can give up and retreat. The Lord has provided help for us in His Word so we can begin to make strides against our sin, rather than be sidelined by our sinful responses when things don't happen in the way we expect.

My purpose in this chapter is to set the table for the feast to come. There is no need to keep eating the fruit of discontentment when the Lord has promised us the bounty of His kingdom! By identifying areas of discontentment and how they may show up in our lives, we will be more prepared to overcome those ungodly responses, even when life seems to go contrary to our expectations. And that's only the first part. Peering into the abyss of discontentment in our hearts won't do us much good if that's all we intend to do.

Proverbs 28:26 says, "He who trusts in his own heart is a fool, but he who walks wisely will be delivered." That is a blunt, but helpful verse! Trying to remedy our hearts on our own won't work. When we respond sinfully to the unmet expectations in our lives, deliverance only comes when we wisely turn to the Lord, repenting of our sinful responses and relying on Him for help. David's prayer, recorded in Psalm 143:8b, can be the template for our own prayers: "Teach me the way in which I should walk; for to You I lift up my soul." What a picture of faith and trust! "I'm lifting my soul up to You, Lord. I'm not hiding anything from You. You see all my struggles. You see my many sins and weaknesses. I am turning from my wrong responses, but it's not enough! I need Your help! Please take my soul and teach me the way I should walk."

You will have expectations as long as you live. You can also expect to struggle at times when things don't proceed the way you had hoped or planned. You will need to confess your sin to the Lord, and desire to turn away from it. Your *initial* response doesn't have to remain your *continual* response. Be encouraged, though, for you can always expect the Lord to help you grow in faith and wisdom, so that it can be said of you, "Strength and dignity are her clothing, and she smiles at the future" (Prov. 31:25). Keep reading for there is hope!

All right, my fellow pioneer girl, retie your bonnet strings, brush the dust off your face, and let's get moving.

QUESTIONS for REFLECTION

Chapter 2: Take Discontentment Off the Menu

"He who trusts in his own heart is a fool, but he who walks wisely will be delivered"
(Prov. 28:26).

1.   What is the first thing we learn from Proverbs 28:26?

2.   Being told we're a "fool" or acting "foolishly" may seem inappropriate until we gain a clearer understanding of a fool's ways. Look up the following verses, then describe the characteristics of a fool: Psalms 53:1; 107:17; Proverbs 1:7, 22, 32; 12:15, 16; 14:16; 15:5; 18:2, 6, 7.

3.   Identify the characteristics of the human heart that make trusting it a foolish thing to do. See Genesis 6:5; 8:21; Jeremiah 17:9; Matthew 15:18–20; Romans 1:21.

4.   What does it mean to trust in our own hearts? See Psalm 18:21; Proverbs 3:5–8; Jeremiah 17:5; Romans 12:16; Philippians 3:3.

5.   What is the result of trusting in ourselves? See Psalms 20:7–8; 112:6–9; Isaiah 47:10–11; Jeremiah 17:6.

6.   What does the second half of Proverbs 28:26 teach us?

7.   Looking only at Proverbs 28:26, what do you learn about walking wisely?

8.   What are some practical ways we can walk wisely and not trust our own hearts when it comes to unmet expectations? See also Psalm 9:7–10; 57:1–11; 2 Thessalonians 1:11–12; Hebrews 11:6; James 1:5.

3

Thorns, Weakness, and All-Sufficient Grace

If I become content by having my desire satisfied, that is only self-love, but when I am contented with the hand of God, and am willing to be at His disposal, that comes from my love to God.
Jeremiah Burroughs[9]

9 Jeremiah Burroughs, *The Rare Jewel of Christian Contentment* (Edinburgh: The Banner of Truth Trust, 1981), 54.

It's time to be up front with you—this chapter is about contentment. I want to warn you because there's something about seeing *contentment* and *unmet expectations* placed side by side that stirs up an incredulous response in our hearts of "Are you kidding? How is that even possible?" I think it's because we know that if we are going to truly grow in contentment, it's going to cost us. Yet it's my hope that you'll come away encouraged and convinced of the value of contentment.

Our study includes the fundamental and "oh so very necessary" instructions from God about contentment. Learning to live with unmet expectations isn't painless—at least, it hasn't been for me. Getting from Point A, where we leave the hurt, confusion, grief, fear, or anger about our unmet expectations, and arriving at Point B, where we accept God's unfolding plan for our lives as good and glorifying to Him, can be a painstaking and painful process. Yet the rule of all travel is to keep moving. Merely looking at and acknowledging that we have unmet expectations is a hollow exercise. We want to learn how we can gratefully accept God's work in our lives as good so that we can bring Him glory.

God Intends Us to Find Our Contentment in Him

Getting everything we ever hoped for or wanted doesn't guarantee contentment. In fact, getting everything we ever wanted is a sure recipe for discontentment, depression, and hopelessness, as a peek at the lives of those who have all that money can buy clearly reveals. Remember Proverbs 27:20? "Sheol and Abaddon are never satisfied, nor are the eyes of man ever satisfied." More money, more stuff, more love doesn't satisfy our hearts. So, what does?

Oh, what a question to think about! It's grand in its implications. What has the ability to satisfy the human heart that constantly desires more? *Only the Lord is big enough, wise enough, grand enough, deep enough to fill our hearts up and ease the continual longing that resides within.*

Stuff or no stuff, met expectations or unmet ones, God desires our souls be satisfied with Him. It's been His plan from the very beginning. From the time that Adam fellowshipped with God in the Garden of Eden to this very day, the perfect, Creator God of the Universe desires His children to know Him in a very real and tangible way. Unmet expectations play their part in herding us toward the Lord for heart-satisfaction.

Think about what the Lord did for the Israelites: "Yet I have been the LORD your God since the land of Egypt; and you were not to know any god except Me, for there is no savior besides Me. I cared for you in the wilderness, in the land of drought. As they had their pasture, they became satisfied, and being satisfied, their heart became proud; therefore they forgot Me" (Hosea 13:4–6). He showered them with good things so they would learn *where* to look whenever they had a need of any kind.

The same is true for us. God *gives and withholds* things in our lives to teach us not only about contentment but also that we will discover that He is enough for our souls. According to Hosea 13:4–6, the key to finding our satisfaction in the Lord is to *remember Him.* It's His desire that we look past His gifts to *Him* to fill the longings of our hearts. Jesus not only reminds us of this truth, but He also teaches that it's fully possible to be satisfied in God alone. He states this in Matthew 5:6: "Blessed are those who hunger and thirst for righteousness, for they shall be satisfied." *They shall be satisfied.* What a promise! No longer will our souls gnaw away in hunger for the Lord; He will assuage our longing for Him.

But how do we get there?

The Cure for Discontentment

The cure for this chronically recurring disease called discontentment lies in taking our prescribed doses of heart penicillin—and that antibiotic for our hearts means a consistent regimen of Jesus. Contentment means to be "satisfied, to find things sufficient" for your soul. Growing in contentment is the first step to overcoming our sinful responses when life just doesn't match up to our notions of how it should proceed.

The word "contentment" carries with it the idea of having more than enough. Think of when Moses asked the people to give toward the building of the tabernacle. He ended up receiving so much gold and supplies from the people that the leaders actually had to tell them to stop giving. Exodus 36:6b–7 states: "Thus the people were restrained from bringing any more. For the material they had was *sufficient and more than enough* for all the work, to perform it" (emphasis added). That's a perfect picture of contentment, when your soul is so full of Jesus that it overflows into every part of your life. He's enough; you don't need anything else.

One child, misquoting Psalm 23, said, "The Lord is my shepherd, that's all I want."[10] That's contentment in a nutshell. The little one may not have won any prizes for his imprecise recitation, but he did nail the concept of contentment in a profoundly biblical and doctrinally precise way.

We're always going to have longings—longings for this thing or that, longings for our lives to be different, longings for more, longings for less—which is why we need a longing that supersedes all other longings,

---

10 Mark Water, *The New Encyclopedia of Christian Quotations* (Grand Rapids, MI: Baker Book House, 2000), 223.

something that is pre-eminent and stands above all our other heart's desires. God created us so that true heart contentment and soul satisfaction can only be found in Jesus Christ. He is the anchor and answer for our souls (Heb. 6:19).

We all know that when we're content, we're not looking for things or people or different circumstances to make us happy. That concept is really what is at the heart of this whole issue of unmet expectations. Expecting some*thing* or some*one* to some*how* provide deep and lasting contentment sets us up for a fall—and more discontentment. Pastor Carey Hardy has said, "Desire for certain things is okay, but not when it becomes the only means of happiness."[11] True contentment begins when we humbly accept that our circumstances come from the Lord. Contentment then continues to grow when we see things from His point of view. That's when we're able to say with Job, "The LORD gave and the LORD has taken away. Blessed be the name of the LORD" (1:21b). We may desire things, but the all-consuming "I've just got to have it" is tamed as our hearts look to the Lord.

Maintaining true contentment comes when we understand that the Lord is enough to satisfy our souls. If only we would believe it.

Contentment: Easier Said Than Done

Paul wrote in Philippians 1:21: "For to me, to live is Christ and to die is gain." If ever there was a quick and easy way to describe what contentment looks like in our lives, this verse in Philippians gives us a good summary. Paul states that living equals Christ and dying equals gain. He describes his life as *living for* Christ. That's why dying was gain for him because it meant he would depart his earthly body and be *with Christ* in heaven. Living or dying, Paul was content because, ultimately, he wasn't looking to anything else to bring him joy, comfort, or hope. He was looking only to Jesus—no matter what his need.

Paul explained his motivation in more detail in 2 Corinthians 5:14–15: "For the love of Christ controls us, having concluded this, that one died for all, therefore all died; and He died for all so that they who live might no longer live for themselves, but for Him who died and rose again on their behalf." Here Paul revealed that he was controlled, compelled, even constrained by the immense love of Christ toward him and of his love toward the Lord Jesus. That great love *for* Christ and *from* Christ *motivated everything* Paul did, *everything* he said, and *everything* he was. Christ dying in his place on the cross inspired Paul. In fact, Christ's sacrifice affected

---

11 Pastor Carey Hardy speaking on "The Heart of the Matter" at the 2013 Shepherds' Conference. https://www.gracechurch.org/sermons/7606

Paul to such a degree that he determined he would no longer live for himself, but for the blessed One who took the punishment for his sins.

Living for Jesus led to contentment for Paul, which means such a life is possible for us as well. Like Paul, contentment can live in our hearts when we recognize the great gift Jesus gave us when He paid the debt of our sin with His own life. His sacrifice on our behalf motivates us and changes everything.

Did you know that *every* believer is filled with longings to live for Jesus Christ? If we don't desire to live for Him, then we may not truly be saved. He gave His life for us and we *want* to live for Him. Yet, if we're really honest, we have to admit that our desires to live for Him aren't consistent every day. Living wholly for Him isn't always our main concern. We struggle to be completely content in the Lord. More often than not, we find ourselves hanging on to our "if only" list, that fade-away-like-the-mist "if only" list—if only I were thin, if only I were married, if only my family were different, if only this particular event hadn't happened to me—rather than pursuing contentment in the Lord.

Learning to Battle the "If Only" of Your Heart

The apostle Paul had a few "if only" skirmishes that he has recorded in the Scriptures for us. Thankfully, he won the battle by choosing to find his satisfaction in God rather than in his expectations. And if Paul could do it, then there's hope for us too! Look at what he said about it in Philippians 4:10–13:

> But I rejoiced in the Lord greatly, that now at last you have revived your concern for me; indeed, you were concerned before, but you lacked opportunity. Not that I speak from want, for I have learned to be content in whatever circumstances I am. I know how to get along with humble means, and I also know how to live in prosperity; in any and every circumstance I have learned the secret of being filled and going hungry, both of having abundance and suffering need. I can do all things through Him who strengthens me.

Here we gain a picture of what Paul's life looked like at times. There were times when he experienced great need. In fact, in 2 Corinthians 11:27 he writes: "I have been in labor and hardship, through many sleepless nights, in hunger and thirst, often without food, in cold and exposure." Doesn't that break your heart to think of the apostle Paul going to bed hungry or needing a place to sleep? However, rather than focusing on his circumstances, he focused on Christ and found contentment: "I have learned to be content in whatever circumstances I am."

How did he grow to have this marvelous, unshakeable contentment? If we look at Philippians 4:10–13 again, we get the idea that he learned contentment by going through tough times. This may sound all too familiar when we think of what's happening in our lives. Our wise and loving heavenly Father enrolls all His children in the same school. Can't you just imagine someone asking the apostle, "What did you learn today, Paul?" And he replied, "Well, today I learned how to get along with humble means." Many of us can say with a sardonic roll of our eyes, "Oh yeah, I learned that lesson too!" We begrudge learning from hard times. When we suffer want and difficulty, are we able to say that we are content? Have we really learned the lesson that Paul writes about in Philippians 4:11: "I have learned to be content in whatever circumstances I am"?

Then Paul said, "I also know how to live in prosperity" (Phil. 4:12). We love the idea of learning contentment through prosperity. But Paul said there were lessons he needed to learn about living contentedly when he had enough. Contentment in prosperity allows us to rejoice in God's blessings because *God gave them*, instead of being distracted by them. Contentment focuses on the Lord Himself, rather than on circumstances.

Paul tells us that the secret to contented living lies in knowing that "I can do all things through Him who strengthens me" (Phil. 4:13). Living for the Lord, desiring to obey Him, and accepting His will isn't possible unless we apply Philippians 4:13. We can never be content in plenty or in want, in met or unmet expectations until we turn to the Lord for His strength to do so.

Lessons We Learn About Contentment

From Philippians 4:10–13, we can make some stunning and life-changing observations. We learn:

- Contentment can be learned.
- Contentment isn't static. It can grow.
- Contentment can flourish in *any* environment.
- Contentment can also fluctuate, depending on where we place our focus.
- Contentment isn't dependent on our circumstances or our feelings.
- Maintaining a contented spirit isn't something we can do on our own. Only as we continually go to the Lord for help can we grow in contentment.

- The Lord Jesus Himself helps and strengthens us to grow in contentment.

Paul's Big "If Only" And How He Grew in Contentment

At another point in his life, we see the process Paul went through to learn contentment and trust the Lord in an extremely trying situation. He shows us how to combat the "if only" longings of our hearts, so we too can learn contentment in the not-so-fun times of life.

In 2 Corinthians 12:7–10, Paul is defending himself against false teachers who were constantly criticizing him, saying that he wasn't a true apostle. They wanted to discredit and hijack his ministry to the Corinthian church. For the sake of the believers there, Paul humbly reveals his apostolic credentials by recounting in 2 Corinthians 12:1–6 how the Lord Jesus personally taught him—one of the criteria for those claiming to be an apostle. Paul explains that he wasn't sure how Jesus accomplished this, whether he, Paul, had been transported to heaven or if Jesus had appeared to him in a dream.

What Paul does know is that his experience with Jesus was so glorious that God sought to protect him from pridefully boasting about it. Paul explains, "Because of the surpassing greatness of the revelations, for this reason, *to keep me from exalting myself*, there was given me a thorn in the flesh, a messenger of Satan to torment me—*to keep me from exalting myself!*" (2 Cor. 12:7, emphasis added). The Lord gave Paul a "thorn in the flesh, a messenger of Satan" to keep his heart humble.

Paul's thorn was so painful that he begged the Lord three times to remove the trial (2 Cor. 12:8). This was Paul's "if only" moment. *If only this thorn in the flesh were removed, then I could really minister to these* people. *If only* I were freed from this painful trial, just think of all I could do for the Lord! *If only, Lord. . .*

After hearing Paul's petition three times, God answered Paul with these powerful, heart-strengthening words: "My grace is sufficient for you, for power is perfected in weakness" (2 Cor. 12:9). God's answer for Paul was "My grace is enough for you. In fact, your limitations are ultimately better for your ministry, for My power will be seen through your weakness."

God's Grace is Enough

Reflect on what this means! God's grace is sufficient. It is enough. It is ample and more than abundant *for you*. That sounds perfectly lovely, but how exactly does it work? How can God's grace help us when we're up to our eyeballs in unmet expectations or when life has taken such a sharp left turn that we're suffering from whiplash?

The Scriptures teach us some life-changing truths about the grace of God. We're told in Hebrews 4:16 to "draw near with confidence to the throne of grace, so that we may receive mercy and find grace to help in time of need." Just think! As we draw near to God, seeking Him, we will find grace, abundant grace that will help us in our time of need. Grace is not passive. It's active in a believer's life. It's so active that it actually strengthens us when we need help.

When we look at 1 Corinthians 15:10, we learn even more about the grace of God. Paul writes, "But by the grace of God I am what I am, and His grace toward me did not prove vain; but I labored even more than all of them, yet not I, but the grace of God with me." Paul is saying that God's grace made him into the man he was, that as he took steps to seek and obey the Lord, God's grace was at work in him. Paul even goes so far as to say that it really wasn't his efforts as much as it was the grace of God working in and through him that accomplished his ministry and made it what it was. Again, we see the *active* nature of grace. It *works* in us.

So, when God says, "My grace is sufficient for you," we can take those words of assurance to heart, especially when it comes to dealing with unmet expectations in life. You may not have the marriage you thought you were going to have, but *God's grace is sufficient for you.* You may not have perfect health or an easy life, but *God's grace is enough for you right now.* You may not have the financial stability you'd always hoped for, but *God's grace is amply supplied for you.*

God's grace is enough to help you through this situation or that painful circumstance or any other thing God ordains as the method to teach you to live by His grace each moment of every day. I had known this in a somewhat practical way, but this truth became even more real in my experience when our daughter's headache first began. She had to learn to live with ongoing and uninterrupted daily pain, while I needed to accept God's will for her. The Lord lovingly helped us both through the trial by teaching us more about 2 Corinthians 12:9–10. It became our life-breath. We lived it. We spoke it. We prayed it. Every day. All day.

> *God's grace is sufficient for this minute. Let's rely on Him for this minute. Okay, now let's get through the next minute. His grace is sufficient here. And in this minute too.*

And so, we encouraged each other, through the minutes, through the hours, until we made it through the day, living upon the grace of God. And then we began all over again the next day, when His grace again *actively strengthened* us. Each day became a testimony to the Lord's sustaining and all-sufficient grace.

God's Power is Made Perfect in Weakness

After Paul had asked the Lord to remove his thorn in the flesh and God responded by saying, "No," God told Paul something else, which is recorded for us in 2 Corinthians 12:9. He told Paul that the reason He wanted his affliction and suffering to remain was because power is made perfect in weakness. The Lord was saying specifically that it was good that Paul was feeling weak because then the Lord's strength would be evident. Most of us don't like feeling weak, and Paul was no exception. It's so much nicer to serve the Lord when we feel strong and able and all put together. But more often than not, the Lord brings things into our lives that make us feel vulnerable and in need of help.

That's when we're right where the Lord wants us. Why? Because *His power is made perfect through our weakness.* When we're weak, so "less than," so hindered, then God's power is put on display. It's humbling when this happens. It's also awe-inspiring to see God at work, strengthening us when we feel so ill-equipped, inadequate, and unbelieving.

Grab on to Grace with Gusto

Take note of how Paul responded when God told him it was actually better for him to remain in his weak and vulnerable state: "Most gladly, therefore, I will rather boast about my weaknesses, so that the power of Christ may dwell in me. Therefore I am well content with weaknesses, with insults, with distresses, with persecutions, with difficulties, for Christ's sake; for when I am weak, then I am strong" (2 Cor. 12:9b–10).

For Paul, learning to live by God's grace was sufficient for the circumstances in which he found himself, and the fact that God's strength would be on display through his weakness, was enough for him to enthusiastically embrace God's good plan for his life. Paul's "if only" was transformed into contentment about his circumstances: content with *weaknesses* and *insults*, content with *distresses* and *persecutions*, content with *difficulties.* Paul trusted God's plan for His life and, therefore, he humbly accepted whatever God ordained for him.

It's so easy to say, "I'm content," until we find ourselves in distress. Then a steady stream of "Lord, deliver me" rises to heaven. We can ask the Lord to deliver us, and He may do so. Yet God wants us to learn the lessons of contentment—to find His grace sufficient and trust Him in our weakness. Rather than growing vexed and discontent, the next time we find ourselves feeling weak, hampered, thwarted, or misused, what truths do we need to focus on so we can respond with trust in God's good plan for us? We should consciously reflect on the following:

- God's grace is sufficient for us—right now and for however long the Lord allows these unmet expectations to remain.
- God has a plan for the present difficulty that includes teaching us about His powerful grace. It also includes teaching us that weakness is a means of receiving His blessing, for when we are weak, His power strengthens us.
- It is possible to be content in any situation; in less than perfect circumstances; in painful, distressing times; when life is different than expected.

The Lord's Presence Brings Contentment

Paul is not the only one who learned contentment. More clues to long-lasting contentment can be found in the first part of Hebrews 13:5 where we are given this admonition: "Make sure that your character is free from the love of money, being content with what you have." That's great counsel for us to keep in mind when examining our hearts. You may well think that money is not an issue for you, which may certainly be true. But don't stop there. Consider the encouragement that comes next in that verse: "being content with what you have." You may be content with what you have because you're not into "stuff." But what about being content with the less tangible things? What about being content with your life *just as it is* or with your job or with your health? *If nothing in your life ever changed again, would you be content?*

Five-Dollar Questions with the Million-Dollar Answer

Be content. But how? In Hebrews 13:5–6, the author of Hebrews provides us with practical help for contentment when he tells us, "For He Himself has said, 'I will never desert you, nor will I ever forsake you,' so that we confidently say, 'The LORD is my helper, I will not be afraid. What will man do to me?'"

Let's further examine the point the author of Hebrews is making. We struggle with discontentment when our focus shifts from Christ to our "if only" as the answer to our hearts' needs. When we remember that our Beloved One is near, that our Great God and Savior, the Lord Jesus Christ promises never to leave us, then our eyes are lifted back to Him and off people, off changes in our circumstances, and off our hopes and dreams. Our hearts gain courage to face any situation packed with unmet expectations because the Lord will help us. We don't have to be afraid. *The Lord is near.*

Puritan pastor, George Swinnock, said, "God is the happiness of man because of His suitableness to the soul. A hungry man finds his stomach craving. Give him music or honour and he is hungry still. These are not suitable to his appetite. Give him food and his craving is over. So it is with a man's soul. Give it honour, profits, and the pleasures of the world, and these cannot abate its desire; it craves still. These do not answer the soul's nature, and therefore cannot answer its needs. Set God before it just once, and let it feed on Him; it is satisfied, and its inordinate, dogged appetite after the world is cured."[12]

Are you struggling with unmet expectations? Are you battling discontentment in your heart? If so, take courage! There is hope! The longings of your heart can be met and satisfied in Jesus.

---

12 George Swinnock, *Works*, IV:2-7 quoted in *Voices from the Past*, vol. 1, 169.

QUESTIONS for REFLECTION

Chapter 3: Thorns, Weakness, and All-Sufficient Grace

1. Read 2 Corinthians 12:7. What was the purpose of Paul's thorn in the flesh according to verse 7?

2. How can that *big-picture perspective* from 2 Corinthians 12:7 encourage you, when you consider your own batch of unmet expectations?

3. Though Paul greatly desired to be delivered from his painful trial, what was God's answer for him? See the beginning of 2 Corinthians 12:9.

4. How can the truth of verse 9 be an encouragement to you if the Lord allows your circumstances to remain unchanged?

5. For further study: Read 1 Corinthians 15:10; Philippians 4:13; Colossians 1:29; and Hebrews 4:16 to gain a clearer picture of what the active grace of God looks like in a believer's life.

6. Once Paul understood God's purpose in allowing his painful and trying circumstances, how did he respond according to 2 Corinthians 12:9–10?

7. How can Paul's example, and the truths you learn about God in 2 Corinthians 12:7–10, help you entrust yourself to the Lord when He allows unmet expectations to come into your life?

The Soul Cheering Promise

We know not the trials before us,
But Jesus takes thought for them all,
And trusting the aid of His counsel,
We never, no, never can fall;
We know not the trials before us,
Or what on the morrow may be,
But sweet is the soul cheering promise,
My grace is sufficient for thee.

Then cleave to the Savior, cleave to Him,
Whatever the conflict may be,
Remember the soul cheering promise,
My grace is sufficient for thee.

We know not the trials before us,
But why should we tremble or fear?
The arm of the Lord will protect us,
The ark of His mercy is near;
We know not the trials before us,
Or what our temptations may be,
But stronger than death is the promise,
My grace is sufficient for thee.

Then cleave to the Savior, cleave to Him,
Whatever the conflict may be,
Remember the soul cheering promise,
My grace is sufficient for thee.

We know not the trials before us,
The sorrows and cares we shall meet,
But oh there's a refuge in Jesus,
Though surges may break at our feet;
How blessed, that refuge forever
Where safe from the storm we shall be,
The password to life is the promise,
My grace is sufficient for thee.[13]

---

13   Fanny Crosby, "The Soul Cheering Promise," *The Young People's Hymnal: Adapted to the Use of Sunday Schools, Epworth Leagues, Prayer Meetings, and Revivals* (Nashville, TN: Publishing House, Methodist Episcopal Church, 1897), 95.

4

Snapshots of an Ungrateful Heart

Gratitude is the memory of the heart.
Unknown[14]

If God hath taken away one of your children, he hath left you more; he might have stripped you of all. He took away all Job's comforts, his estate, his children; and indeed his wife was left but as a cross. Satan made a bow of this rib, as Chrysostom speaks, and shot a temptation by her at Job, thinking to have shot him to the heart, "Curse God, and die" but Job had upon him the breastplate of integrity; and though his children were taken away, yet not his graces, still he is content, still he blesses God. O think how many mercies you still enjoy; yet our base hearts are more discontent at one loss, than thankful for a hundred mercies. God hath plucked one bunch of grapes from you; but how many precious clusters are left behind!
Thomas Watson[15]

14   Josiah H. Gilbert, *The Dictionary of Burning Words* (New York: Wilbur B. Ketchum, 1895), 290.
15   Thomas Watson, *The Art of Divine Contentment* (1835; reprint, Morgan, PA: Soli Deo Gloria Publications, 1995), 54-55.

A Christian should keep two books always by him, one in which to write his sins, that he may be made humble; the other in which to write his mercies, that he may be kept thankful.
Thomas Watson[16]

O ur son, Nate, uses his digital camera with skill, combining a naturally artistic eye with an innate sense of how to achieve the look he wants in a photograph. I've had yearnings toward photography myself, which is why, a couple of years ago, I asked Nate if I could use his camera for a while. He had been working so much, he hadn't used it in months. Like the generous man that he is, he quickly sent it to me and taught me how to use it. We had all kinds of phone chats about apertures, ISOs, shutter speeds, and the art of capturing images on camera. I loved it!

And then, one day, Nate asked for his camera back, as he had the right to do. After all, it was his camera. But I developed a very bad case of "gimme hands."[17] I didn't want to give it back to him. Yep, you're reading that right. Nate's mom didn't want to give her son's camera back to him. My soul whined, "I want to keep it!" You see, I didn't really expect him to ask for it back. I thought that by the time he got around to taking pictures again, he would be ready for something better. And then the camera would be *mine, mine, mine* by right of possession.

My, those expectations can stir up some gnarly sin issues! I wasn't thankful that my son had allowed me to use his camera for as long as he did. If the super, ugly truth be told, I was pouting because he wasn't letting me keep it. I still wanted it, even though, toward the end of my tenure with it, I hadn't been using it much. Thankfully, by the time I mailed the camera back to my son, I had repented wholeheartedly of my sinful responses and was properly grateful for Nate's kindness, as I should have been all along.

I was shocked by my expectations in this little episode and the sinful, harmful attitude they produced in my heart. I guess it's safe to say our expectations can surprise us and cause us to respond differently than we might under "normal" circumstances. One of Israel's kings found that out for himself. Let's look at his story to see what we can learn about being surprised by unmet expectations.

---

16   Thomas Watson, *Light From Old Paths,* vol. 2, ed. C. Matthew McMahon (Crossville, TN: Puritan Publications, 2005), 90, Kindle.

17   This reference comes from a book we read to our kids: Michael P. Waite, *Buzzle Billy: A Book About Sharing* (Chariot Family Publishing, 1987). In the book, one of the characters didn't want to share and developed "gimme hands."

Hezekiah, the Man of the Hour

Hezekiah was one of Israel's good kings. He sought to do what was "good, right and true before the LORD his God" (2 Chron. 31:20). In the fourteenth year of Hezekiah's reign, Sennacherib, the king of the Assyrians, began to lay waste to Israel, conquering and consuming city after city. Sennacherib sent his lackey, Rabshakeh, to Jerusalem to let them know they were next on the "destroy" list. In response, Hezekiah threw himself upon the mercies of the Lord. Rather than giving in to the Assyrians' fear-inducing campaign, he urgently called upon the Lord for help and the safety of his people.[18]

Second Chronicles 32:21 says the Lord "destroyed every mighty warrior, commander and officer in the camp of the king of Assyria"—185,000 of them, according to Isaiah 37:36. The Assyrian king was so demoralized by this defeat that he went home in shame (2 Chron. 32:21). "So the LORD saved Hezekiah and the inhabitants of Jerusalem from the hand of Sennacherib the king of Assyria" (2 Chron. 32:22). Sennacherib's wicked blaspheming against God showed itself empty and false, while Hezekiah's faith in God proved completely sufficient.

Yet more dangerous to Hezekiah than the Assyrian king and his conquering army was what happened next. Hezekiah, the man of faith and trust in the Lord, found himself the hero of Israel and a marvel to the surrounding nations. Second Chronicles 32:23 tells us, "Many were bringing gifts to the LORD at Jerusalem and choice presents to Hezekiah king of Judah, *so that he was exalted in the sight of all nations thereafter*" (emphasis added).

It's a rare man who isn't the least bit tempted to pride by the adulation of the world. Hezekiah was no exception to this rule. After experiencing the highs of his faith-building trial, God brought a different kind of test to Hezekiah's door. Sadly, Hezekiah's sinful response shows how quickly we can descend from the heights of trust and obedience to the lows of unbelief. Studying these events will help us guard against giving into selfish pride and ingratitude when God tests our hearts.

Surprised by Expectations

Second Chronicles 32:24 and Isaiah 38:1 both say the same thing: "In those days Hezekiah became mortally ill." Not only was he sick, but the prophet Isaiah told him, "Thus says the LORD, 'Set your house in order, for you shall die and not live.'" Those would be hard words to hear! For

---

18   This event is recorded in 2 Kings 18-20, Isaiah 36-39, and 2 Chronicles 29-32.

Hezekiah, they were certainly surprising and most definitely unexpected. God graciously told him the news beforehand so he could prepare himself and the nation for his death. Yet, rather than motivate him, knowing that he wouldn't recover from his illness threw Hezekiah into a tailspin of rebellion against the Lord's plan.

Most people in Israel, and it appears even Hezekiah, believed that if a person suffered some long-term sickness or calamity, it was an indication of God's displeasure with that person. This was the same mindset Job encountered among his friends when he was overwhelmed by his trials. Job was known by all as a man of integrity and righteousness. Yet his friends accused him of harboring secret sins. They reasoned that Job must have engaged in sin of some kind, otherwise all those terrible things wouldn't have happened to him.[19]

Most commentators believe Hezekiah was around thirty-nine years old when the Lord struck him with his sickness. To make things even more humiliating, at that time, it was also commonly considered a judgment to die young. For Hezekiah, coming down with a mortal illness in the prime of life after his victory over the Assyrians, would have felt like the Lord was declaring to all the world that Hezekiah had been sinning or had displeased Him.

Isaiah 38:2–3 tells us that when Hezekiah found out he would die from his sickness, he "turned his face to the wall and prayed to the LORD, and said, 'Remember now, O LORD, I beseech You, how I have walked before You in truth and with a whole heart, and have done what is good in Your sight.' And Hezekiah wept bitterly."

It says of Hezekiah in 2 Kings 18:3–6:

> He did right in the sight of the LORD, according to all that his father David had done. He removed the high places and broke down the sacred pillars and cut down the Asherah. He also broke in pieces the bronze serpent that Moses had made, for until those days the sons of Israel burned incense to it; and it was called Nehushtan. He trusted in the LORD, the God of Israel; so that after him there was none like him among all the kings of Judah, nor among those who were before him. For he clung to the LORD; he did not depart from following Him, but kept His commandments, which the LORD had commanded Moses.

Hezekiah found God's plan devastating because he expected the Lord to reward him for his faithfulness rather than "punish" him, which is how he viewed his death sentence. In Hezekiah's view, he had been faithful to

---

19 The backstory to Job's calamities can be found in Job 1-2.

honor and obey the Lord in all he had done. That explains why we read in Isaiah 38:2–3 that he turned his face to the wall, praying and pleading his integrity before the Lord, and weeping bitterly over his circumstances. His response begins to make some sense in light of his worldview.

Coming Face to Face with Unmet Expectations

Hezekiah never imagined that scenario for his life. *Die young? Die having people think that he had sinned in some way? No way! He wasn't having it, not a bit.* Rather than respond willingly and well to the Lord, Hezekiah struggled. He was not content with God's will, plain and simple. But God showed him mercy, answering Hezekiah's prayer for healing and delaying his death by fifteen years (Isa. 38:4–5). Where it gets interesting, and what instructs us today, is Hezekiah's response to the Lord's mercy toward him.

What Ingratitude Says About You

The Lord mercifully healed Hezekiah. Yet we're told in 2 Chronicles 32:25 that "Hezekiah gave no return for the benefit he received." The NIV puts it this way: "He did not respond to the kindness shown him." Oh my! Not good! Hezekiah's ingratitude is shocking, considering the kindness the Lord had shown him.

If we're going to benefit from Hezekiah's life, we must ask ourselves, "Why wasn't Hezekiah grateful for the Lord's mercies?" What hidden expectations lurked in his heart that fueled his ingratitude? Second Chronicles 32:25 provides us with the insight we need. Hezekiah wasn't thankful for the Lord's kindness to him *because his heart was proud.*

Pride: The Gratitude Killer

The well-traveled path between pride and ingratitude is littered with expectations that God owes us something, or that He should do something for us because we have somehow earned it or deserve it. We get a bit stiff and stubborn inside at this point. So, even when the Lord does show us mercy (just as He did to Hezekiah), we receive His kindness with an attitude that says, "It's about time God was nice to me." Hezekiah had reached that stage in his heart. When God healed him, he responded with pride rather than gratitude for the kindness shown to him.

Stubbornly clinging to a sense of entitlement places us in a precarious position. "Danger, No Fishing" signs need to be posted around that particular puddle in our hearts. Sometimes, we can feel our thoughts creeping near the edge, so we veer away from the peril and retreat into right thinking about our circumstances. Other times, we've fished far too long in Ungrateful Pond, largely due to our pride. Henry Ward Beecher said, "Pride slays thanksgiving, but a humble mind is the soil of which thanks naturally grow. A proud man is seldom a grateful man, for he never thinks he gets much as he deserves."[20]

You probably know how the Lord feels about pride, but it's always good to review it. Proverbs 16:5 tells us, "Everyone who is proud in heart is an abomination to the LORD; assuredly, he will not be unpunished." "Pride goes before destruction, and a haughty spirit before stumbling" (Prov. 16:18). While Proverbs 21:24 calls it what it is, "'Proud,' 'Haughty,' 'Scoffer,' are his names, who acts with insolent pride." Our ingratitude and sullen spirit hide the pride tucked away in our hearts. *Our pride leads us to think we deserve something different than what God has given us.*

J. C. Ryle writes: "The widespread thanklessness of Christians is a scandal. It reveals our lack of humility. So, we must pray for a deeper sense of our own sinfulness and admit how unworthy we are. This, after all, is the true secret for a grateful heart. It is the person who daily feels his debt to grace and daily remembers that in reality he deserves nothing but hell who will be blessing and praising God every day. Thankfulness only blossoms from a root of deep humility."[21] Basically, Ryle tells us that if we want to become more grateful, then we need to put our pride to death. The way to do so is to ask the Lord to give us a "deeper sense of our own sinfulness and admit how unworthy we are,"[22] remembering that we don't deserve anything from the Lord.

If we don't like that counsel, I guess we could go with Nebuchadnezzar's plan. You remember what happened to him, don't you? God warned him to humble his heart, but ol' Neb didn't take heed and, before he knew it, he was eating grass in the field like a cow (Dan. 4:28–33). If anyone can affirm that the Lord knows how to handle the proud, it is Nebuchadnezzar. Do you remember his testimony in Daniel 4:37? "Now I, Nebuchadnezzar, praise, exalt and honor the King of heaven, for all His works are true and His ways just, *and He is able to humble those who walk in pride*" (emphasis added).

Neb's life plan proved quite painful. It is far wiser to follow Peter's counsel on how to deal with pride: "You younger men, likewise, be subject to your elders; and all of you, clothe yourselves with humility toward one

20 Henry Ward Beecher. (n.d.). BrainyQuote.com. Retrieved August 31, 2016, from BrainyQuote.com web site: http://www.brainyquote.com/quotes/authors/h/henry_ward_beecher.html

21 J. C. Ryle, *Luke: The Crossway Classic Commentaries*, eds. Alister Begg and J. I. Packer (Wheaton, IL: Crossway Books, 1997), 222-23.

22 Ibid.

another, for God is opposed to the proud, but gives grace to the humble. Therefore humble yourselves under the mighty hand of God, that He may exalt you at the proper time, casting all your anxiety on Him, because He cares for you" (1 Peter 5:5–7).

Peter reminds us of the subtle connection between pride and anxiety. Often, we resort to pride because we're fearful of waiting humbly upon the Lord. Understanding the connection between pride and anxiety helps us see what was going on with Hezekiah when God struck him with sickness. Hezekiah's prideful response was tied to his fear of what people would think when they learned of his mortal sickness.

It is good to pause and ask ourselves the question: *"Can my pride be traced back to fear or anxiety about something?"* Certainly, this is something to consider. Yet, no matter what your answer, 1 Peter 5:6–7 provides guidelines on how to respond. Humble yourself; trust the Lord that He'll take care of exalting you at the proper time. Give all your worries to the Lord and remember that He cares for you.

The Dark Side of Forgetfulness

J. C. Ryle wrote, "Murmurings, and complainings, and discontent abound on every side of us. Few indeed are to be found who are not continually hiding their mercies under a bushel, and setting their needs and trials on a hill."[23] We often focus on what we don't have, in effect, hiding God's mercies under a basket, rather than emphasizing all that we do have because of His kindness to us. And when we forget all the Lord has done for us, discontentment abounds—and where discontentment abounds, gratitude fades.

It seems that God has often had to deal with pride and forgetfulness in His children. Deuteronomy 8 teaches us this. God used the Israelites' forty-year wandering in the wilderness to teach His children obedience and dependence upon Him. It was crucial to their training that they remember the Lord, as forgetting Him would result in pride of every different shape and size. Take a look at Deuteronomy 8:11–14:

> Beware that you do not forget the LORD your God by not keeping His commandments and His ordinances and His statutes which I am commanding you today; *otherwise*, when you have eaten and are satisfied, and have built good houses and lived in them, and when your herds and your flocks multiply, and your silver and gold multiply, and

23   J. C. Ryle, *Expository Thoughts on the Gospels: St. Luke,* vol. II (London: William Hunt and Company, 1859), 234.

all that you have multiplies, *then your heart will become proud and you will forget the LORD your God* who brought you out from the land of Egypt, out of the house of slavery (emphasis added).

The antidote to pride lies in remembering the Lord and all He has done for us. That's why Moses goes on to explain God's plan for building humility and thankfulness in them. We read this in Deuteronomy 8:15–17:

He led you through the great and terrible wilderness, with its fiery serpents and scorpions and thirsty ground where there was no water; He brought water for you out of the rock of flint. In the wilderness He fed you manna which your fathers did not know, *that He might humble you and that He might test you, to do good for you in the end. Otherwise, you may say in your heart, "My power and the strength of my hand made me this wealth"* (emphasis added).

We forget that the Lord allows unmet expectations and difficulties and trials "to do good for [us] in the end." Oh, if only we would *remember* His intentions, it would help so much! John Bunyan wisely counseled, "Fear, lest, by forgetting what you are by nature, you also forget the need that you have of continual pardon, support, and supplies from the Spirit of grace, and so grow proud of your own abilities, or of what you have received from God."[24] The Lord is so kind to us! We must choose to lean on Him by turning away from sinful pride.

Our continual need to remember all that the Lord has done for us makes the admonition from Psalm 103:2 crucial for us to put into practice: "Bless the LORD, O my soul, and *forget none of His benefits*" (emphasis added). Don't forget *any* of the Lord's blessings. The next few verses of the psalm remind us of some of our benefits. He pardons *all* our sins (v. 3); heals our diseases (v. 3); redeems our life from the pit (v. 4); crowns us with lovingkindness and compassion (v. 4); and satisfies our years with good things, so that our youth is renewed like the eagle (v. 5).

Will we learn from Hezekiah's folly or follow in his ungrateful footsteps? What will our response be the next time we struggle with the unmet expectations in our lives? We always have a choice to make when it comes to dealing with our sin. Remember the Lord's encouragement in 1 Corinthians 10:13: "No temptation has overtaken you but such as is common to man; and God is faithful, who will not allow you to be tempted beyond what you are able, but with the temptation will provide the way of

---

24   John Bunyan, *The Fear of God* (London: The Religious Tract Society, 1839), 94.

escape also, so that you will be able to endure it." The Lord always helps us respond well, if we would only avail ourselves of His help.

A Step-by-Step Guide to Gratitude

Realizing that you need to be thankful doesn't make it any easier to be thankful, does it? *So, what can you do, if you're struggling to be thankful?*

- *Plead with God to make you thankful.* I know it's obvious, but it's the perfect first step. Pastor R. C. Chapman employed this step in his walk too. He said, "The more bitter the cup of discipline, the more reason for our thankfulness. If we be not thankful, let us give God no rest, nor ourselves, until He make us so."[25] We can gain ground on gratitude if we just ask the Lord to build it in us. It is also true that we must keep asking until God supplies our hearts with the needed thankfulness. Genius counsel in its simplicity, but oh so necessary.
- *Put your hope in the Lord, not in your circumstances, and you won't be disappointed.* One of the quickest paths to gain gratitude is to keep our eyes firmly fixed on the Lord. David understood this important measure and wrote of it often in the Psalms. "To You they cried out and were delivered; in You they trusted and were not disappointed" (Ps. 22:5). Psalm 146:5 echoes this encouragement: "How blessed is he whose help is the God of Jacob, whose hope is in the LORD his God." Did you know God finds your hope and trust in Him pleasant? It's true! Psalm 33:18 says, "Behold, the eye of the LORD is on those who fear Him, on those who hope for His lovingkindness." The Lord watches over those who endeavor to hope and trust in Him. Trusting the Lord rather than your circumstances always results in a thankful spirit.
- *Tell yourself the truth about your situation.* Psalm 16:5–6 gets us started on this truth-telling mission. It says, "The LORD is the portion of my inheritance and my cup; You support my lot. The lines have fallen to me in pleasant places; indeed, my heritage is beautiful to me." Just like David, we're guided into a more thankful frame of mind when we remind ourselves that the Lord is the best part of our longed-for "inheritance." Every line marking out our present situation has been carefully chosen by the Lord Himself for our good and blessing, and for His own glory. No wonder David proclaimed his circumstances pleasant and beautiful, which is all the more amazing considering that his life was often in upheaval and less than ideal. If

---

25 Chapman, *Choice Sayings*, 72.

David could tell himself the truth about his circumstances, then we can follow his example and slay the giant of unmet expectations with the stone of gratitude.

- *Give thanks by faith.* George Matheson, a well-known preacher in Scotland from a by-gone era, born with poor eyesight that eventually led to complete blindness, once remarked, "My God, I have never thanked Thee for my 'thorn!' I have thanked Thee a thousand times for my roses, but never once for my 'thorn;' I have been looking forward to a world where I shall get compensation for my cross as itself a present glory. Teach me the glory of my cross; teach me the value of my 'thorn.' Show me that I have climbed to Thee by the path of pain. Show me that my tears have made my rainbow."[26] Whether he was addressing his blindness or not, I'm not sure, but Matheson sought to thank the Lord by faith for the thorn in his life.

- *Thanking the Lord for a painful trial, a currently unmet expectation, or a difficult situation honors the Lord in a unique way and allows us to exercise faith in Him.* Hebrews 11:6 reminds us: "And without faith it is impossible to please Him, for he who comes to God must believe that He is and that He is a rewarder of those who seek Him." As you seek the Lord, entrusting yourself to Him, He rewards you with Himself, with grace, with strength, and with hope. Psalm 27:13–14 focuses on this truth—believing God when everything else in our lives would lead us to despair and unbelief. David wrote, "I would have despaired unless I had believed that I would see the goodness of the LORD in the land of the living. Wait for the LORD; be strong and let your heart take courage; yes, wait for the LORD." Will you trust Him even though your circumstances seem to cry out that God is not doing you good? Will you *choose* to trust His character and thank Him by faith? It takes courage to do so, but this response of trust pleases God. "How great is Your goodness, which You have stored up for those who fear You, which You have wrought for those who take refuge in You, before the sons of men!" (Ps. 31:19).

- *Give God glory through the simple act of thanking Him.* Ten lepers waited outside the village for any mercy a passerby might extend to them. When they saw Jesus and remembered what they had heard about Him, they called out, saying, "Jesus, Master, have mercy on us!" The Bible then records these details: When He saw them, He said to them, "Go and show yourselves to the priests." And as they were going, they were cleansed. Now one of them, when he saw that he had

---

26   George Matheson, *Streams in the Desert*, ed. L. B. Cowman (Grand Rapids, MI: Zondervan Publishing House, 1996), 147.

been healed, turned back, glorifying God with a loud voice, and he fell on his face at His feet, giving thanks to Him. And he was a Samaritan. Then Jesus answered and said, "Were there not ten cleansed? But the nine—where are they? Was no one found who returned to give glory to God, except this foreigner?" And He said to him, "Stand up and go; your faith has made you well" (Luke 17:14–19). Only one of the healed lepers returned to give glory to God by thanking Jesus for curing him. Every believer desires to give God glory. Here we've been given a surefire, easy sneezy way to do that. Thank the Lord, and as you do, give Him glory for what He has done, is doing, and will do in your life, unmet expectations and all. Belshazzar could have followed this tried-and-true method of giving God glory, but he didn't. The Lord had given him life and breath. Yet gratitude to God wasn't on Belshazzar's bucket list. Daniel 5:23b says, "But the God in whose hand are your life-breath and your ways, you have not glorified." May the Lord help us to respond to our unmet expectations like the healed leper, rather than Belshazzar.

Thanking God for His Wisdom

God, in His perfect, fatherly wisdom, doesn't always give us everything we want or think we need. We've all encountered those little ones who want what they want when they want it. If they can't have it, they try to make life as miserable as possible for everyone around them. Generally, there is an ungrateful, petulant, selfish spirit about them. God says in Proverbs 29:15, "The rod and reproof give wisdom, but a child who gets his own way brings shame to his mother." God reminds us that parents who continually cater to their little one's wants and whims without giving direction, guidance, or correction will find themselves shamed by their offspring's self-centered focus. And we know from Proverbs 27:20[27] that a child who often gets his own way, only wants his way *more* often, not less.

When it comes to our own desires, we become like a runaway horse who wants his own way. Trying to rein them in becomes nearly impossible when our appetite cries out for more, more, *more*. That's why our perfectly wise and loving Father doesn't always supply all our wants, hopes, and dreams when we want them. God knows what we often wish He would forget. He knows we would bring shame to Him, if He always gave us everything we prayed for. Can you imagine how petulant and peevish we would be, if we always got our way?

27 Proverbs 27:20, "Sheol and Abaddon are never satisfied, nor are the eyes of man ever satisfied."

Moving from Gratitude in Theory to Practical Thankfulness

How can I grow more thankful when I don't really feel it? What if I'm not thankful for the unmet expectations God has allowed me to have? Those questions get to the crux of the issue. Here are some ways we can practically move toward gratitude, when our lives don't match up to our expectations.

Eight Surefire Ways to Grow More Grateful, No Matter What Your Circumstances

1. *Read, study, and think on the Scriptures.* You will never truly be thankful unless you gain a greater understanding of God. The doctrines of man, sin, and salvation are crucial for all of us to understand because it's only as we understand how incredibly generous God has been with us that we begin to see our circumstances in their right perspective. I would highly recommend Jerry Bridges' timeless classic, *Trusting God,* as an introduction to these truths.

2. *Pay attention to what God is doing.* This proactive approach to thankfulness cultivates an attitude of noticing the big things and the little things God does. Do you remember Psalm 103:2 from earlier in the chapter? Even the smallest things God does, deserve notice and thanks. It's certainly what David had in mind when he penned these words: "Bless the LORD, O my soul, and forget none of His benefits." Pastor R. C. Chapman said, "Mercies reviewed and pondered are even sweeter than when first bestowed."[28] Chapman echoes the psalmist who stated, "Praise the LORD! I will give thanks to the LORD with all my heart, in the company of the upright and in the assembly. Great are the works of the LORD; *they are studied by all who delight in them*" (Ps. 111:1–2, emphasis added).

3. *Pay attention to the attitudes in your heart.* It's really rather simple. If you struggle with a critical spirit, you need to practice *thankfulness.* If you struggle with discouragement or depression, you need to *practice* thankfulness. If you struggle with anxiety, apathy, or anger, you need to *practice thankfulness.* Start by confessing and repenting of your sins and then you can begin to *practice thankfulness.* Without repenting first of your sinful responses, you will never be able to do this.

---

28 Chapman, *Choice Sayings*, 116.

4. *Remember God's promises.* Meditating on the promises of God develops a thankful spirit. The promises of God reveal truths about God's character, which is cause for giving thanks. Notice how Psalm 145:17–19 is full of truths that produce gratitude: "The LORD is righteous in all His ways and kind in all His deeds. The LORD is near to all who call upon Him, to all who call upon Him in truth. He will fulfill the desire of those who fear Him; He will also hear their cry and will save them." Just think, every way, every deed of the Lord rests in His righteousness and kindness. This has tremendous bearing upon your life. Every aspect of your life comes from His righteousness and kindness toward you. Or think on the Lord's nearness to those who call upon Him. Talk to the Lord about your burdens, worries, hurts, or fears. And as you do so, remember that the Lord is always near to those who call upon Him. Such sweetness to consider!

5. *Remember your salvation and heaven too.* Sometimes we need a good dose of the basics to cultivate a thankful spirit, especially when pain and sorrow fill our days. Peter understood the need to think on our salvation and the inheritance that awaits us when everything around us seems gray and full of despair. That's why he exuberantly writes about these truths in 1 Peter 1: God, according to His mercy, has caused us to be born again (v. 3); we have a living hope because of Christ's resurrection (v. 3); we have an inheritance which is imperishable and undefiled and will not fade away, reserved in heaven for us (v. 4); our salvation is protected by God (v. 5); and one day that salvation will be revealed in its fullness (v. 5). And there's more where that came from in 1 Peter! You can also read Revelation 21 and 22 where John eloquently writes about the heavenly city where we will see Jesus face to face! Hopes for that day fill us with gratitude for today.

6. *Trust the Lord to do good for you.* Romans 8:28 has been the "go to" verse for believers through the centuries. Its many truths encourage and strengthen our hearts as we consider that "God causes all things to work together for good to those who love God, to those who are called according to His purpose." Trusting the Lord to bring good out of painful or trying circumstances produces thankfulness in us. Talk to the Lord about any area of difficulty in your life; do so in faith, and thankfully pray through Romans 8:28. Your prayer may look something like this: *Lord, thank You for actively working in my life; thank You for orchestrating*

every detail to bring about good for me; thank You for the assurance that You will bring good out of these difficulties somehow, some way, some day. Amen.

7. *Be thankful by faith.* Showing faith, living by faith, acting in faith is always a good idea. How pleased and blessed the Lord is when His children live in faith (Heb. 11:6; 2 Cor. 4:16–18; 1 Peter 1:6–9). God affirms in Psalm 50:23 that offering a sacrifice of thanksgiving to Him honors Him. Sometimes, our grateful offering feels more full of sacrifice than joy, more barren than abundant. Yet even then, God is glorified in that faith-filled basket of gratitude.

8. *Remember that gratitude must be cultivated.* Gratitude isn't a static thing that we obtain and possess forever. Even the most grateful person today can turn into a Grumpy Gus tomorrow. So, we must recognize its fragile nature and cultivate it. Just look at what we learn about maintaining a spirit of gratitude from the children of Israel:

So their sons entered and possessed the land. And You subdued before them the inhabitants of the land, the Canaanites, and You gave them into their hand, with their kings and the peoples of the land, to do with them as they desired. They captured fortified cities and a fertile land. They took possession of houses full of every good thing, hewn cisterns, vineyards, olive groves, fruit trees in abundance. So they ate, were filled and grew fat, *and reveled in Your great goodness.* But they became disobedient and rebelled against You, and cast Your law behind their backs and killed Your prophets who had admonished them so that they might return to You, and they committed great blasphemies (Neh. 9:24–26, emphasis added).

What a tremendous attitude of heart to consider for ourselves: "Am I reveling in God's great goodness? Are His works so sweet to my heart that joy overflows in my speech and actions? However, the Israelites' praiseworthy response to God's kindness soon turned into a stubborn refusal to trust and obey Him. Fellow pioneer girls, let us learn this lesson in seeking the Lord's help for a grateful heart.

Ingratitude Doesn't Have to Be the End of Your Story

Second Chronicles 32:25 says, "But Hezekiah gave no return for the benefit he received, because his heart was proud; therefore wrath came on him and on Judah and Jerusalem." Thankfully, Hezekiah's story didn't end there. The next verse goes on to say, "However, Hezekiah humbled the pride of his heart, both he and the inhabitants of Jerusalem, so that the wrath of the LORD did not come on them in the days of Hezekiah." Hezekiah's pride got in the way of his gratitude. Yet, when he humbled himself before the Lord for his wrong attitudes, then he was able to proceed to a place of thankfulness.

One woman wisely commented, "You don't realize you have expectations until they're not met." Choosing to thank the Lord catapults us into the realm of trusting in the Lord's good plan for our lives. God wisely and lovingly shifts our plans and stymies our efforts, all for a purpose. He knows it's challenging to be thankful when we are faced with dashed hopes and derailed designs. Yet each unmet expectation comes to us from God's sovereign hand, and presents us with an opportunity to give Him glory by responding in a spirit of gratitude.

John Newton said, "It is indeed natural to us to wish and to plan, and it is merciful in the Lord to disappoint our plans, and to cross our wishes. For we cannot be safe, much less happy, but in proportion as we are weaned from our own wills, and made simply desirous of being directed by His guidance."[29] Psalm 92:4 describes a grateful spirit: "For You, O LORD, have made me glad by what You have done, I will sing for joy at the works of Your hands." My fellow pioneer girl, are you "glad" at what the Lord has done in your life? Are you willing to "sing for joy" at His works in your life?

---

29   John Newton, *The Amazing Works of John Newton*, ed. Harold Chadwick (Alachua, FL: Bridge-Logos, 2009), 158-59.

QUESTIONS for REFLECTION

Chapter 4: Snapshots of an Ungrateful Heart

1. We're instructed in Psalm 103:2 to bless the Lord by remembering His benefits (meaning acts, services, rewards) to us. How many benefits should we remember according to Psalm 103:2? What are some ways you might remember His benefits?

2. What benefits have we received from the Lord according to Psalm 103:3–5?

3. What do you learn about the Lord's character in Psalm 103:6–8? How are those things a *benefit* for which you can thank the Lord?

4. What do you learn about the Lord's forgiveness from Psalm 103:9–12?

5. What does the Lord remember about you according to Psalm 103:13–18? What do you learn about Him from these verses?

6. The psalm ends as it began with encouragements to bless the Lord. How would remembering the Lord's many blessings and kindnesses to us help us overcome any wrong responses we may have toward unmet expectations in our lives?

7. R.C. Chapman, a pastor in nineteenth-century England, asked this: "Look back on the last seven days of your life: how much of thanksgiving and praise has your heart rendered to God?"[30] I would ask, "What kinds of things have you thanked Him for? And even more instructive than the answer to that question is your answer to this one: What things have you *not* thanked Him for? Why do you think that this is?

---

30 Chapman, *Choice Sayings*, 117.

My God, I Thank Thee

My God, I thank Thee, who hast made the earth so bright,
So full of splendor and of joy, beauty and light;
So many glorious things are here, noble and right.

I thank Thee, too, that Thou hast made joy to abound;
So many gentle thoughts and deeds circling us round,
That in the darkest spot of earth some love is found.

I thank Thee more that all our joy is touched with pain,
That shadows fall on brightest hours, that thorns remain;
So that earth's bliss may be our guide, and not our chain.

For thou who knowest, Lord, how soon our weak heart clings,
Hast given us joys, tender and true, yet all with wings;
So that we see gleaming on high diviner things.

I thank Thee, Lord, that Thou hast kept the best in store;
We have enough, yet not too much, so we long for more:
That yearning for a deeper peace not known before.

I thank Thee, Lord, that here our souls though amply blessed,
Can never find, although they seek a perfect rest;
Nor ever shall [find it], until they lean on Jesus' breast. [31]

---

31 Adelaide Proctor, "My God, I Thank Thee," http://www.hymntime.com/tch/htm/m/y/g/mygoditt.
htm.

PART 2: PACKING FOR THE TRAIL

The Pioneers packed their wagons with everything they would need for their new life in the West. Many overloaded their wagons, only to discover that life on the trail necessitated an even greater amount of narrowing down than they had previously thought. Places along the Oregon Trail were littered with the "necessities" that weren't essential for survival. Cluttered biblical thinking can impede our progress. So, we start with indispensable truths in our journey of unmet expectations.

• • • • • • • • • • • • • • • • •

5

The King and
the Traitor

Heaven is not here; it's there. If we were given all we wanted here, our hearts would settle for this world rather than the next. God is forever luring us up and away from this one, wooing us to Himself and His still invisible Kingdom, where we will certainly find what we so keenly long for.
Elisabeth Elliot[32]

If we want proof of God's love for us, then we must look first at the Cross where God offered up His Son as a sacrifice for our sins. Calvary is the one objective, absolute, irrefutable proof of God's love for us.
Jerry Bridges[33]

32   Elisabeth Elliot, *Keep a Quiet Heart* (Grand Rapids: Revell, 2004), 28.
33   Jerry Bridges, *Trusting God* (Colorado Springs, CO: NavPress, 1988), 138.

A temporary living arrangement is so different than a real-life, more permanent one! When my husband was called to pastor a church in Louisville, Kentucky, we decided to rent an apartment for a short while in order to focus on getting to know the people at our church without the distraction of setting up house. We also wanted to get to know the Louisville area better so we could make a more informed decision about where to eventually look for a home. With those two goals in mind, our moving, which had already taken a lot of mental planning and preparation, grew to Goliath-sized proportions as we considered which items were needed for living in our small apartment for a few months. Choosing what to keep and what to pack away meant engaging in bare-minimum, survival-mode thinking. What did we *absolutely need* for a few months? And conversely, what could we *live without* for a few months, even up to half a year?

There's something helpful and soul-simplifying in getting things narrowed down to the essentials. In this section, bottom-line thinking is the name of the game when it comes to gaining a right perspective on our unmet expectations. In previous chapters, we've looked at problems that can arise when life is different than we thought it would be. We discussed the pitfalls of expectations and how they can become stumbling blocks if we don't recognize discontentment in our hearts. And then we started to look at ways to combat our discontentment.

Notice I said "started" battling discontentment, for our flesh is a wily opponent, well able to parry our death blows. When we don't like how things are turning out in our lives, we complain or rage or grow morose—all fancy terms that say we're discontent. Yet the tide turns in our battle with our flesh when we respond with gratitude to the Lord. A thankful heart says, "I trust you, Lord." It also says, "Your will, not mine, be done." That thankful heart says, "Lord, I may not understand *why*. But I know You are good and wise in all Your ways. So, thank You for what You have given."

Gratitude—Our Soul's Immunization

Gratitude is the antidote to the poison of discontentment. Understanding that truth gets us on the right track to overcoming the battles we have with discontentment. In many ways, gratitude is like that little mom-and-pop corner grocery store that stocks all the basics. The grocery store staples we find at Grateful Grocery keep us going. Yet there are times when we need some specialty items mom and pop don't sell at their little corner grocery. That's when we travel to the big city and trolley up and down the aisles of "MegaMart" to find everything else we might ever need. Having shopped the basics at mom-and-pop's corner grocery in the previous chapters, the rest of this book is MegaMart for us. There are specialty ingredients and supplies in the coming chapters to fill our soul-pantries with what we need to live life well for God's glory. God trains our hearts in a variety of ways and means, and our foray into unmet expectations is no exception. Hence our trip to shop for those specialty items at MegaMart!

Survival-Mode Living

In the upcoming chapters, we're going to tweak our attitudes and find help for our responses to unmet expectations by poring over God's Word. Yet, before we do that, we need to make sure our minds are packed with the truths tucked away in our "don't-leave-home-without-it" survival-mode backpack. Our backpack needs to be stocked with the essentials that will enable us to give God glory, even when our journey includes the unexpected.

During the course of everyday life, my purse contains those items I need for running errands and doing ministry—a wallet, cell phone, gum, keys, lipstick, floss, and that's pretty much it. But when I travel, I fill my handy-dandy backpack with a few more helpful items for life away from home. I take my Bible and my laptop, charging cables for my electronic gadgets, toothpicks and bobby pins, snacks, medicine, throat lozenges, tea, and a toothbrush, along with a change of underthings. Having traveled by air a fair bit in recent years, I've found that these items make all the difference to "surviving" the unexpected when flying. Not only are my backpack items helpful for traveling, but I continue to use them when I get home. Why? Because those narrowed-down, survive-while-traveling items are needed for my everyday life at home too.

When battling unmet expectations, we need to fill our *mental* backpack with truths *essential* for responding well and giving God glory. Survival-mode truths help us stand firm when our lives and circumstances are different than we thought. Though we may add more items to our survival-mode-thinking backpack, we must ensure that we take along the most important ones. Filling our minds with solid, biblical truths will comfort and strengthen us when we encounter the unexpected.

By this point in your reading, you may have identified some areas, or potential areas, of unmet expectations. You may have also identified some sinful fruit in your life that needs to be plucked from the tree through repentance. You may have also discovered tiny seeds of discontentment springing up in your heart that need your attention because large or small, sin is still sin.

What We Think Matters

Sinful responses indicate that somehow, in some way, we're not thinking rightly about God, ourselves, or our circumstances. When we struggle with unmet expectations, no matter what they are, we can be assured that some of our underlying thoughts aren't entirely biblical. It's important we understand that whether our thoughts are off just a smidge or a mile, whenever we *struggle* (which is a nice way of saying, "have a sinful response") with unmet expectations, it is because of problematic thinking.

This is huge! When we see little struggles deep in our hearts or give way to overtly sinful responses, we know we're thinking wrongly somewhere and to some degree. In that moment, we can say with complete confidence that we aren't thinking correctly about the Lord, our circumstances, or other people. It may encourage you to know that this happens to everyone. Let's look at the first part of 1 Corinthians 10:13: "No temptation has overtaken you but such as is common to man. . ." All of us fall prey to wrong thinking at times. Yet the Lord is ever ready to help us! He will provide a way of escape from our temptation to think wrongly about things. Just read the remainder of 1 Corinthians 10:13: "And God is faithful, who will not allow you to be tempted beyond what you are able, but with the temptation will provide the way of escape also, so that you will be able to endure it." We're all in this together. And, more importantly, God is in it with us to strengthen and help us. It's when we look to sources other than God to satisfy our souls that we run into trouble.

D. A. Carson has said, "One of the major causes of devastating grief and confusion among Christians is that our expectations are false. We do not give the subject of evil and suffering the thought it deserves until we ourselves are confronted with tragedy. If by that point our beliefs—not well thought out, but deeply ingrained—are largely out of step with the God who has disclosed Himself in the Bible and supremely in Jesus, then the pain from the personal tragedy may be multiplied many times over as we begin to question the very foundations of our faith."[34] Carson is simply saying that if we're not careful to align our thoughts with biblical truths about God and His ways, then our faith will suffer.

---

34   D. A. Carson, *How Long, O Lord? Reflections on Suffering and Evil* (Grand Rapids, MI: Baker Academic, 1990, 2006), 11-12.

Some Clues That Show We May Not Be Thinking Biblically

The key to a strong and vibrant faith is to make sure that we are scripturally sound in our thinking, even when encountering unmet expectations, trials, grief, and confusion. Yet, sometimes, it can take us a while to realize that we're not thinking rightly. Pain and grief can cloud our judgment, so that we aren't immediately aware of our unbiblical thoughts.

Here is a little test we can apply to our thinking. If we hear ourselves say or think things like the following, then we know we're in danger of being "out of step with the God who has disclosed Himself in the Bible" as Carson says above.

- I don't deserve this.
- God doesn't care what happens to me.
- That's the last straw!
- I can't be expected to put up with this anymore.
- It's not my fault.
- God doesn't know what's happening to me.
- I have it all worked out in the best way.
- God doesn't love me because if He did, He would. . .
- Or anything in a similar vein to the above.

It has been said that every sin we commit can be traced back to a wrong view of God. If that's the case—and it is—then we need to build a foundation of right thinking about God's work in our lives, so that we don't respond sinfully.

Bottom-Line Thinking #1

Bottom-line thinking works for me. I find it a useful way of removing anything extraneous and superfluous in my thoughts by starting with the most biblically helpful ones. Getting back to the basics helps me consider, "What do I need to meditate on that will get me back on the path of right thinking?"

I've come up with four non-negotiable, don't-leave-home-without-it, foundational truths from the Scriptures we must be sure to live on. The first one effectively levels the playing field. So, without further ado, here it is: *I am a sinner and I don't receive what I deserve.* Now you might be saying, "Huh? I was expecting something a bit more encouraging. How is being told I'm a sinner helpful?" My fellow pioneer girls, this one truth alone can quickly correct any deviations in our thinking, keep us from veering off track, and heal many of the wounds in our hearts.

I'm a Sinner; You're a Sinner

Some people don't like the idea of wearing the label *sinner*. They might agree to it in theory, applying it to everyone else, while not accepting it for themselves. Yet, if we're going to get anywhere in overcoming our struggle with unmet expectations, we must come to terms with this truth. My husband explains sin in this way: "Sin is anything we do in thought or deed that departs in any degree from God's perfect, revealed will." Well, that makes me a sinner, for sure. God's revealed will in His Word tells me I'm not to lie, (um, I've done that); it tells me not to fear or be anxious (yikes, I've done that too); it reminds me that if I've been angry, I am akin to a murderer, for anger is simply murder in its infancy (guilty again).

Every one of us is a sinner, plain and simple. As Yoda would say, "Hmm. . .perfect, we are not." We've all sinned, which means we are in dire need of a Savior. Let's test this right now. Think of a time when you sinned, something like, when you lost your temper or gossiped, or literally lusted over that chocolate fudge cupcake with salted caramel buttercream frosting. I'm not kidding. It happens! Now, mentally hold onto that particular sin. Don't worry about any others that may come to mind. Just mentally hold onto that one.

Our Sin Has Consequences

Even one sin of rebellion against God causes trouble for us. Romans 6:23 tells us that "the wages of sin is death." Unlike the fiction the world creates about death, the Bible is clear about the kind of death we earn for ourselves with just one sin. We learn that death is separation from God (Eph. 4:18; Col. 1:21), a place of eternal torment and pain (Matt. 13:41–42; Rev. 20:10), a place of fiery judgment (Matt. 5:22; 18:9), and a place of destruction and darkness (John 3:19–20; 2 Thess. 1:9; 2 Peter 3:7) where the fire is never quenched (Mark 9:43–48). My husband, Jack, has said, "Hell is far worse than any words mere mortals can use to describe it." Our sin has consequences of eternal proportions.

It began simply enough. God created a perfectly glorious world, full of wonder and variety beyond imagination. Into that world He placed the first people, Adam and Eve. Now, as Creator, Author, and Completer of all things, God gets to make the rules for His world and its inhabitants. God told Adam not to eat of the tree of the knowledge of good and evil (Gen. 2:17; 3:1). And then, the unimaginable happened. The created ones turned their hearts away from their loving Creator, sinning against Him in the process. They had been warned that defying God's command would usher in death. But still they rebelled because they thought they were missing out. They were discontent with God's way, and they thought they knew better than God. Oh my! This seems so much like my own heart's reasoning when I sin. Mankind's rebellion hasn't changed since Adam and Eve fell in the garden.

Though death entered the perfect world God had created, He lovingly spared His created ones from instantaneous destruction. *Though they had sinned against God's clearly communicated command, and experienced consequences for their sin, they still didn't receive what they really deserved from God.*

And neither have we.

Wondrously Experiencing God's Mercy

Romans 6:23 reminds us we all deserve death if we've committed even *one* sin. Yet we've committed innumerable sins. Amazingly, in spite of our many and ongoing sins, we're still living and breathing, enjoying the blessings of this earth, such as sunshine, fresh fruit, changing seasons, the laughter of little children, family, friends. Even more astounding is that *everyone* enjoys these blessings, whether they call God their Father or not. The Lord shows mercy to *all*. The sun shines and the rain falls on the just and the unjust. The first time I sinned, I should have died and faced the consequences of my sin. But God, in His mercy, withheld the death I had earned for myself. That's why our first stop in bottom-line thinking is *"I am a sinner and I am not receiving what I deserve."*

The fact that we are still alive, breathing, and enjoying the blessings of this world speaks to the infinite mercy we receive from God. Even more wondrous is the fact that God extends a greater mercy toward us for an express purpose. As my husband often says, "If sin has no consequences, then there is no need for a Savior." Romans 2:4 tells us that God's kindness, tolerance, and patience have always been intended *to lead us to repentance*.

Ephesians 2:1–3 reveals to us that we are in a sorry state; we are spiritually dead and children of wrath. We need help and rescue! As sinners living under the peril of God's righteous and holy judgment, we cannot help ourselves. That's why the words of Ephesians 2:4–9 should melt our hearts:

> But God, being rich in mercy, because of His great love with which He loved us, even *when we were dead in our transgressions*, made us alive together with Christ (by grace you have been saved), and raised us up with Him, and seated us with Him in the heavenly places in Christ

Jesus, so that in the ages to come He might show the surpassing riches of His grace in kindness toward us in Christ Jesus. *For by grace you have been saved through faith*; and that not of yourselves, it is the gift of God; not as a result of works, so that no one may boast (Eph. 2:8, emphasis added).

By nature, we are dead in sin. We hate God and indulge ourselves in sin. We truly deserve death. And yet God, out of infinite love, has chosen to do good to us. Even as unbelievers with no chance of ever pleasing Him or knowing Him, God has made it possible for us to escape judgment through the One and Only Savior, Jesus Christ. By turning to Christ in faith and repenting of our independence and rebellion against God, we can be forgiven through Jesus Christ. Our salvation is complete and perfect because of Jesus alone. No works or efforts of our own can help us gain salvation. Salvation is only through Jesus Christ.

My husband commented on the mercy of God in a sermon on Titus 3:4: "If you watch or read science fiction, there are those times when a forcefield is turned on to protect the ship or the city from attack. God's lovingkindness is a force field that keeps His own justice from attacking the sinner."[35] The bottom line? *I am a sinner and I am most certainly not receiving what I deserve.* In fact, I've been given life! Eternal, abundant, satisfying life! "Amazing love, how can it be that Thou, my God, shouldst die for me!"[36]

Adding Balance to an Unbalanced View of Our Circumstances

Maurice Roberts has stated: "A man's theology always determines his view of providence."[37] Simply put, our doctrine, that is, our understanding of God and His ways, *affects our response* to our circumstances. Charles Spurgeon insightfully remarked, "Just get one small error into your minds, get one small evil into your thoughts, commit one small act of sin in your life, permit these things to be handled, and fondled, favored, petted, and treated with respect, and you cannot tell what they may grow into. They are small in their infancy: they will be giants when they come to their full growth. You little know how near your soul may be to destruction, when you indiscriminately indulge in the smallest act of sin!"[38] What wise

35   Jack Hughes, in his sermon titled, "God's Kindness Offers You Salvation!" on Titus 3:4. You can contact www.drivennails.com if you'd like more information on the sermon.

36   Charles Wesley, "And Can It Be That I Should Gain?" *Hymns for the Family of God* (Nashville, TN: Paragon Associates, Inc., 1976), 260.

37   Maurice Roberts, *The Thought of God* (Edinburgh: The Banner of Truth Trust, 1993), 34.

38   C. H. Spurgeon, "Little Sins" in *The New Park Street Pulpit Sermons*, vol. 5 (London: Passmore & Alabaster, 1859), 187.

words! Spurgeon is right in stating that unbiblical thinking, if left unchecked, can lead to further and greater sin.

Why We Need to Be Reminded of These Truths

If we're not truly biblical in our understanding of God, then, of course, it's going to show up in our lives. We might respond with fear, lack of trust, or anger, if we think God doesn't care about the details of our lives. Even a simple misunderstanding of the gift of salvation can morph into a sinful attitude, affecting how we respond to our circumstances and causing us to think that somehow God is indebted to us. A stubborn, hard-hearted spirit toward the Lord reveals that we haven't submitted to His majesty and kingly right to govern our lives. *How we think matters*. A foundation of thinking must be laid that is biblically correct concerning ourselves, our circumstances, our hopes, and even our trials, if we want to give God the glory.

The truth is we often feel that God has somehow got it wrong when things in our lives don't match our plans. We may be tempted to wonder if God needs more information from us, so He'll change things for our good. We are completely forgetting that God is *always* good in everything He does. He's *always* faultless in His wisdom. He judges and puts into place the details of our lives *perfectly*. Jerry Bridges writes: "We must see our circumstances through God's love instead of, as we are prone to do, seeing God's love through our circumstances."[39] Simple truths, yet they are groundbreaking in their ability to define and shape how we live and respond to the Lord's work in us.

Jerry Bridges hit the nail on the head when he discerned that we interpret God's love for us through our circumstances. All too often, we consider the difficulties, hurts, and frustrations in our lives as an indication that God doesn't love us. We think that if He did truly love us, then He would allow us to have everything we want, the way we want it, when we want it! That certainly wouldn't be good for us. Jerry Bridges helpfully counsels us again, when he says, "Anytime we are tempted to doubt God's love for us, we should go back to the Cross."[40]

All the good that unbelievers will ever experience is given to them here on earth. For believers, all the bad we will ever experience occurs here—in this life only. Understanding the powerful truth summed up in *"I'm a sinner and I'm not receiving what I deserve"* helps us balance our thinking when we feel that we deserve better than what we're experiencing. God's

39 Bridges, *Trusting God*, 149.
40 Ibid., 140.

great grace and our complete unworthiness are the bottom-line thinking we all need to enable us to assess our circumstances from God's point of view.

My husband told this story as an illustration of God's incredible mercy. It fits perfectly with what we've been discussing in this chapter:

> Let's say you commit treason against your king. You are caught, tried, and found guilty. The king, being kind and merciful, decides not to have you beheaded right away, but chooses to stay your execution and offer you pardon.
>
> As all in the king's court look on, you say in boldness, 'King, I understand I deserve swift execution for committing treason, but I would prefer to wait and commit treason against you a while longer, and then, after I have worn out my days trying to overthrow your rule, then on my death bed, I would like to have the mercy you now offer me and the pardon that comes with it.'
>
> *What do you think would be the chances of that kind and merciful king granting that traitor his request?* Surely, the man will die for his crimes. Without mercy, justice will have its day. This is the exact position of every unconverted person in the world. God extends loving-kindness and mercy to them, every moment of every day.[41]

"I'm a sinner and I have never received what I deserve" humbles our hearts so we can learn what God wants to teach us.

---

41 Jack Hughes, from a sermon titled, "What Grace Teaches Us to Deny" from Titus 2:12. You can contact www.drivennails.com if you'd like more information on the sermon.

QUESTIONS for REFLECTION

Chapter 5: The King and the Traitor

1. Responding in a God-glorifying way to the unmet expectations in our lives means first coming to terms with our complete lack of rights or privileges. Clinging to a sense that we deserve something better impedes our growth in grace. We are to live a life given to God, completely subject to Him. He calls the shots because it is His right and privilege to do so, not ours. Getting that firmly fixed in our heads is the order of the day if we're going to gain traction against our grumpy, fussy, little pity-party selves. What foundational truth does Ephesians 2:1 establish for us?

2. Why does Paul say people are dead in Ephesians 2:1? See Genesis 2:17; John 5:24; and Romans 5:12; 6:23.

3. What are people doing in their deadness according to Ephesians 2:2–3? According to verse 3, what will be the outcome of that way of living for those who die unconverted?

4. What hope is there for a spiritually dead person, deserving only God's wrath? What did God do for us according to Ephesians 2:4–5?

5. What motivated God to respond in grace toward those who believe? See Ephesians 2:4. What things did they do to "catch God's eye" in order to receive His grace? Review verses 1–5 for your answer.

6. Spiritually dead people can't respond or do anything. But God's children see the active and continual working of God on their behalf. List the things He has done. See verses 5–7.

7. How did believers move from spiritual deadness to life? See verses 8–9.

8. Read 2 Corinthians 5:14–15 and consider the debt believers owe their great God. How should the truths in 2 Corinthians 5:14–15 and Ephesians 2:1–9 shape their thinking and their responses when life turns out differently than they expected?

*Every sin deserves God's wrath and curse,
both in this life and that which is to come.*[42]
Westminster Shorter Catechism, Q. 84

*In our fluctuations of feeling, it is well to remember that Jesus admits no
change in His affections; your heart is not the compass Jesus sails by.*[43]
Samuel Rutherford

42 Westminster Shorter Catechism "Sin," *Dictionary of Burning Words*, ed. Josiah H. Gilbert (New York: Wilbur B. Ketcham Publishers, 1895), 551.
43 Ibid., 93.

6

The Downside of
Keeping Score

Thou hast done for me all things well,
hast remembered,
distinguished,
indulged me.
All my desires have not been gratified,
but Thy love denied them to me
when fulfillment of my wishes would have proved my ruin or injury.
My trials have been fewer than my sins,
and when I have kissed the rod it has fallen from Thy hands.
Thou hast often wiped away my tears,
restored peace to my mourning heart,
chastened me for my profit.
All Thy work for me is perfect, and I praise Thee.[44]

44   *The Valley of Vision: A Collection of Puritan Prayers and Devotions*, ed. Arthur Bennett (Edinburgh: The Banner of Truth Trust, 1999), 105.

Margaret Thatcher once famously remarked, "I'm extraordinarily patient, provided I get my own way in the end."[45] That quote makes me smile, and I'd like to let Margaret Thatcher own it. But I must confess it's true of me too. It's probably true of most of us, which raises a question that begs to be asked, "What happens if, or when, you *don't get your own way in the end*? What then?" Most likely, the answer would be that it depends on what you're looking for. If all you're looking for is to get your own way in the end, then a life of responses like Margaret Thatcher's will probably do. But, if you want something more, such as a response that gives glory to God, then this chapter is for you. We will look at the next item to be packed in our don't-leave-home-without-it, survival-mode-thinking backpack. What a name! But every syllable is essential.

Speaking of survival-mode thinking, Psalm 73 contains some valuable pointers as we forge ahead into the realm of unmet expectations. In verses 1–3, the psalmist, Asaph, confesses his struggles with envy and bitterness when he sees the wicked prospering. In verse 1, he states his fundamental premise that "God is good to Israel, to those who are pure in heart!" Nothing wrong with that expectation at all! It is absolutely true; God truly *is* good to Israel and to those who are pure in heart.

For Asaph, the trouble came when he noticed the blessing and favor the arrogant and wicked enjoyed. That didn't seem to add up to what he thought he knew of God's character. His expectation of how things should proceed in life wasn't matching up to what he was observing.

Apparently, it got to be "a thing" for him, so much so, that he admits in verses 2–3, "But as for me, my feet came close to stumbling, my steps had almost slipped. For I was envious of the arrogant as I saw the prosperity of the wicked." Asaph knew he was in a spiritual danger zone when he realized that "[his] feet came close to stumbling, [his] steps had almost slipped."

Later, he explained his struggles and disillusionment in verses 13–14 when he murmured, "Surely in vain I have kept my heart pure and washed my hands in innocence. For I have been stricken all day long and chastened every morning." However, the temptation to continue in that downward spiral was checked when he considered how his embittered attitudes would affect the faith of others. He confided in verse 15, "If I had said, 'I will speak thus,' Behold, I would have betrayed the generation of Your children." He realized that his sour attitudes would have been a bad example for those watching his life.

Asaph was at a crossroad of unmet expectations. He had a choice to make and he knew it. Would he continue down the road of envy and

45 Quoted from a March 1982 European Council meeting.

bitterness? Or would he cling to the bedrock truths of God's character, while entrusting the *seemingly* unjust details of his trying circumstances to God? It was time for Asaph to engage in survival-mode thinking. The same get-to-the-bottom-of-it kind of thinking protects us when our feet come close to stumbling and almost slip when our own expectations aren't met (Ps. 73:2).

What Theology Guides Our Hearts?

The essence of our heart's theology is *how we think about God when circumstances are different than we expected*. We saw Asaph's heart theology in Psalm 73 as he struggled to understand God's kindness toward the wicked. Naomi's heart theology was on display in the book of Ruth shortly after her daughters-in-law, Ruth and Orpah, were suddenly widowed. Naomi's own unmet expectations colored her view of God so that she saw every circumstance, every so-called setback, as proof that God had turned against her (Ruth 1:13; 2:20–21).

After experiencing devastating trials, Job's wife responded similarly in Job 2:9 when she told Job he should just curse God and die because it wasn't worth trusting God any longer. Proverbs 19:3 says, "The foolishness of man ruins his way, and his heart rages against the LORD." Man gets himself into trouble and then gets angry at God. Those pesky unmet expectations strike again! But, as we have learned, unmet expectations aren't the problem. When we don't get our own way, it is our unbiblical way of thinking that is the trouble!

Anchoring our thoughts upon a biblical view of our circumstances enables us to joyfully submit to God's plan. It's humbling to realize that our sinful responses to our unmet expectations reveal the true condition of our hearts. Unlike any other time in our lives, it's when we're *not receiving* whatever it is that we think we need or deserve that the theology of our hearts is lit up like a billboard on Route 66 in the middle of the Mojave Desert.

Even the most mature of saints succumb at times to a doctrinal disparity between their hearts and their heads. We'll all find ourselves at this place of theological discrepancy at some point. We know the *biblical* thing to do, the *God-glorifying* way to respond, the *right* way to think, but our hearts stubbornly insist on seeking their own desire. Survival-mode thinking, that is, counseling ourselves with bottom-line thinking from the Scriptures, helps us respond with the truths we know from God's Word.

Jeremiah's survival-mode thinking was on display when he penned Lamentations 3:39: "Why should any living mortal, or any man, offer complaint in view of his sins?" Jeremiah counsels himself—and us—by eliminating our sense of entitlement, by reminding us of the debt we owe God, though we can never repay it. He helps us understand who we are in relation to God. In the last chapter, we looked at the oh-so-necessary truth that God has mercifully withheld the judgment we deserve as sinners who have defied our Creator, not once, but many times every day. Jeremiah's perceptive question is another brick in building a foundation of right thinking. *Who of us can complain about our circumstances when we consider our numerous sins?*

Let's continue to shop for the next item to stock our "don't-leave-home-without-it" bag.

One of the Few Times It's Good to Compare

Most of the time, it's not a good idea to engage in the comparison game. But the next item we need to add to our "don't-leave-home-without-it" bag requires us to make a comparison. Consider this statement: *My trials are fewer than my sins.*[46] This was coined by one of the Puritan writers included in Arthur Bennett's book *The Valley of Vision*. I've latched onto the expression "my trials are fewer than my sins" because it aptly summarizes the kind of thinking we need to have about our circumstances, especially when we don't get our own way.

"My trials are fewer than my sins" instantly invites us to compare the number of our sins with the number of our trials. It gently helps us realize that what we're experiencing is still far less than what we deserve, no matter how difficult or drastic our situation may seem to be. When we find ourselves complaining about our circumstances, we need to remind ourselves again of the first stage of our survival-mode thinking: "I'm a sinner, not receiving what I deserve." We need to add to that the notion that "my trials are fewer than my sins."

Psalm 103:10 says something similar: "He has not dealt with us according to our sins, nor rewarded us according to our iniquities." Meditating on this truth develops humility and gratitude in place of attitudes of entitlement, anger, bitterness, or whatever else we've conjured up. God hasn't dealt with us according to our sins. If He did, we would be in hell—even if we had only committed *one* sin. Think about that! James says, "For whoever keeps the whole law and yet stumbles in one point, he has become guilty of all" (2:10).

We get so bent out of shape thinking about how we *should be treated*, that we don't see things as they really are. We certainly don't see the riches

46 *The Valley of Vision*, 105.

of God's mercy and grace, which He has showered upon us—things like family, friends, sunshine, rain, the changing of the seasons, mountains, music, art, sunsets, little children, salvation in Jesus Christ. *If there were any way that the Lord has not dealt with us as we deserve, it's His saving us by His grace.*

Remember Ephesians 2:1–3[47] instructs us that we were God's enemies; we hated Him. Yet, even in the midst of our hating and rejecting God, He didn't stop intervening in our lives and drawing us to Himself. Why? Because Ephesians 2:4 tells us that God is *rich in mercy* and full of love toward us, *even when* we weren't looking or wanting to please Him.

His Mercies Never End

Even after the Lord mercifully and amazingly saves us and gives us all we need to obey Him, we continue to sin against Him. *How many times have you sinned against the Lord since He transferred you into the kingdom of His dear Son?* For me, there have been far too many times to count when I have stumbled into sin, purposely chosen my own way, or rebelliously hardened my heart against His will. Yet, even in this, the Lord has not dealt with me according to my sins. What are some of the ways God has shown mercy and kindness to you, even when you knew you deserved a "spanking" from the Lord?

When I compare my trials to my sins, it's easy to see how good and merciful the Lord has been to me. He certainly hasn't treated me as my sins deserve. Even if I am experiencing trials and unmet expectations, they are still far fewer in number than the many sins I have committed against the Lord. Though I may prefer to be in different circumstances, it goes without saying that God has shown incredible mercy to me.

What if the Lord Kept a Balance Sheet?

Mene, mene, tekel upharsin (Dan. 5:25). Daniel read those words to King Belshazzar after God's finger wrote them on the wall. The words meant that Belshazzar's kingdom would soon come to an end because God had weighed him and found him wanting. Talk about an awkward moment at a drinking party! The words on the wall struck fear into Belshazzar's heart. There's not one of us who feels comfortable when our offenses are put on display. We feel so incredibly naked and ashamed.

---

47 Ephesians 2:1-3: "And you were dead in your trespasses and sins, in which you formerly walked according to the course of this world, according to the prince of the power of the air, of the spirit that is now working in the sons of disobedience. Among them we too all formerly lived in the lusts of our flesh, indulging the desires of the flesh and of the mind, and were by nature children of wrath, even as the rest."

As believers, we count on the fact that Christ's perfect sacrifice has taken away all our sin, so that there is no longer a need for our sins and lawless deeds to be trotted out for all to see. None of that awful, naked feeling. But just think for a moment what it would be like for us if the Lord did indeed mete out a trial every time we sinned. *You sin? You get a trial. Sinned again? Trial. Sin. Trial. Sin, sin, sin—trial, trial, trial.* Our days would be filled with fear, dread, and shame. There would be no escape from trials, for we sin at least once every day (though that's a conservative estimate). Consider this amazing truth that, even if God did measure out our trials in relation to our sins, the number of our trials would still be far fewer than we deserve.

Think about what that means: I am a sinner. I deserve death. Even after experiencing new life in Jesus Christ, I still sin constantly, offending my Savior. But He hasn't dealt with me as my sins deserve; He hasn't rewarded me with punishment. Instead, He pardons my sin and passes over my rebellious acts. No matter how difficult, painful, frequent, or great my trials, they are still fewer in number than the sins I have committed against the One who gave His life for me.

Comfortable truths? No. *Essential*, survival-mode thinking? Absolutely.

Fifteen-Hundred Ways Truth Helps Us Think Rightly

All right, maybe not fifteen-hundred ways, but close! That's why it is essential to ask, "How does the simple little statement 'my trials are fewer than my sins' bring balance to my thoughts and responses when life turns out differently than I expected?" First, it removes the sense of entitlement that we deserve something different or have somehow earned better treatment than we are receiving. Second, it humbles our hearts by reminding us that God is the great King, who reigns over His kingdom—and us—with perfect wisdom and righteousness. Third, it reminds us to live humbly and gratefully before God, who has been so kind to us. And fourth, it is just the thing we need to change our hearts' theology.

Have you ever stood on the beach only to be knocked over by a wave you didn't see coming? And then, when you tried to get up, another one crashed right on top of you, keeping you flat on the sand? Finally, as the wave washed back out, did you struggle to stand, coughing up seawater, pushing hair away from your eyes, feeling bedraggled and in need of help, only to have another wave rush in and knock you over again? Well, it's a treat, let me tell you.

You may never have experienced the particular joy of being turned into a burrito for Poseidon. It's probably more likely that you have experienced its spiritual counterpart: wave after wave of trials coming upon you, to the point that you wonder if you'll ever find your way to safety and comfort again. I've had seasons like that and most likely will have them again. During one particularly heart-numbing time of testing, our daughter had an unrelenting headache, our son injured his knee, my husband's mother passed away, our brakes went out on the freeway causing us to plow into the back of another vehicle, totaling our van, and Jack badly injured his shoulder in a bike riding accident. I remember feeling knocked down and bedraggled spiritually. Yet, even then, God's wisdom was never in question. We knew the continuous barrage of trials produced gold in our souls that wouldn't have been formed any other way.

Counseling Ourselves or Unpacking Our Survival-Mode-Thinking Backpack

Imagine you receive a nice, actually, *really* nice, blouse from your Aunt Greta for your birthday. You wear it once and throw it in the wash. Then, to your utter dismay, while it's spinning in the wash cycle, it comes into contact with the pen your husband forgot to take out of his pocket. Splotches of ink adorn your lovely blouse. How do you respond? Do you yell at your husband, cry, or turn into a grumbly mess for the rest of the day, all because the circumstances in which you find yourself aren't what you expected? Are your circumstances disappointing? Absolutely. You know the ink-stained blouse isn't a huge trial. But it bothers you just the same, to the point that everything feels awful! You find yourself grumbling, "Lord! You know how much I love this blouse! Why didn't You prevent it from getting ruined?"

This is the time to start rummaging through our survival-mode-thinking backpack and finding what we need to counsel ourselves through our unbiblical expectation. Our hearts might murmur, "I thought I would enjoy my new blouse for a long time. I'm so disappointed I only got to wear it once. Now, I have to try to get the ink stains out, which are notoriously difficult to remove."

You wisely reply back to yourself, "Yes, I am experiencing disappointment and frustration. Yes, there are difficulties I have to deal with in this situation. But my trials, if you can call the addition of this pint-sized episode by that name, are still far fewer than my sins. In fact, I've already committed many sins, but have only faced one trial."

Your biblical counsel rises to the surface so that you're willing to submit your circumstances, desires, and even your expectations to God's good and perfect will. "Lord, I know you know what is best for me and that, in your wisdom, you have allowed this difficulty to come about for my good. I don't understand how my blouse being ruined is helpful to my spiritual growth, but You do. Lord, how I respond to the roadblocks and upsetting circumstances in my life is more important than my blouse. Father, would You enable me to have a cheerful spirit no matter what the outcome, to trust you in the process, leaning on You for grace to respond well? Thank you, Lord, that my trials are far fewer than my sins. Thank you for reminding me that You are God, and I am not."

"Blouses, shmouses," you might exclaim. "What if my situation isn't that simple?" Yes, what do we do when we find ourselves face to face with heart-wrenchingly personal and painful unmet expectations? Survival-mode thinking still applies—and works—whether we're dealing with inconvenient things like spilt milk or heart-shattering things like miscarriage or debilitating illness. Could it be that you lost your job and have been out of work for two years? Or your husband left you for your best friend? Or there seems to be no end to your years as a single? Or your siblings have conspired against you in dividing up your parents' estate? Any one of those scenarios is laden with sorrow and dashed expectations. Those are the times to counsel yourself with the truths of God's Word.

Back to Asaph and His Unmet Expectations

Remember Asaph in Psalm 73? We left him hanging at the beginning of the chapter, languishing under the weight of his unmet expectations. Thankfully, though he faced initial struggles, he did work through them and came to realize the kindness God continued to show him. His gaining the right perspective serves as an example for us, as we seek to correct the responses of our hearts. Look at what he said in Psalm 73:21–22: "When my heart was embittered and I was pierced within, then I was senseless and ignorant; I was like a beast before You." He saw his responses as God saw them. "I was so bitter because of my circumstances that I really wasn't thinking, and then, when I did think, it was uninformed and instinctive rather than biblical."

You might wonder why God continues to be patient with us when we respond like that. Asaph surely expected God to turn His back on him. But God is not a man, nor does He respond like a man. Asaph marveled, saying, "*Nevertheless* I am continually with You; You have taken hold of my right hand. With Your counsel You will guide me, and afterward receive me to glory" (Ps. 73:23–24, emphasis added). Such is the remarkable kindness of God to His children. He doesn't abandon us. Amazingly, He actively engages with us *when we are at our worst* and takes hold of us.

Within God's grip is fatherly counsel that guides all the way to heaven. Oh yes, my trials are far fewer than my sins.

Dr. Martyn Lloyd-Jones teaches us the art of counseling ourselves. We'll spend more time on this topic later. But, for now, let's glean from his wisdom:

> The main art in the matter of spiritual living is to know how to handle yourself. You have to take yourself in hand, you have to address yourself, preach to yourself, question yourself. You must say to your soul: "Why art thou cast down"– what business have you to be disquieted?
>
> You must turn on yourself, upbraid yourself, condemn yourself, exhort yourself, and say to yourself: "Hope thou in God"– instead of muttering in this depressed, unhappy way. And then you must go on to remind yourself of God, who God is, and what God is and what God has done, and what God has pledged Himself to do.
>
> Then having done that, end on this great note: defy yourself, and defy other people, and defy the devil and the whole world, and say with this man: "I shall yet praise Him for the help of His countenance, who is also the health of my countenance and my God."[48]

It is easy to see how helpful Dr. Lloyd-Jones' advice is while we search through our survival-mode-thinking backpack. He's placed his "exhort yourself" counsel on top of all our gear, where it waits neatly folded for us to shake it out and put it on. Keep talking to yourself! But it's not just any kind of talk. It must be a truly biblical conversation with your heart. As you counsel yourself with Scripture, you'll discover a renewed willingness to trust the Lord. You will have peace in your circumstances and hope for the future.

And we still have more goodies to pack into our survival-mode-thinking backpack!

---

48   D. Martyn Lloyd-Jones, *Spiritual Depression: Its Causes and Cures* (Grand Rapids, MI: W. M. B. Eerdmans, 1965), 20-21.

QUESTIONS for REFLECTION

Chapter 6: The Downside of Keeping Score

1. In order to understand our targeted text, we need to back up a bit and read the verses leading up to it. Briefly explain the focus of 1 Corinthians 15:1–8.

2. How does Paul describe himself in 1 Corinthians 15:8–9? See also Galatians 1:13–16; Ephesians 3:8; 1 Timothy 1:12–17 to develop your answer.

3. What explanation does Paul give in 1 Corinthians 15:9 for the way he describes himself?

4. Paul's life, and our own, reveals God's kindness in transforming sinners into useful subjects of His kingdom. Look up the following verses and explain how our lives change because of Jesus Christ: 1 Corinthians 6:9–11; 2 Corinthians 5:17, 21; Ephesians 5:8; Colossians 3:5–7.

5. Though forgiven, Paul never forgot the debt he owed to Christ for his rescue from sin. Understanding our own debt helps us respond with thankfulness to the Lord. Look up the following verses, then assess them in light of the kindness the Lord has shown you in forgiving your sin: 1 Corinthians 15:10; 2 Corinthians 5:14–15, 21; Philippians 3:6–11.

6. We will never respond rightly to the unmet expectations in our lives, if we don't see how undeserving we are of God's rescue and redemption. When we understand what we've been saved from, we will be less likely to chafe against the sanctification process God chooses for us. How do the following Scriptures help us gain a right perspective and enable us to truly affirm the statement: "My trials are fewer than my sins"? See Psalms 86:11–13; 103:2–3; 116:12–13, 16–17; Romans 12:1; 1 Corinthians 6:20.

O thou, my soul, forget no more
The friend who all thy misery bore;
Let every idol be forgot,
But, O my soul, forget Him not.

Jesus, for thou, a body takes,
Thy guilt assumes, thy fetters breaks,
Discharging all thy dreadful debt;
And canst thou e'er such love forget?

Renounce thy works and ways with grief,
And fly to this most sure relief;
Nor Him forget, who left His throne,
And for thy life gave up His own.[49]

By Krishna Pal, translated from Bengali into English by Joshua Marshman

49 Krishna Pal, translated from Bengali to English by Joshua Marshman, "O Thou, My Soul, Forget No More," http://www.hymntime.com/tch/htm/o/t/h/othoumys.htm.

7

A Crossing Guard's Guide to Life

In Pastures Green
by H. H. Barry[50]

"In pastures green?" - Not always. Sometimes
He, who knoweth best, in kindness leadeth me
In weary ways, where heavy shadows be;
Out of the sunshine warm and soft and bright,
Out of the sunshine into darkest night;
I oft would faint with sorrow and affright,
Only for this, I know He holds my hand;
So whether led in green or desert land,
I trust, although I may not understand.

"And by still waters?" - No, not always so.
Ofttimes the heavy tempests round me blow,
And o'er my soul the waves and billows go.
But when the storm beats loudest, and I cry
Aloud for help, the Master standeth by,
And whispers to my soul, "Lo, it is I!"
Above the tempest wild I hear Him say,
"Beyond the darkness lies the perfect day;
In every path of thine I lead the way."

So, whether on the hilltops high and fair
I dwell, or in the sunless valleys where
The shadows lie, what matter? He is there;
And more than this, where'er the pathway
Lead He gives to me no helpless broken reed,
But His own hand, sufficient for my need.
So where He leads me I can safely go;
And in the blest hereafter I shall know
Why, in His wisdom, He hath led me so.

50   H. H. Barry, "In Pastures Green,"
http://www.saved.com/wis/archive/1998/w1998128.htm.

Amy Carmichael, missionary to India and devoted servant of Jesus Christ, wisely observed, "Sooner or later God meets every trusting child who is following Him up the mountain and says, 'Now prove that you believe this that you have told Me you believe, and that you have taught others to believe.' Then is your opportunity. God knows, and you know, that there was always a hope in your heart that a certain way would not be yours. 'Anything but that, Lord,' had been your earnest prayer. And then, perhaps quite suddenly, you found your feet set on that way, that and no other. Do you still hold fast to your faith that He maketh your way perfect? It does not look perfect. It looks like a road that has lost its sense of direction; a broken road, a wandering road, a strange mistake. And yet, either it is perfect, or all that you have believed crumbles like a rope of sand in your hands. There is no middle choice between faith and despair."[51] "Anything but that, Lord." How often those words have been in my heart as God's unexpected plan for me has unfolded. No doubt, you've whispered similar pleading words to the Lord, which means that you also know that how we respond is key to giving God glory and responding in faith.

What God Deems Good

You might feel as though some of these truths are hard to take in. If you think that, then you are right, for there is nothing easy about the concepts we've been developing so far in our study of unmet expectations. They are stretching truths. They are heart-challenging, soul-searching, and sin-clearing truths. Most likely you've discovered that God is in the constant work of refining and shaping you into His likeness. Certainly, not a terrible concept, and one we're glad for! Yet the rub occurs when we realize that our God, who could fix or bring anything about, chooses not to do so. Learning to accept what God gives us is what we're going to tackle next. Our third don't-leave-home-without-it, survival-mode thinking can be summed up with these words: "If I am experiencing unmet expectations, it is because God has deemed it good for me."

Now admittedly, the word *deem* isn't a particularly trendy word, nor is it a word we use regularly these days. Yet it expresses in a succinct and perfectly relevant way exactly what we need to understand at this stage of our journey in overcoming our unmet expectations. The word *deem* means to judge or consider something. When God *deems* something good, it means He has judged it, considered it, examined all the options and angles and "what ifs," and *still* allowed it. God's perfect wisdom unfolded

---

51 Amy Carmichael, *Gold from Moonlight* (Fort Washington, PA: CLC Publications, 2013), 80-81.

in our lives is what makes Romans 8:28 so appealing to us: "And we know that God causes *all* things to work together for good to those who love God, to those who are called according to His purpose" (emphasis added). We see that there is no part of "all things" that hasn't been considered by God. Nothing is unknown; every consequence is considered. This means that the expectations we so long to have met, *in God's wisdom, remain unmet*, for a time and for a purpose. God has considered our thwarted plans, dashed hopes, difficulties, sorrows, and unmet expectations to be the best thing for us. Yet I must hasten to add that, *although God allows our expectations to remain unmet, He has no intention whatsoever of allowing us to remain the same.*

God Has an Eye for What's Produced

God has something specific He is working toward in our lives. Peter spells out His specific plan for us in 1 Peter 5:10: "After you have suffered for a little while, the God of all grace, who called you to His eternal glory in Christ, will Himself *perfect, confirm, strengthen and establish you*" (emphasis added). What that means is this: If I have expectations that are unmet or trials in my life that I find difficult to endure, it can only mean one thing—God has judged them, considered them, and *deemed* them good for me. He has ordained, *for my good*, this particular set of circumstances for me to go through. As God's plan unfolds, we learn some essential aspects of God's character, such as His sovereign and perfect wisdom in guiding, teaching, and training His children, and His ability to use any and all things to do good to us, to do good for us, because He is good. And that's just the tip of the iceberg!

God has a plan for your growth. If you belong to Him, you can rest, knowing that He will ensure you end up looking more and more like Jesus Christ. Keith and Kristyn Getty eloquently detailed this process in their hymn "The Perfect Wisdom of Our God." After lovingly extolling all the ways the Lord has revealed His wisdom in creation, they wrote, "teach me humbly to receive the sun and rain of Your sovereignty."[52] Knowing God has planned things helps us to receive whatever comes from His hand, whether it is sun or rain. Yet understanding God's wise and kingly dealings with us must be undergirded by a trust in God's character as good, full of love, caring, compassionate, wise, and powerful. That's why the Getty hymn goes on to say:

---

52 Keith and Kristen Getty, "The Perfect Wisdom of Our God," Getty Music, accessed July 22, 2018, https://www.gettymusic.com/the-perfect-wisdom-of-our-god/.

Each strand of sorrow has a place
Within this tapestry of grace;
So through the trials I choose to say:
"Your perfect will in your perfect way."[53]

God thwarts, blocks, and guides. As He does, our souls learn to respond, "Your perfect will in your perfect way." It's good to say, "Lord, let me love your will and plan for my life." But it is an entirely different thing to say it, and *mean it*, when we are in the midst of waiting, wanting, and possibly raging against God's perfect wisdom working in our lives. There have been many times when I have responded with submissive joy to God's will during times of quiet devotion. Yet sweeter still are the times when I've been bowed low by sorrow or trials and responded with acceptance to His unfolding plan for my life. We must have *fixed* in our minds and hearts that God reigns as king over *every* detail, *every* event, *every* circumstance in our lives. We must also firmly settle in our hearts that the all-powerful God is equally and immeasurably full of love and compassion toward His children—in sun or rain.

God's Compassion Permeates His Will for You

Have you ever been asked to do something really difficult that just makes you drag your feet to complete it? I'm sure you have; we all have. Often a willingness to do the hard thing depends on who has asked you to do it. If you are assured of the person's love and desire to do what's best for you, it makes it so much easier to do the hard thing you are being asked to do. Knowing that the person cares for you makes all the difference.

With the Lord, we never have to doubt His care and concern. He goes to great lengths in the Scriptures to assure us that He loves us, as we read in Isaiah 49:14–15: "But Zion said, 'The LORD has forsaken me, and the Lord has forgotten me.' Can a woman forget her nursing child and have no compassion on the son of her womb? Even these may forget, but I will not forget you." Thomas Watson says ". . . we are precious in His sight. He prizes His children above all His treasures. He delights in their company. He loves to see their countenance, and to hear their voice. He is full of sympathy, and pities them in their infirmities."[54] God's compassion undergirds His every interaction with us, even the unmet expectations we may be experiencing.

---

53 Ibid.
54 Thomas Watson, *The Lord's Prayer*, pp. 15-19 quoted in *Voices from the Past*, vol. 1, 228.

God's Righteousness Determines His Will for You

Not only is an understanding of God's unceasing devotion to His children essential, but also an understanding that there is no darkness in God or in anything that He does. He is righteous in all His ways. There may be times when we want to chafe against our circumstances and exclaim, "This isn't right, God!" However, if we have a correct understanding of who God is, then we know He always does what is right. His righteousness permeates His every action, thought, and purpose, even when His plan includes cancer, an adulterous spouse, persecution from family members, or abuse. There are no shadows of unrighteousness or un-right-ness in what He allows for His children. Even when we're experiencing wickedness or injustice at the hands of evil men, God always does what is right for His children.

How can this be? It's the question of the ages. It is one theologians to theologian housewives continue to grapple with: "How can a good God allow evil to be done?" The answer lies in studying His character, which we will continue to do in this chapter and throughout the book, for we will never come to terms with the unmet expectations in our lives unless we see that God is righteous in all His ways, good in His dealings, and sovereign over all.

God's Power Enfolds His Will for You

Over and over again, the Bible proclaims God's power. When Moses was trying to feed the children of Israel in the wilderness, the Lord challenged him to consider whether or not His power was limited (Num. 11:23). In Deuteronomy 4:37, we read how Moses reminded the Israelites of the fact that God brought them out of Egypt "by His great power." Jesus Himself affirmed God's power to be so great that all things are possible with Him (Mark 10:27). Deuteronomy 33:26 paints a picture of God mightily coming to the aid of His children: "There is none like the God of Jeshurun, who rides the heavens to your help, and through the skies in His majesty."

When we pull all the pieces together, we see the immense value of knowing and understanding God's character when it comes to moving past hurts and struggles with unmet expectations.

- God is *completely righteous* in all His ways. This means no fault or complaint can be brought against Him because we consider that what we are experiencing is not right.
- God is *all powerful*. This means that if He didn't want us to experi-

ence a particular thing, He could have changed it or averted it.

- God is *all wise*. This means that if He didn't think our circumstances would do us good, then He most certainly wouldn't have allowed them to arise.
- God is *all knowing*. He understands how our disappointments and unmet expectations will affect us.
- And God is *abounding in lovingkindness*. This means that everything that comes into our lives has been filtered first through His love.

These truths draw us to the conclusion that if God, being righteous, powerful, holy, wise, and compassionate in every part of His being, still allows the trial or the difficulty, it is because He, in His perfect wisdom and judgment, decided that it was best. *He has deemed it good for us.*

Living on the Truths Jeremiah Knew

The prophet Jeremiah worked through these issues. In the Book of Lamentations, he poured out his sorrow and despair after the destruction of Jerusalem by the Babylonians. Yet, even while experiencing God's chastisement on the nation, Jeremiah found hope as he remembered the Lord's unceasing lovingkindnesses and ongoing compassions. If God's chosen prophet needed to fix his mind on God's character, then certainly we need to as well. Disappointment, discouragement, sorrow, fearful or angry responses to our circumstances can be tamed as we dwell upon the truths of God's character, just like Jeremiah did. Jeremiah grew encouraged, in spite of his circumstances, by thinking on God's great faithfulness (Lam. 3:22–23). He remembered that God is his portion (v. 24) and that God delights in seeing His children wait on Him alone for rescue (vv. 25–26). Jeremiah reminded himself that it's good to submit in one's heart to God's training regimen (vv. 26–30).

Jeremiah made some unexpected observations. First, in Lamentations 3:31, he reminds us, "The Lord will not reject forever." What does he mean? Sometimes, it feels as though the Lord is rejecting us when things don't go our way, when the unexpected happens, when we're hurt or betrayed or grief-stricken. And sometimes it can feel to us as though we will never again see the Lord smile upon us. That's why Jeremiah reminds us, as he reminded himself, "The Lord will not reject forever." The time of affliction and difficulty will come to an end. It won't last forever. We know that God never rejects His children, as we see in Romans 8:32–39 that *nothing, not a thing*, can separate us from the love of God. Nor will He ever leave us or forsake us (Heb. 13:5). Yet, in times of testing, training, and unmet expectations, it can *feel* as though God has rejected us. Nothing could be further from the truth! In fact, Hebrews 12:5–6 tells us that God disciplines every son whom He loves.

Jeremiah counsels his heart because he felt rejected and punished by the Lord. He says, "for if He causes grief, then He will have compassion." Have your circumstances caused you grief? Are you hurting because your hopes and dreams aren't met? Do you find your situation discouraging? Consider the truth Jeremiah shines upon your despair in verse 32, "if He causes grief, then He will have compassion according to His abundant lovingkindness."

Jesus Wept—and Other Tales of Compassion

One of the most endearing stories of Jesus' life on earth was when His friend, Lazarus, had died and Lazarus' sisters, Mary and Martha, were grieved and distraught over losing their brother. They had asked Jesus to come to them when they realized their brother was getting sicker. But Jesus tarried two extra days and, during that time, Lazarus died. Jesus' interactions with His disciples in John 11:11–16 indicate that His delay in healing Lazarus had a greater purpose than Lazarus' physical cure. The disciples were surprised that Jesus didn't rush off to heal their friend—unmet expectations. Mary and Martha were dismayed that Jesus didn't arrive in time to prevent Lazarus' death—unmet expectations. Lazarus was dead and in his tomb for four days before Jesus arrived on the scene—four days of unmet expectations.

Jesus arrived in Bethany to witness the great sorrow of His friends. Even though He knew that Mary and Martha's grief would soon be turned to joy, John 11:33 and 11:38 both record that Jesus was deeply moved by His friends' grief. John 11:35 tells us that "Jesus wept." He wept because Lazarus' body had succumbed to the wages of sin and the curse. He wept for His friends' sadness and for the griefs they were enduring. He wept—even though He knew their grief would be temporary. He would soon raise Lazarus from the dead, but that didn't prevent Him from weeping out of His great love and compassion.

When Moses received the Ten Commandments, God said, "The LORD, the LORD God, compassionate and gracious, slow to anger, and abounding in lovingkindness and truth" (Exod. 34:6). I think it's fascinating that of all the ways God could have introduced Himself to mankind, He chose to describe Himself first as "compassionate." The Lord has compassion on us in our griefs, sorrows, and trials. Never doubt this truth! He knows the distress that will come to our souls when He says no to our expectations. But He unfailingly shows compassion to us. If we look again at Lamentations 3, we learn in verse 33: "For He does not afflict willingly or grieve the sons of men." There are treasures here. But what is Jeremiah getting at?

Jeremiah means that God isn't capricious in His dealings with His children, nor is He using our circumstances in a careless or uncaring manner. When we face trying circumstances and painful trials, *it's because there is no other way.* In verse 33, the picture Jeremiah paints is one in which it is almost as if God's arm is being twisted. God doesn't want to cause grief or sorrow to His beloved ones. But He will allow it because it is the best way to produce the desired character and faith in us.

Thomas Watson said, "He will not lay upon us more than we are able to bear. He deals gently and will not over-afflict."[55] This is "Goldilocks and the Three Bears" theology—it's not too much affliction so that we sink under it. The trials, pressures, and unmet expectations are not so small that they don't produce grace in us; rather, they are just right, for God knows what is necessary for our growth. Joni Eareckson Tada said something similar as she reflected on living most of her life as a quadriplegic as a result of a diving accident. She said, "God permits what He hates to accomplish what He loves."[56] Simple. Succinct. Stark in its truth and blindingly beautiful. God permits unmet expectations, and all the attendant situations that go with them, to produce godliness in us. Every detail is sovereignly guided and perfectly placed to make us more like Christ.

Trials are Good for You—No, Really, They Are!

The psalmist said, "It is good for me that I was afflicted, that I may learn Your statutes" (Ps. 119:71). Do you understand what the psalmist is telling us? He is saying that trials are good for us. Isn't it nice to remind other people of that truth? We can affirm it so heartily and urge them to receive their difficulties with gratefulness—until it's our turn. Trials don't feel so good for us then, do they?

The Christian life is a life of faith. It's about seeing what is unseen, about believing what God says, even when the circumstances may scream the exact opposite. James opens his letter to his beloved ones with these words: "Consider it all joy, my brethren, when you encounter various trials, knowing that the testing of your faith produces endurance. And let endurance have its perfect result, so that you may be perfect and

---

55 Ibid.
56 Joni Eareckson Tada, "Reflections on the 50th Anniversary of My Diving Accident," The Gospel Coalition, accessed July 22, 2018, https://www.thegospelcoalition.org/article/reflections-on-50th-anniversary-of-my-diving-accident.

complete, lacking in nothing" (1:2–4). Trials test our faith. They not only reveal whether our faith is genuine, but they also reveal the depth of our faith—where its roots lie—as well as its strengths and weaknesses. Moving from one trial to the next, we learn to persevere in trusting God. Steadfastness and endurance are built into our faith.

When I was a new believer and learning some of these truths, I romanticized endurance. The endurance needed in the Christian life seemed very much like my little-girl imaginings of being a pioneer on the Oregon Trail, trudging across the Snake River Valley of Idaho with my bonnet pulled down around my face to protect me from the beating sun, while I covered my nose and mouth with my apron to keep out the choking dust of the wagon train. As a young believer, in my understanding of the Christian life and what it might be like, I simply switched my traveling companions and destination, exchanging Ma and Pa and oxen for fellow saints on the the way to the *real* Promised Land. I knew the path toward heaven would require endurance and courage, although my imagination imbued it with rosy glow.

Neither a rosy glow nor a swelling orchestral theme accompanies real-life endurance. It's hard, gritty, often distressing, and physically, emotionally and spiritually taxing. Real-life enduring rarely feels victorious, at least not while you're in the middle of it. Yet trials produce a strong faith, a faith that perseveres, a faith that's been tried and tested. Faith produced through trials endures and results in a perfected, complete godliness that lacks nothing. No wonder James tells us to rejoice!

The end of the journey produces thankfulness for the lessons learned along the way. It's like the swelling, rolling, crescendo of music at the end of the movie that gives us the kind of closure we love. For the believer, joy in God's work doesn't have to be deferred because we believe God and live by faith. Of course, there is that little word "let" in James 1:4 that gives us some insight into how we might stymie the process of grace. James 1:4 says, "And *let* endurance have its perfect result, so that you may be perfect and complete, lacking in nothing" (emphasis added).

Letting God Have His Way in Training Our Souls

We're told to let endurance have its perfect result in us. It is the same when a parent tells a child, "Let your sister have the toy now." The parent knows there could be the moment of quiet acquiescence and a cheerful, "Yes, Mommy. Here, sissy, it's your turn now. You can have it." Or there could be the pouting lip and the unwillingness to give anything to anyone, no matter who is asking. More often than not, we're a little too close to the pouting lip stage when we need to endure unmet expectations. We need the gentle reminder from James not to get in the way of endurance doing its perfecting work.

When our youngest was little, he loved playing "crossing guard," holding up his hands to stop traffic. All too often I've played crossing guard, standing in the way of God's training regimen for my soul. I've fought against it at times. I've complained and moped and even been stubbornly defiant. When we see all the benefits James lists to letting endurance do its perfect work, it's hard to understand *why we wouldn't let it* have its way. I think sometimes we forget the bigger picture. All too often, we only think about our comfort, pleasure, or happiness. But God doesn't forget His purposes. He *always* has our sanctification in mind.

Thankfully, God always gets us to the place He wants us to go. Maurice Roberts explains it this way: "All the time the Christian is on earth God takes steps to limit his happiness and to put a brake on his pleasures. This is because we are now in a state of preparation and progressive sanctification. If we had too much pleasure here we should be content with our present lot. We should 'reign as kings' (1 Corinthians 4:8) without God and should make an idol of this life. Hence He wisely and kindly puts a thorn in the nest and a crook in the lot. He skillfully breaks our foolish schemes over and over again until we learn at last to seek our true happiness only and always in Him. Here on earth, God empties us out from vessel to vessel."[57]

Tucking Away Precious Truths

We've been painstakingly tucking away soul-nourishing truths in our little survival-mode-thinking backpack. These don't-leave-home-without-it truths fortify our soul's health, which is why we first packed, *"I am a sinner and don't receive what I deserve"*; then we added, *"My trials are fewer than my sins"*; and now next to the previous two, we lay, *"If I am experiencing unmet expectations, it is because God has deemed it good for me."* Our growth in grace and our spiritual health depend upon our understanding and adhering to these truths. Our latest item reminds us that, no matter what is happening in our lives, it is God's will for us, which He intends to use for our good (Rom. 8:28), to perfect, confirm, strengthen, and establish us (1 Peter 5:10), and to equip us for every good thing (Heb. 13:20–21).

When our son, Mark, was a little guy, his "Tweety" blanket was his "precious." I couldn't understand why he liked that blanket so much. I kept trying to introduce him to other ones, but he preferred the bright green

---

57 Roberts, *The Thought of God*, 226.

one decorated with yellow canary Tweety birds all over it. As he got a bit older, and it was not cool to sleep with a Tweety blankie, we discovered how ingenious little boys can be when it comes to their beloved snuggly thing. We noticed Tweety finding its way into Mark's little suitcase when we would go on trips. Or we would find Tweety neatly layered in between the blankets of his bed. Well, just like Tweety blankie, the next item for our survival-mode backpack brings with it all the comfort that Tweety brought our sweet boy. And just like Mark, we definitely don't want to leave home without it.[58]

---

58 Mark is now a grown man, who no longer sleeps with Tweety.

QUESTIONS for REFLECTION

Chapter 7: A Crossing Guard's Guide to Life

1. The theme of the book of James is that true faith, saving faith, is life-transforming faith. Saving faith changes every action and reaction we have, including our response to trials. James begins his letter on that very topic in James 1:2–4. What are you to do when you encounter trials according to verse 2?

2. The Greek word translated "encounter" in the NASB has also been translated "meet" or "fall into" in other Bible translations. The word describes the action of walking along, minding your own business, when all of a sudden you fall into a trial or run right into the middle of one. What are trials supposed to do according to verse 3?

3. What is significant about the plural use of the word "trials" in verse 2? Which word describes trials in James 1:2?

4. We have seen that trials are the means God uses to *test* our faith. That same Greek word is used in 1 Peter 1:7. What do you learn about the meaning of the word "testing" by looking at both James 1:3 and 1 Peter 1:7?

5. The time of testing produces a steadfast, enduring, unwavering faith. What role do we play in that process according to James 1:4?

6. What would be the result if we got in the way of the process or stubbornly refused to submit to God's good plan? See James 1:4.

7. After looking at James 1:2–4, what do we need to be convinced of to consider trials as "all" joy or "pure" joy? See also Job 23:10; Psalm 145:17; Proverbs 17:3.

8. How does having our eyes on the bigger picture help us trust the Lord's process in using trials—and unmet expectations—to perfect our faith?

Men make more haste to get their afflictions removed than to be sanctified in them.
Thomas Case[59]

Let us search and try our ways. Let us consider that the present condition is best for us, and learn in whatever state we are, to be content (Philippians 4:11).
Thomas Case[60]

---

59 Thomas Case, *Selected Works, A Treatise of Afflictions*, pp. 65-67 quoted in *Voices from the Past,* vol. 1, 172.
60 Ibid.

8

Flaky Prom Dates and the Faithfulness of God

If your view of God is shaped by Scripture, it is impossible to have anything but holy and loyal thoughts of God.
William Gurnall[61]

---

61   William Gurnall, *The Christian in Complete Armour*, 11:91-97 quoted in *Voices from the Past*, vol. 1, 310.

My high-school-prom date stood me up. Fun stuff. There I waited in the dress I had made myself just for the dance. My friend and her date waited. My family waited. Finally, my friend and her date left for the dance. There's not too much you can say or do in a situation like that to cover over the embarrassment of being stood up. I tried to be brave and put on a good face. This happened a long time ago, in the seventies, in the days before cell phones or emails or those helpful "find my date" apps, which meant I had no idea where my date might be hiding. That he didn't show was certain. It was a little humiliating, definitely disappointing, though I have to admit, not too emotionally damaging. My darling dad, in an effort to salvage the evening for me, took me to a movie. The movie was nothing to speak of, but my dad's loving care brought solace.

The next year, the young man I was then dating stood me up for my high-school graduation. Yes, stood up a *second* time by an entirely different guy! We'd been seeing each other for a couple of months. But the prospect of meeting all the extended family who had gathered for the grand occasion apparently freaked him out, so he didn't show. Most likely, a high-school graduation didn't seem like that big of a deal to him. He had already graduated from high school; however, the ceremony was still important to me. I was crushed when he didn't show up. Even crying through most of the night didn't diminish my sense of loss and betrayal.

Yet the Lord was gracious in using this last episode as a key event in drawing me to Himself. I yearned for someone I could depend on. I longed for security. As the Lord worked in my heart, it slowly began to dawn on me that no guy could ever fill the emptiness of my soul the way the Lord would.

The Lord Will Never Disappoint Us

We've all been disappointed in life, even if we made it through high school without being stood up. We've all experienced that moment when someone or something didn't quite meet up to our expectations. And most of us have also experienced, at least once, a time when our hopes were absolutely crushed. While people or circumstances may disappoint us, there is good news! God tells us that He will never fail us (Isa. 49:14–16; 2 Cor. 4:9; Heb. 13:5). And because He cannot lie, we can believe it when the Bible states that God is completely trustworthy (Titus 1:2). This truth is the fourth item we're going to pack into our survival-mode-thinking backpack: *the Lord will never disappoint you*. Reminding ourselves of this truth will go a long way in helping us to think correctly about our circumstances when unmet expectations arise.

Psalm 22:5 tells us, "To You they cried out and were delivered; in You they trusted and were not disappointed." The ESV and the NKJV translate this verse so that it reads: "In You they trusted and were not put to shame [ashamed]." We learn from Psalm 22:5 that when we trust in the Lord and call upon Him for help, we will not be disappointed or ashamed of our hope in Him. *He will help us.* He will do good to His children. In fact, He always does what is good, which is why it's safe to say, "You won't be sorry that you trusted the Lord."

To say *the Lord will never disappoint you* means first of all that you won't be disappointed when you trust the Lord for salvation. Paul explains this in Romans 10:9–11: "If you *confess* with your mouth Jesus as Lord, and *believe* in your heart that God raised Him from the dead, *you will be saved*; for with the heart a person believes, resulting in righteousness, and with the mouth he confesses, resulting in salvation. For the Scripture says, 'Whoever believes in Him will not be disappointed'" (emphasis added). Basically, Paul is saying, "The Bible says you will be saved if you put your trust in Jesus alone for salvation. You won't be disappointed that you put your hope in God because He always keeps His promises."

Second, the Scriptures affirm that *anytime* we put our trust in the Lord, we won't regret hoping in Him for rescue and help. God Himself backs up His promise in Isaiah 49:23b: "And you will know that I am the LORD; those who hopefully wait for Me will not be put to shame." God's reputation is on the line here. He says that we won't be sorry for leaning on Him in times of trial or difficulty. In fact, Jeremiah reminds us that just the opposite is true. We will find ourselves sad and sorry for *not* trusting in the Lord. Jeremiah wrote, "O LORD, the hope of Israel, all who forsake You will be put to shame. Those who turn away on earth will be written down, because they have forsaken the fountain of living water, even the LORD" (Jer. 17:13).

The Value of Knowing the Lord's Character

Psalm 34:9–10 proclaims, "O fear the LORD, you His saints; for to those who fear Him there is no want. The young lions do lack and suffer hunger; but they who seek the LORD shall not be in want of any good thing." In Psalm 34 David exults in God's complete care for His children. In fact, God's care is so comprehensive that those who seek Him won't be missing out on anything that's good for them. Certainly, that truth helps us say, "The Lord will never disappoint me." But you may be thinking to yourself (though you might not ever say it), "If I'm honest here, I would have to say that there have been times when I've felt disappointed with God. I thought

He would rescue me. I thought He would answer my prayer. I thought He would do things differently. I didn't think I would go through the things I've had to go through. So, is something wrong with me? What does it mean when the Bible tells me the Lord won't disappoint me?"

Before we discuss that, let me assure you that we'll all trudge through the Valley of Disappointment at some stage in our lives. Beginning with wrong presuppositions is one reason that this is so. This is why we need to get back to the basics in our thinking. Do you remember the items we neatly tucked into our survival-mode-thinking backpack in the previous chapters? Let's pull them out and look at them again: *I'm a sinner and I'm not receiving what I deserve; My trials are fewer than my sins; If I am experiencing unmet expectations, it is because God has deemed it good for me.* These essential presuppositions help us, if and when, we find ourselves feeling disappointed with the Lord.

Another reason for finding ourselves in the Valley of Disappointment comes from God Himself! Wait! What? Yes, it's true. God sanctifies us when our faith scrapes the bottom of the barrel. The gunk and gook in the depths of our hearts needs to be brought to the surface and cleaned out so that we'll grow in holiness. We know God uses trials and difficulties to test, refine, and strengthen our faith (James 1:3; 1 Peter 1:7), and cause our relationship with Him to grow in the process. However, to do that means He must strip away any false views of Himself that we may harbor—and we all harbor some in one form or another. *Any disappointment we may harbor toward the Lord stems from a wrong view of Him, His work, or who we are in relation to Him.* These are painful truths to acknowledge. But it is necessary for us to do so.

Counteracting any wrong views we have of the Lord must become our primary business if we truly want to overcome our struggles with unmet expectations. Thankfully, the Lord provides all the help we need in His Word, for it's there that He reveals His character to us. Counseling your soul might sound something like this: "The Bible says the Lord will not disappoint me. But I have to admit that I'm feeling disappointed. That means either I'm wrong in my thinking somewhere or the Bible is wrong. Hmm. . .I wonder which is wrong?"

Standing at the crossroads in counseling your soul, you now have some choices to make. Will you believe God rather than your feelings? Will you trust what God says in His Word, even if your circumstances scream the opposite? Choosing to believe God means embarking on an adventure of discovery in which you will learn where you are wrong in your thinking and then, more importantly, appropriate an accurate view of the Lord of glory.

The Reward of Seeing God Accurately

In Psalm 34:4–7 David recounts, "I sought the LORD, and He answered me, and delivered me from all my fears. They looked to Him and were radiant, and their faces will never be ashamed. This poor man cried, and the LORD heard him and saved him out of all his troubles. The angel of the LORD encamps around those who fear Him, and rescues them." David's trials and troubles propelled him toward the Lord, leaving us with a portrait of a grateful man. No regret dogged his heels. Why? David explains that when he sought the Lord, the Lord answered his prayer for help by delivering him from his fears. Not only that, David said that the Lord heard his cry for help and saved him from *all* his troubles. He was able to look back at his circumstances and see God's unequivocal rescue. He wasn't sorry that he had trusted in the Lord. God's deliverance may have been different than he expected, and it may have taken longer, but the Lord was faithful to fulfill His promises of help to His child who had called out to Him.

Learning to say, "The Lord will never disappoint me," brings its own reward. It means you are seeing God for who He is—not for who you want Him to be. Reminding yourself that the Lord won't disappoint you teaches you to see your unmet expectations within the envelope of God's wisdom and love. Your unmet expectations become tools for your sanctification, rather than something to escape from, or a right to which you're entitled, a "must have," or a privilege you feel you've earned. Psalm 119:75 reveals this truth when the psalmist proclaims, "I know, O LORD, that Your judgments are righteous, and that in faithfulness You have afflicted me." Any affliction that comes to you finds its origin in God's faithfulness in doing good to those who trust Him. God has judged your situation righteously—perfectly. He isn't showing partiality to others and being mean to you. He is perfectly righteous in what He is allowing in your life, even if He portions out unmet expectations. *What you know and take to heart about God and His character helps you think rightly about your current circumstances.*

Counsel Yourself with These Truths

Psalm 25:8–10 contains some of my favorite "get my head on straight" truths. Psalm 25:8 says, "Good and upright is the LORD." Right from the start we're told vital truths for thinking correctly, no matter what circumstances we face. Whether we're enduring storms or enjoying sunshine, we can remind ourselves that God is *good* and *upright* in everything. He never does anything wrong, mean, or unrighteous. To further illustrate

God's good and upright character, David tells us, "He instructs sinners in the way." The Lord doesn't just leave us—sinners—to our own devices. He teaches us how to walk in His paths.

David continues extolling the Lord's virtues in verse 9: "He leads the humble in justice, and He teaches the humble His way." When the psalmist refers to "the humble," he's talking about those who love the Lord and obey Him, the very ones the Lord leads and teaches in His ways! And to make sure we get how amazing God is, the psalmist gives us even more details. In verse 10, we're told: "All the paths of the LORD are lovingkindness and truth to those who keep His covenant and His testimonies." Did you catch what he said? *All* God's paths are "lovingkindness and truth." No matter what path you're on, smooth or rocky, it is God's path for you, paved with His love and faithfulness.

The Word of God promises and assures us of God's good intentions toward His children. In fact, He stores up goodness toward those who fear Him (Ps. 31:19). Psalm 84:11 tells us that the Lord never withholds anything good from His children. We might not understand His methods or His ways, but we can cling to this one thing: "I won't be disappointed or ashamed to put my trust in Him. He may say no. He may allow very difficult things in my life. But, if I put my trust in Him, I won't be sorry." "How blessed is the man who trusts in you!" (Ps. 84:12).

Psalm 9:10 says, "And those who know Your name will put their trust in You, for You, O LORD, have not forsaken those who seek You." Reflect on what Psalm 9 says about the Lord's care for His children. How ungrateful we can be at times! Notice, too, that it's God's children who trust Him. Of course, not perfectly, and often not right away, but eventually, all those, who know the Lord and call Him Father, will trust Him. And He, in His perfect faithfulness, will not abandon them.

Psalm 145 trumpets God's praises and proclaims how wonderful and faithful He is. It's the perfect psalm for a study of God's character as one attribute after another is extolled. Let's consider verse 17. It says that "the LORD is righteous in all His ways and kind in all His deeds." Notice the word "all" in these verses. The Lord is righteous in *all* His ways, which includes His sovereign dealings in our lives. That means that right now, we can view our circumstances and say, "The Lord is acting with perfect righteous judgment and wisdom in all that He's allowed in our lives and given us." No wonder each one of us is able to marvel and respond with these words: "The Lord will never disappoint me."

Notice, too, how Psalm 145:17 reminds us of the Lord's kindness. *All* His deeds are kind. That means every single one. We may collide with this truth when we're feeling a bit hurt or put out because of the difficulties or trials in our lives. But no injury will result if we accept the Bible's bold claims that the Lord's kindness is directed toward us *always* and in *every* way. Reflecting upon God's character changes us so that our response is: "With a God like that, how can I ever doubt His goodness? I will never be disappointed by putting my trust in Him."

If It's Not Working, Here's Why

If we are disappointed in the Lord, it's not the Lord's fault. It's ours. Something has become muddled somewhere in our thinking, if that's where we've ended up. It means there's a disconnect, some kind of missing link between point A and point B. How can I say that? I can because the Bible itself tells us that *God is trustworthy*. We can't just believe the parts of Scripture that work for us and disregard the others. God's Word is all true and perfectly reliable. God Himself can be trusted, which means we'll never be ashamed of waiting, hoping, and believing in the Lord. Is it easy to do so? No, definitely not. If we trust Him, will He give us everything we desire? No, certainly not. But, as we place our hope in Him, we will take part in the great adventure of knowing Him. Charles Spurgeon wrote, "We shall not be ashamed of our hope. It shall be even as the Lord has said. We shall be fed, led, blest and rested. Our Lord will come, and then the days of our mourning shall be ended. How we shall glory in the Lord who first gave us lively hope, and then gave us that which we hoped for!"[62]

Changing Your Response Begins Here

Moving from a place of disappointment to one that is in line with Scripture's proclamation of the Lord's trustworthiness begins with this plea: "Sustain me according to Your word, that I may live; and do not let me be ashamed of my hope" (Ps. 119:116). The Lord quickly responds to our cries for help, especially when we correctly view His glory and splendid kindness. Oh, let us pray with the same resolve as the psalmist: "In You, O LORD, I have taken refuge; let me never be ashamed" (Ps. 71:1). Stepping away from a sense of injustice or injury begins with asking the Lord for His help, just as we do in everything else in the Christian life. We can't save ourselves, so we plead with the Lord to redeem us and rescue us from our sin. We can't sanctify ourselves, so we beg the Lord to complete the work He began in us. We can't obey well or love God wholeheartedly, unless we lean on Him for help.

---

62 C. H. Spurgeon, *The Cheque Book of the Bank of Faith: Being Precious Promises Arranged for Daily Use with Brief Comments* (New York: American Tract Society, 1893), 163.

Computers garner little things called "cookies." Nearly every time you go to a website or click on a link, you pick up a "cookie" that stays on your computer. Most of the time those cookies are harmless little tracking devices that speed up your ability to search the internet quickly. They can become pesky when you start getting bombarded with advertising because a site you visited used cookies. Thankfully, you can do a little computer maintenance and clean up your "cookie" cache, if it gets bothersome. Similarly, through the Lord's wise and loving use of unmet expectations, God cleans out any "cookies" we've accumulated along the way. He skillfully uses unmet expectations to reveal some of the heretofore unknown attitudes or presuppositions that have accumulated in our hearts. Like computers, our hearts need to be checked over regularly and maintained biblically, or our wrong thinking will cause trouble and slow us down spiritually.

David didn't know a thing about computer "cookies," but he did know how to counter the damage we do to ourselves when our thoughts about the Lord aren't biblical. He wrote in Psalm 27:13: "I would have despaired unless I had believed that I would see the goodness of the LORD in the land of the living." Despair, fear, bitterness, anger, anxiety are all ways which bring harm to our souls, if our thinking is wrong. That's why David explains that he could have easily found himself in trouble if he had not applied the correct thinking to his situation. He says, "I believe I will see God's goodness while I'm living." He believed the Scriptures in spite of, and in the face of, his circumstances. Practical David then counsels us to "wait for the LORD; be strong and let your heart take courage; yes, wait for the LORD" (Ps. 27:14). Living out those wise words means believing, just as David did, that God is good, wise, loving, and perfect in all He does, even when everything—or even some things—in our lives seem to say something different.

William Gurnall wisely observed the importance of thinking rightly and accurately about the Lord, when he said:

> Faith will not harbor unworthy thoughts of God in the heart. If your view of God is shaped by Scripture, it is impossible to have anything but holy and loyal thoughts of God. Satan seeks to encourage hard thoughts of God when His providence is hard to understand. Some have questioned God's justice because He does not judge speedily. Others have questioned His care and faithfulness in not providing better for His servants or in allowing their afflictions. Satan seeks for us to view God through these broken glasses.
>
> Job quenched this dart: "You speak as a foolish woman." What

God takes from me is less than I owe Him, and what He leaves me is more than I deserve. Unbecoming thoughts or words about God are the product of a rash and hasty spirit. It is fitting for Christians to bless God in the saddest condition that can befall them. Faith finds mercy in the greatest affliction and in the saddest mixture of providence. Praise God for past mercies and it will not be long before you have a new song in your mouth for the present mercy.[63]

What have we learned?

- I'm a sinner and I'm not receiving what I deserve.
- My trials are fewer than my sins.
- If I am experiencing unmet expectations, it is because God has deemed it good for me.
- The Lord will never disappoint me.

Tuck these truths away in your survival-mode-thinking backpack. Use their no-nonsense wisdom to reveal any wayward thinking or unbiblical presuppositions you may have picked up along the way. Survival-mode thinking strengthens your faith and provides the foundation you need to bring glory to God.

This is so exciting! We're well on our way to finding the hope and help we need to respond well to life's unmet expectations. Our goal remains—to give God glory in all His dealings with us. In the next chapters, we'll examine the Scriptures and gain godly wisdom and strength for the times when unmet expectations impact our relationships with others, ourselves, and the Lord.

---

63   William Gurnall, *The Christian in Complete Armour*, 11:91-97 quoted in *Voices from the Past*, vol. 1, 310.

QUESTIONS for REFLECTION

Chapter 8: Flaky Prom Dates and the Faithfulness of God

1. What truths about God do you see in Psalm 33:1–5?

2. How would reflecting on the truths from Psalm 33:4–5 help us to come to terms with God's dealings with us and our unmet expectations?

3. For further study, see Deuteronomy 32:4; Psalms 25:10; 119:75–76; and Romans 8:28. What insights do you gain from these verses about the Lord's dealings with you, especially when it comes to areas of unmet expectations?

4. In Psalm 33:6–12, we learn of God's complete sovereignty and power over all things. What insight does verse 10 give you into some of the surprises you might encounter throughout the day?

5. Psalm 33:11 reveals one of the reasons why God may not answer our prayers in the affirmative or allow our plans to move forward. What do you learn from Psalm 33:11; Proverbs 16:9; Isaiah 46:10?

6. Though we may feel small and forgotten, what can we be assured of according to Psalm 33:13–15?

7. What kinds of things are we tempted to put our hope in according to Psalm 33:16–17? Can you think of other things to add to that list?

8. Why is the Lord the One we should hope in according to Psalm 33:18–22? For further encouragement see also Psalms 34:15, 18–20; 147:11; Lamentations 3:25–33.

Many plans are in a man's heart, but the counsel of the Lord will stand.
Proverbs 19:21

PART 3: LIFE ON THE TRAIL

Most of the pioneers had no knowledge of the terrain or the route to their hoped-for destination in the West. They relied heavily upon the experience of the trail boss, knowing their survival depended upon his wisdom. When it comes to unmet expectations, we can trust our good Guide who leads us to the place of peace, rest, and joy.

• • • • • • • • • • • • • • • • •

9

Soul Mates and Other Myths

Sin makes us super-sensitive to the faults of others and insensitive to our own.
Maurice Roberts[64]

Pride nourishes the remembrance of injuries:
humility forgets as well as forgives them.
R. C. Chapman[65]

64   Roberts, *The Thought of God*, 137.
65   Chapman, *Choice Sayings*, 59.

I'm an avid hiker—in my *mind*! I love the outdoors. I love walking and hiking, though I must admit I haven't done much *real* hiking at all. It seems, from what I've gleaned and from the vast sum of my non-hiking experience, that "enjoying the journey" is a hiker's main goal, unlike a runner who competes in a race, and whose main motivation is to finish and, preferably, to win. Hikers venture out into the woods, trudge up mountains, and traipse all over the countryside for a variety of reasons. The primary goal for most seems to be more about the experience of being outside, savoring glorious views, breathing fresh air, getting exercise, and enjoying time with others or time alone. I've also noticed that serious hikers often use a hiking pole or stick to keep them from stumbling as they march over uneven terrain. It makes sense to bring along such a helpful hiking accouterment because, if the goal is to enjoy the journey, then getting skinned up in the process doesn't quite fit the bill. Generally, hikers seem to prepare well for their expedition, taking into consideration what they might need along the way for their comfort, protection, and survival.

Thus far in our journey over the daunting Unmet Expectations' Mountain Range, we've done some pre-hike training and conditioning in Part 1 by identifying unmet expectations. In Part 2, we filled our backpacks with the essentials we need for our "comfort, protection, and survival" along the way. Now, in Part 3, we're ready to head out and traverse mountains! As we look at specific ways unmet expectations affect us and our relationships, we'll navigate the uneven terrain with the sturdy walking sticks God provides in His Word to prevent us from stumbling or falling.

Like a little band of supporters cheering us on toward heaven, encouragement and help wait for us in the pages to come. Hikers, from the Lewis and Clark Expedition to today's adventurers, know the compelling lure to see what's over the next hill or around the river bend. It's my prayer that you'll straighten your bonnet strings, pick up your hiking pole, tug on your survival-mode backpack, and answer the call to discover the goodness of God. In the chapters ahead, we'll fine-tune our responses to the unmet expectations we face, while applying the truths we've learned from the previous chapters. So, tighten the laces on your hiking boots and let's go. Oh hey, wait for me!

If Only They'd Do Things My Way!

People aren't going to meet our expectations and we won't meet theirs, plain and simple. Unlike Mary Poppins, we're not "practically perfect in every way," which means we'll let one another down—frequently, possibly daily. Without a doubt, some disappointments are easier to deal with than others. Though we may heartily concur with those very rational state-ments, we may still struggle at times when others don't meet up to our expectations. It's so easy to default to blaming others, becoming bitter, arguing, or feeling anxious when we are living with unmet expectations. Since it's so natural to end up responding. . .well. . .*naturally,* rather than *spiritually,* we need a bit of pre-hike training to prepare our hearts in the art of overcoming our disappointments. Much like we did in packing our don't-leave-home-without-it-survival-mode-thinking backpack, we'll dis-cover the help God provides in His Word to enable us to respond in a way that gives Him glory—even when we do feel let down or hurt in some way by others.

Dancing with a Dream

One of the quickest ways to dispel expectations, especially the crip-pling, soul-stumbling unmet ones, is to remember that no individual person can ever meet all of our needs. Our earthly friendships are giv-en to us as a blessing from God. But no earthly friend, no matter how godly and wonderful that person is, can be "all" to us in the way that God can. Often, without realizing it, we expect our friends, family, and loved ones to know how to meet our needs, whether they are physi-cal, mental, emotional, or spiritual. This is too big a burden to place on anyone. Yet we often have expectations for others, without even realizing we have them; that is, *until* our anticipations and desires go unnoticed and unmet.

We so long to be understood that we cling to the concept that somewhere out there, there will be that single individual who "gets" us. The idea of a soul mate rests on this very desire. And just like Anne Shirley in *Anne of Green Gables,* we long for a kindred spirit who will understand us and intrinsically "get" who we are. We especially long to find a romantic counterpart who is perfectly suited to us. The concept of a soul mate is romantic, but unattainable. When we find ourselves dancing with that desire, we need to switch partners! Dancing with a dream leaves our arms and hearts empty because dreams are unable to satisfy our heart's desires.

In truth, when we look to others to fulfill every need, we find ourselves in a far more dangerous place than waltzing with a dream. Jeremiah 17:5 states: "Thus says the LORD, 'Cursed is the man who trusts in mankind and makes flesh his strength, and whose heart turns away from the LORD.'" Jeremiah reminds us that anytime we put our trust in people, such as our friends and family, we're trusting in "flesh." It's so easy to fall into this trap. And whether we realize it or not, it means that we're putting our trust in people, rather than in God. Jeremiah tells us there is blessing when we trust the Lord: "Blessed is the man who trusts in the LORD and whose trust is the LORD" (Jer. 17:7).

Like Jesus, Only Taller

One day I was talking with our son, Nate, about some of the expectations for romantic relationships that he's encountered. He summed it up by quoting what a wise pastor once told him, "You sometimes feel like what a girl is looking for is someone just like Jesus, *only taller*." That, my sweet friends, perfectly sums up the heart of discontentment. We want someone who's perfect in every way. But, even then, we have an idea of something *better*, something *more*, something *different* than the real person standing directly in front of us.

If we enter a relationship expecting the person to be "just like Jesus, *only taller*," then we're in for a surprise and, probably, a big letdown, as no individual can live up to that perfect standard. There will be times when our dear ones and friends will fail us, hurt us, and, possibly, even betray us in some way. But all is not lost! God has provided everything we need to extend love and forgiveness, no matter what the situation. Because Jesus died on the cross for our sins, His forgiveness makes it possible for us to forgive others.

When You're Dealing with Others, Expectations Can Creep Up on You!

"I thought you would take out the trash every day." "I really did expect you to change the dirty diapers like my dad did." "I thought you'd want to talk about *all* these details for decorating the family room." "I guess I expected that you'd like doing anything with me, even if it means going to a ballet." Sometimes our loved ones' reactions to our expectations leave us feeling wounded when they have no desire to fulfill our hopes, wants, or even needs. That doesn't mean we have to stay in a cycle of hurt, frustration, bitterness, or irritation. The Lord is more than sufficient to comfort our distresses as we go to Him with our hopes and expectations.

It's important to recognize that, even though we may hope for certain things, our unmet expectations can be used by the Lord to draw our hearts nearer to Him. Sometimes, the best response is not to make our expectation known, to demand our rights, or to clarify our position, but to take our little bundle of dashed hopes and dreams to the Lord first, asking

Him to bind up our wounds, seeking Him for the best way to respond, and then resting in His provision.

We live in a fallen world among fallen people, and we ourselves are fallen and broken. The things that happen to us or go on around us will have an effect upon us, no doubt about it. Yet, before we sinfully default to hurt and frustration, let's consider how to respond in a God-glorifying way.

First, We Deal with Our Own Hearts

It may be appropriate to talk to your spouse, your friend, or your family member about your hurt feelings. But, before you do, start by putting your hope in the Lord. Cry out like David did when his expectations were dashed and his friends let him down: "I cried out to You, O LORD; I said, 'You are my refuge, My portion in the land of the living'" (Ps. 142:5). With the Lord as your portion in this life, even if your circumstances remain unchanged, you can move past the hurt, irritation, fretting, even any bitterness or unforgiveness that can arise when it feels as though others have failed you. One of the cardinal rules of biblical counseling is that you can't fix the other person; you can only fix yourself. This is certainly true as we tackle the underpinnings of unmet expectations.

Next, We Must Extend Forgiveness

When we're dealing with other people, we will need to extend forgiveness at some point. It's just the way it is. We're sinners—I am, you are, they are—which means that at some time or another, we will sin. People may get exasperated or become angry. They may steal from you or deceitfully use you. They may criticize, gossip, or slanderously malign you. A spouse may betray your trust by flirting with a co-worker, engage in pornography, commit adultery, or a trusted family member may sexually abuse you.

We will fail others and they will fail us. It's right to expect our spouse to remain faithful to us, our loved ones to stand by us, and other believers to do what's right. In each of these situations, we expect others to treat us well, to treat us right, to love us. But what if they don't do what is right? What then? We extend forgiveness. This is much easier to say than it is to do. Extending forgiveness may be challenging, but it's not impossible— certainly not impossible for someone who's been redeemed from her own sins by the blood of Jesus Christ. Basically, Paul teaches us that an unforgiving spirit is incompatible with the redeemed spirit in a believer. In Ephesians 4:32, he wrote: "Be kind to one another, tender-hearted, forgiving each other, just as God in Christ also has forgiven you."

We see Jesus modeling forgiveness, even before He went to the cross to die for our sins. John 13:1 reads, "Now before the Feast of the Passover, Jesus knowing that His hour had come that He would depart out of this world to the Father, having loved His own who were in the world, He loved them to the end." He kept loving His sin-filled, temptation-prone, self-seeking disciples to the very end. He didn't quit. He loved them completely, to the fullest extent. He showed that He did by washing their feet—including Judas'. Jesus knew Judas would betray Him (John 6:70; 13:27). He knew Peter and the other disciples would also (Matt. 26:56; Luke 22:31–34). Oh yes, Jesus knew about extending forgiveness in the face of unmet expectations. And we are to follow His example.

The Struggle to Forgive

Sometimes, it can be extremely difficult to forgive, even when the offense is small. Sometimes, those so-called "smaller" offenses can be tougher to overlook than the larger ones. Yet, no matter what the offense, your heavenly Father knows what He's asking of you when He tells you to forgive others the way He has forgiven you. If you've experienced the full and free forgiveness of your sins because you've placed your faith in the perfect and complete work of Christ to cover your sins, then you are called by God to forgive others for the "lesser" sins they have committed against you.

Which is greater in terms of offense? The offense given when one sinner sins against another sinner? Or the offense given when we sin against a perfect and holy God? If we *compare the sins* we commit in our horizontal relationships with others *to the sins* we commit against God in the vertical relationship between us and Him, *they don't match up*. As God is holy and always does what is right, when God extends forgiveness to any sinner, it is from a far greater "distance" than that which separates two sinners.

The sins that are committed against us—though some are awful and wicked beyond description—still pale in comparison to the sins we ourselves have committed against a most holy God. And yet, God in His infinite kindness and mercy, sent His Son to die, to be the means of wiping away the stain of our offenses against Him. In Christ, He has forgiven us. *That's why we're told to forgive one another, because the Lord has so completely forgiven us.* "So, as those who have been chosen of God, holy and beloved, put on a heart of compassion, kindness, humility, gentleness and patience; bearing with one another, and forgiving each other, whoever has a complaint against anyone; just as the Lord forgave you, so also should you" (Col. 3:12–13).

Opening Up Our Survival-Mode-Thinking Backpack

When people don't meet our expectations, we can return good for evil, forgive and cover over a wrong done to us, be gracious and merciful to them because we are applying the truths we tucked away in our survival-mode-thinking backpack:

1. I'm a sinner and don't receive what I deserve. So, when it comes to dealing with others, I need to see my circumstances from God's point of view. *The Lord has been more than kind in His dealings with me. Though I'd prefer things to be different, I need to remember I am living on the mercy of a gracious God.*

2. My trials are fewer than my sins. Again, when it comes to dealing with the hurt or trauma of someone's sin against you, in order for healing to take place and to give God glory in your response, you must remember these foundational truths. Our sense of justice often cries out for an accounting. An accounting would certainly be just, but not really what we're looking for. If we really want God to take note of another person's sin against us, then it's only right and just that our sins against someone else, or even against Him, should also be made accountable. Justice operates on an even playing field, one which holds all to the same standard of holiness. *So, though the trials I'm experiencing may be rough, the trials in no way match up to the consequences I should experience because of the sins I've already committed.*

3. If I am experiencing unmet expectations, it is because God has deemed them good for me. *Even the hurts, the frustrations, or the betrayals will be used by God and result in good for me.* He will strengthen, help, sanctify, and draw me into deeper and closer fellowship with Himself. His wisdom, love, and sovereignty cause my trials to make me more holy. If they weren't helpful in causing me to become more holy, I wouldn't experience them. Plain and simple. God's ways are not my ways, nor are His plans my plans.

4. The Lord will never disappoint me. I can trust Him even if others aren't trustworthy. Even if they are wonderful, attentive, and caring, because they're not omniscient, they still won't meet all my expectations. *Even when dealing with disappointment, the Lord is trustworthy.*

Other people cannot meet our every need. Even the closest and most nurturing of relationships will, at times, leave us wanting more, needing more, because mankind cannot meet the deepest yearnings of our hearts. *That role of meeting our needs belongs to God, and God alone.* In the next two chapters, we'll look specifically at how unmet expectations can lead to conflict in our relationships with other believers. We will also pinpoint areas within marriage that can fall prey to unmet expectations.

We started this journey by taking a look at unmet expectations and the undetected fallout they can sometimes bring to our lives. Yet the goal has never been to stay there just looking and assessing. *The goal is to gain wisdom from God and to learn from Him how to respond well when life doesn't go as planned, when we encounter the unexpected, and when we have a hard time accepting these things from the Lord.* As we consider our ways and apply biblical wisdom from God to them, it's my prayer that we'll fall more in love with Him, as our unmet expectations draw us nearer to Him.

QUESTIONS for REFLECTION

Chapter 9: Soul Mates and Other Myths

1. Read Colossians 3:1–11 and briefly explain what Paul discusses in these verses.

2. How do verses 1–11 of this chapter provide the framework for Paul's comments in verse 12?

3. What are the "chosen of God, holy and beloved" supposed to do according to verse 12?

4. Identify an additional two godly actions that are listed at the beginning of Colossians 3:13.

5. According to verse 13, what else should those godly responses include? Why should we show this mercy to others?

6. The situations for extending forgiveness can be varied and complex. Oftentimes, they require specific biblical counsel, so it's difficult to address every circumstance where forgiveness is needed. Yet, generally, when it comes to extending forgiveness, we have two basic scenarios. There are times when someone doesn't meet our expectations and we're irked or hurt about it. We need to realize that, in order to give God glory and not become bitter, we must forgive and move on. Colossians 3:12–14 provides perfect counsel for this type of situation. How would you counsel someone who needs to extend forgiveness based on what you learn from Colossians 3:12–14?

7. We also have scenarios in which we've been sinned *against*. Whether the offending party asks for forgiveness or not, God still calls us to forgive them. Summarize what you learn from the following Scriptures: Matthew 6:12–15; Luke 17:3–4, and Ephesians 4:30–32; 5:1–2.

8. How do the following Scriptures guide us in forgiving others when our hearts cry out for justice? Read Proverbs 20:22; Romans 12:17–21; 1 Thessalonians 5:15; Hebrews 12:14–15.

"Three Promises of Forgiveness"
1. I will not bring the matter up again.
2. I will not bring the matter up to others.
3. I will not bring the matter up to myself.[66]

"If I have been injured by another, let me bethink myself—How much better to be the sufferer than the wrong-doer!"
R. C. Chapman[67]

---

66 From "Peacemaking: An introduction to Biblical Conflict Resolution" by Janie Street from the "Women Discipling Women Conference" 2011, Used by permission.
67 Chapman, *Choice Sayings*, 81.

10

Stories from the Choir Loft

Those who are much acquainted with the cross of Christ, and with their own hearts, will be slow to take the reprover's office: if they do reprove, they will make it a solemn matter, knowing how much evil comes of the unwise handling of a fault.
Robert C. Chapman[68]

68 Chapman, *Choice Sayings*, 81.

Ellen and Sophie were founding members of their church. In the church's early days, they worked tirelessly with their pastor to share the gospel and train members of the congregation. Lately, little cracks have emerged in their relationship. A few months ago, Ellen was asked to plan a women's retreat for the church. Sophie fully expected Ellen to ask her to help on the committee. But, when Ellen didn't approach her about it, Sophie's feelings were hurt.

To make matters worse, Sophie learned through the church grapevine that Ellen was actually glad for the opportunity to lead the committee without Sophie taking the limelight. Wounded by this news, Sophie found she had trouble thinking kind thoughts about Ellen. Soon little disparaging comments about Ellen began to leap from her lips when she talked with other women in the foyer. When Ellen heard what Sophie was saying, she became hurt and withdrew from social contact with Sophie.

Because both women were well-liked, influential members in the church, what started as hurt over some unmet expectations escalated to a full-scale schism in the church. While Ellen and Sophie's story is fiction, we know it is more common than we'd like to admit! For some of us, their story is our story. It doesn't take a rocket scientist to connect the dots between our unmet expectations and the ensuing conflict in our relationships. Even if a relationship becomes strained or suffers from conflict, it doesn't mean it has to stay that way. God always provides a way for us to respond in a godly manner. That's why it's imperative that we consider how to respond well when unmet expectations, hurt, or conflict arise.

We Don't Intuitively Know How to Resolve Conflict

When her darling progeny have run to her one too many times, each eager to tell their tales of woe and outrage against a sibling, many a tired-out mommy has replied, "You two just go up to your room and figure it out. And don't come down until you're ready to play nice." While that may seem to calm the conflict, it doesn't provide a real solution to the problem; for children, if left to themselves, rarely know how to promote peace. The same holds true for grown-ups.

Left to ourselves, we rarely know how to gain control of sinful responses or bring a peaceful solution to a dispute. Thankfully, the Lord gives us everything we need to guide us in the process. Life and unmet expectations go hand in hand. So, until we go home to be with the Lord, or He returns in glory, we'll have unmet expectations in our relationships. However, we can apply godly wisdom to the situation and the conflict can be healed in a way that brings glory to God.

Everyone Will Get Along—In Heaven

One *expectation* we often have as Christians is that we won't have conflict. We expect all who claim to be Christians to get along. I battle this expectation—often. Yet that expectation doesn't take into account the depth or pervasiveness of sin in each of us. We need to understand that among the best and brightest of God's people, misunderstandings, mistrust, and disunity can occur. Even when we're trying to do what's right and bless others, conflict can arise. This gives us another reason why we need to understand and guard against letting expectations turn into an opportunity for conflict. How can we protect our relationships so that conflict doesn't escalate and bring dishonor to the name of Christ?

We'll find the answers we're looking for tucked into the book of Philippians. Philippians is the perfect place to start because, as Paul wrote to the believers, he revealed that doing all for Jesus Christ was to be their primary motivation.

Living for Jesus then becomes our guide in overcoming unmet expectations. The book of Philippians calls us to see Jesus Christ in His glory and to live for Him. Paul summed it up by saying in Philippians 3:8, "I count all things to be loss in view of the surpassing value of knowing Christ Jesus my Lord, for whom I have suffered the loss of all things, and count them but rubbish so that I may gain Christ." All the hopes, thoughts, and desires that are bound up in our relationship with the Lord are pulled together in that verse. *Jesus* is our reason for striving for unity, even when hurt by unmet expectations.

The Philippians Dealt with Many Kinds of Conflict

It's apparent as you read the book of Philippians that the church was dealing with conflict on a number of levels. In Philippians 1:27–30, Paul writes:

> Only conduct yourselves in a manner worthy of the gospel of Christ, so that whether I come and see you or remain absent, I will hear of you that you are standing firm in one spirit, with one mind striving together for the faith of the gospel; in no way alarmed by your opponents—which is a sign of destruction for them, but of salvation for you, and that too, from God. For to you it has been granted for Christ's sake, not only to believe in Him, but also to suffer for His sake, experiencing the same conflict, which you saw in me, and now hear to be in me.

The church had enemies on the outside who were stirring up trouble, so Paul instructed the people to be godly in their responses and to maintain unity. He reminded them that, though they had enemies *outside* the church, they needed to live in harmony *inside* the church.

The Need for Unity

We see Paul addressing the issue of unity again in chapter 2:3–4: "Do nothing from selfishness or empty conceit, but with humility of mind regard one another as more important than yourselves; do not merely look out for your own personal interests, but also for the interests of others." It's clear from these verses that there was an unholy competition among the people in the Philippian church. They were being selfish and proud in their dealings with one another and needed reminders to live with one another in humility and love. Yet those admonitions and encouragements are for us too, and are meant to shape our responses when our unmet expectations inject discord into our relationships.

Paul is so concerned about their problem that he sends Timothy to check on their condition (Phil. 2:19–30). He understood the damage that could be done to the fledgling church if those factions and fractures were allowed to continue. Paul urged the Philippians to follow his example, as there were many who had turned away from Christ and had become enemies of Christ (3:17–19). Those who had turned away from following Christ revealed that their god was their appetite and that they gloried in their shame, as they set their minds on earthly things. By contrast, he reminded the Philippians that "our citizenship is in heaven, from which also we eagerly wait for a Savior, the Lord Jesus Christ; who will transform the body of our humble state into conformity with the body of His glory, by the exertion of the power that He has even to subject all things to Himself" (Phil. 3:20–21).

The Need to Stand Firm

So, when we come to Philippians 4:1 and we read the first word "therefore," it comes loaded with Paul's previous admonitions to fight for peace and live for the glory of Jesus Christ. He writes, *"Therefore"*—because our citizenship is in heaven, because we are going to be transformed, because we are going soon to be with our Savior—*"therefore, my beloved brethren whom I long to see, my joy and crown"* (emphasis added). It is easy to imagine the whole crowd leaning forward to listen. "Yes. What else? What Paul? Oh, this is going to be good—tell us. We are breathless with anticipation to hear what you are going to tell us next."

So, Paul proceeds, "Therefore, my beloved brethren . . . *stand firm in the Lord*" (emphasis added). The Philippians must have leaned back in their seats and collectively scratched their heads. Huh? After all that build up, Paul simply told them to stand firm. Now, that's not quite what we expected to hear. And yet, because Paul spent all that time laying the foundation of thought from chapter 1 to chapter 4, we must take note. What was happening, or was going to happen, that necessitated this admonition to stand firm in the Lord? Paul knew that what was coming down the pike was going to test their mettle, so his exhortation to them was "Stand firm."

What was the thing that would test their faith? It follows in Philippians 4:2–3: "I urge Euodia and I urge Syntyche to live in harmony in the Lord. Indeed, true companion, I ask you also to help these women who have shared my struggle in the cause of the gospel, together with Clement also and the rest of my fellow workers, whose names are in the book of life." Wow! Not what we might have expected after all that buildup.

Yet, as I review the story of Euodia and Syntyche, I realize their conflict could have begun in a very similar way to the story I made up about Ellen and Sophie at the beginning of this chapter. When Paul addresses Euodia and Syntyche, he never mentions any doctrinal heresy or any sin of immorality. These were *normal* women who labored in the ministry together in *normal* ways and somehow something rather *normal* happened, which undermined their unity to the point that Paul had to name them in his letter to the church. Imagine having *your* name and sins recorded in the Bible for all posterity!

The Philippians needed to *stand firm* as Paul called on them to deal with the discord in their church. I find his admonition so interesting! Why would the Philippians need to stand firm? The situation doesn't seem like that big of a deal—simply help two women get their disagreement worked out. Apparently, it was more than that. It may have been that these women were well known and loved in their church. It may have been because the church had put off dealing with their conflict when it was a small thing. By the time Paul wrote to them, it had grown into a big problem. Perhaps the church didn't want to risk offending either of these women as they were both so well known and loved. Perhaps the members didn't want to be accused of meddling. It could even have been that the Philippians were afraid of damaging their relationships with these women or with one another if they took a stand for righteousness. Whatever the reason, it was now time for the Philippians to stand firm in the Lord, as they helped these women work out their differences.

How Did We End Up Here?

Paul gives the Philippians a clear instruction as to what they are to do. This is what standing firm means in practice: "I urge Euodia and I urge Syntyche to live in harmony in the Lord" (4:2). Paul strips away the "let's pretend it's not happening because of who these women are" veneer and calls the whole church to look at the mess this conflict has created. Paul wanted everyone to recognize, acknowledge, and deal with what was happening in their midst. The fact that these two women were named and given specific instruction means that their conflict had moved beyond being a private misunderstanding to a public disagreement and it was threatening the unity of the church.

It must be stated that Paul doesn't have some personal issue with Euodia and Syntyche. They were included in the group he called "beloved" and his "joy and crown." He reminded everyone in verse 3 that Euodia and Syntyche had helped him proclaim the gospel of Christ. His love and affection for them caused him to use winsome language to bring them around. Concerning their conflict, Paul was impartial. He appealed to both women since they each had played a part in their discord.

Uh-oh, This Conflict Could Happen to Me

We don't know what happened between these two women. We only know that it happened—and that's sufficient warning to us. *Conflict can happen at any time to anyone.* Certainly, most of us have experienced a break in a relationship at least once. Disunity can begin in harmless enough ways, which if not dealt with biblically, may grow to epic proportions. Disagreements can arise over every topic conceivable: marriage, parenting, modesty, money, politics, house cleaning, dating, types of schooling for your children, entertainment choices, even the best time to have your devotions. And let's not even enter into the food wars about the virtues and vices of organic, free-range, gluten-free, dairy-free, non-gmo and so on. Little divisions can arise, and if we're not careful, they can become the artillery for a war zone.

Want Your Name in Lights for All to See?

If Paul were writing his letter to your church today, would you be in danger of having your name listed in his letter? Perhaps not. It is also possible that you may not recognize how perilously close you are to turning into a Euodia or a Syntyche. Here are a few questions to help you diagnose the beginnings of a conflict that you might have:

- *Do you avoid a person when you see him or her at church?* For me, avoiding someone is a quick indicator that all is not well in my heart. Rather than avoiding that person and rationalizing my behavior, I need to go to him or her and seek to heal the breach and mend the relationship.

- *Do you rationalize your behavior so you can take communion, rather than going to seek peace with the person?* If you've been in church for any length of time, you know what I'm talking about. We walk into church and discover that it's communion Sunday, the time when we're to examine our hearts, to see if we are harboring any sin, and, if we need to make something right with someone, to "let the elements pass." Rather than going to the person as the Scriptures command, we may simply stop at confessing our sin to the Lord, and skip the part about making things right with our offended brother or sister (Matt. 5:23–24).

- *Do you think ugly thoughts about someone? Do you talk about them in a negative way or with a negative slant?* I don't need to say too much on this one. We know it's wrong for us to do this. The color and nature of our thoughts and words reveals the true state of our hearts. Negative thoughts in our hearts, if not repented of, produce sinful behavior toward others.

- *Do you pray for them?* Certainly, if you're unwilling to pray for someone, then something's going on in your heart. In Matthew 5:44, Jesus tells us that we are to pray for those who persecute us, which includes those who hurt us on a far lesser scale.

- *Are you taking sides or taking note of who is taking your side or theirs?* Anytime you move into a place of "me" versus "the other person," you need to guard against bearing grudges and fostering disunity.

- *Do you notice that you feel more stubborn or unyielding toward that person than other people?* This is another tell-tale sign for me. Often, when my heart isn't right, I find I'm less willing to listen to the other person's ideas.

- *Is it possible that you know you are just plain old, downright unforgiving toward the person? Unwilling to yield? Unrepentant about your actions? Bitter? Resentful?* All things to consider.

- *Is there any way they can ever regain your good graces?* Or are you like Mr. Darcy in Jane Austen's *Pride and Prejudice*, "My good opinion once lost is lost forever."[69] I find this is another good indicator for me. If my heart is right toward the other person, then I won't hold that person at arm's length.

---

69   Jane Austen, *Pride and Prejudice*, (San Diego, CA: Canterbury Classics, a division of Baker and Taylor Publishing Group: San Diego, 2012), 48.

The diagnostic questions above help reveal the true condition of our hearts by poking at the places where we *try* to hide behind our sins of puffed-up pride and self-protection. It's safe to say that if we allow petty jealousy, bitterness, or grudges from unmet expectations to linger, we are in danger of becoming a Euodia or a Syntyche.

From Danger to Deliverance

Can you imagine what it must have been like the Sunday Paul's letter was read to the Philippian church? Perhaps Euodia and her supporters were sitting on one side of the church, while Syntyche and her crew sat on the other. These godly women, who had *together* shared the gospel alongside Paul, who had been transformed by the blood of Jesus, now found themselves entangled in a snarl of sins so knotted that they were dividing the very church they had labored to build up by God's grace. Hurt feelings, unmet expectations, and unresolved issues were wedged in so tightly between them that unforgiveness, rationalizing and blame-shifting had taken root. Oh, the shame of it all!

Even while Paul's letter was being read, even while they were nodding their heads in agreement to its opening chapters, even while murmuring "amen" at its contents, God was x-raying their hearts with His Word, revealing the cancer of their sin. Their conflict was affecting the church to the point that Paul was compelled to name them personally in his letter for all to hear, for all following generations to know! There was no place to hide, no commendation, only shame because they would not live in harmony with each other. Their tiff had turned into a tussle, and their tussle into a cold war. Paul had to get tough with them. We should heed the lessons they needed to learn for our own relationships, so that we live harmoniously with one another.

In previous chapters, we've taken some good hard looks at our own discontentment over unmet expectations. We would certainly be remiss if we didn't spend time examining the fallout we experience when unmet expectations come into our relationships, and consider what we should do when this occurs. By using Euodia and Syntyche as a case study, we will examine the components necessary to keep our relationships healthy and harmonious, and working the way God intends.

In Philippians 4:2, Paul states that we are "to live in harmony." This can also be translated "to be of the same mind, to agree." The same Greek word[70] is used in Philippians 2:2, Romans 12:16, and 2 Corinthians 13:11, to mention a few verses where it occurs. In each instance where the specific Greek

---

70   Strong's Enhanced Greek Lexicon #5426, *phroneo*

word is used, we are urged to be agreeable and like-minded concerning agreed upon truth. That sounds well and good. Yet what will it look like in the day to day? Does being agreeable and like-minded mean that we always agree and may never have a different opinion? To what extent are we to be like-minded? If you like blue, do I need to like blue? If I send my kids to a Christian school, do you need to send your kids to a Christian school? What is really in view when we're told to live harmoniously, agreeably, with like-mindedness? Surely, it can't mean that we become a church of drones with no opinions or differences whatsoever! Thankfully, it doesn't! Biblical unity is not about everything being the same. *Biblical unity is about working together and being in harmony with one another concerning the truth of God's Word. As we won't always agree or have the same opinions about things that are extra biblical, practicing biblical unity is essential.*

The Musical Picture of Harmonious Living

I sang in the choir in junior high and high school. Generally, I was an alto, though at the "zenith" of my singing career I was able to slide into second soprano. In a choir, the altos have the role of singing the harmony to the melody being sung by the sopranos. Generally, once I learned my part, I was a fairly dependable singer, that is, as long as everyone around me was singing the same part. My somewhat inept musical ear could at times usher in harmony headaches for those around me who were endeavoring to sing their part well. That's the thing about a choir. Everyone has a part to sing in order to bring harmony and richness to the melody of the music. Harmonies makes the music richer, more interesting, and more nuanced as each part supports the melody. Not everyone can sing the melody, so the other parts work *with* and *for* the melody, rather than against it, producing something beautiful and enjoyable. They're not fighting against one another, but supporting one another. This provides us with a perfect picture of biblical harmony.

The *Believer's Bible Commentary* states: "It is impossible for us to be united in all things in daily life, but, as far as the things of the Lord are concerned, it is possible for us to submerge our petty, personal differences in order that the Lord may be magnified and His work advanced."[71] Here is the goal. Here is the aim of our like-mindedness— "that the Lord may be magnified." The Lord, His ways, and Word being our focus, our unity with one another gains a framework. The Word of God is the musical score that keeps us from singing our own individualized part or getting off-key.

---

71 William MacDonald, *Believer's Bible Commentary: Old and New Testaments*, ed. Arthur Farstad (Nashville, TN: Thomas Nelson, 1995), 1977.

Caveats to Harmonious Living

Philippians 4:2 says we are to live in harmony "in the Lord," which means in very simplified terms that anything not "in the Lord" isn't helpful for living in unity. With the little caveat of "in the Lord" humming in our heads, we will take a closer look at harmonious living. As we do, we'll gain much needed wisdom and guidance in our day-to-day relationships.

We understand the sense of the phrase "in the Lord," when we look at two other verses of Scripture where it's similarly used. In Ephesians 6:1 we read, "Children, obey your parents in the Lord, for this is right." Children are to obey their parents as if they are obeying the Lord Himself, knowing it's the right and pleasing thing to do. A further insight is given into the meaning of this phrase in Colossians 3:18 where we read, "Wives, be subject to your husbands, as is fitting in the Lord." Here we learn that a wife's submission to her husband is predicated on "the degree that it is fitting and proper in the Lord."[72]

Harmonious Living Requires Turning Away from Sin

Basically, our text in Philippians 4:2 means that it is God's will for us to live in harmony with one another. But that harmony is never to be at the expense of truth. So, we must never fail to address issues that need to be dealt with for fear of disrupting the unity. There is no true, biblical unity when sin is overlooked and God's standards are compromised. Isn't that interesting? We live in a time when *taking a biblical stand* for right and wrong is seen as unloving and divisive. However, harmonious, biblical unity *never* contradicts the Scriptures, nor is biblical unity ever maintained by sinning. Relationships cannot take priority over our obedience to the Lord—even for the sake of getting along with others.

Let's consider: Is it possible to enjoy God-pleasing fellowship with someone who is in a state of ongoing rebellion against the Lord? Not at all. The person living in sin rejects God. The most "harmonious" thing we can do is to lovingly confront the person in sin, praying that God will bring them to repentance. Only when Christians are right before the Lord can harmony reign. James 5:19–20 states: "My brethren, if any among you strays from the truth *and one turns him back*, let him know that he who turns a sinner from the error of his way will save his soul from death and will cover a multitude of sins" (emphasis added). James paints a picture of how to maintain true, biblical, harmonious living—if we see someone

---

72 I deal more with this issue in my book, *God's Priorities for Today's Woman: Discovering His Plan for You* (Eugene, OR: Harvest House, 2011), 205-217. Chapter 14 is on "The Art of Loving Submission," while pages 212 and 213 deal with the issue of when *not* to submit.

caught in sin, we are lovingly to plead with that person, exhorting him or her to turn from that sin. When he or she repents, we are to rejoice in the fact that unity has been restored!

Harmonious Living Requires Turning Away from Doctrinal Heresy

Being nice or not making waves doesn't promote godly unity either, especially when someone is drifting into doctrinal heresy. We need to remember we can never be of one mind, one spirit, and one faith with someone who holds to a different faith. Instead, evangelism is needed. God gives us specific commands on how to handle those who have strayed from the faith: "Now I urge you, brethren, *keep your eye on those who cause dissensions and hindrances contrary to the teaching which you learned, and turn away from them.* For such men are slaves, not of our Lord Christ but of their own appetites; and by their smooth and flattering speech they deceive the hearts of the unsuspecting" (Rom. 16:17–18, emphasis added). Notice we're to take note of people who live in a swirl of doctrinal controversy and chaos. If we discover their teaching is contrary to sound doctrine, then we're to "turn away from them." Keeping our eyes on doctrinal pot-stirrers requires discernment and consideration as to what they're really teaching. If their teaching is dangerous or wickedly heretical, we are to "turn away from them." *Living in harmony with one another in the Lord requires evaluating and judging what is being taught.*[73]

Charles Spurgeon said, "The best way to promote unity is to promote truth. It will not do for us to be all 'united together' by simply yielding to one another's mistakes. We are to love each other in Christ; but we are not to be so united that we are not able to see each other's faults, and especially not able to see our own. No, purge the house of God, and then shall grand and blessed times dawn on us."[74]

Harmonious Living Requires Discernment

We are called to *stand firm*, not to be mindlessly flexible and tolerant when the honor of the Lord and the safety of souls is at stake. Yet, when it comes to things that are extra biblical where "my opinion versus your opinion" or "my conviction versus your conviction" or "my way of doing things versus your way of doing things" apply, then God calls us to strive diligently to maintain harmonious relationships. Again, "harmonious"

---

73 Acts 20:29-31; Ephesians 4:14-16; 1 Timothy 1:3-7; and Titus 1:10-11 all give counsel on how to handle false teaching that may infiltrate the church.

74 C. H. Spurgeon, "Importance of Small Things in Religion," in *The New Park Street Pulpit Sermons*, vol. 6 (London: Passmore & Alabaster, 1860), 171.

doesn't mean identical. We're not cookie-cutter Christians, drones without thought, opinion, or ideas. However, we must have unity in doctrines essential to salvation. Our differences will make us prone to conflict, unmet expectations, and divergent opinions. This is all the more reason to practice unity and to guard our relationships.

A little preparation and ongoing vigilance in the areas just discussed can make a great difference in responding well to unmet expectations and avoiding harmony busters. Proactive thinking asks, "How should I respond the next time my feelings get hurt, when my pride gets in the way? What should I do when a misunderstanding occurs, or I find myself competing with or feeling resentful toward someone? Will I allow the little ripple created by my unmet expectations turn into a tidal wave of destruction and misery?"

A Little Preparation Makes a Difference

It's helpful to remember you can only prepare *your* heart. You'll have to leave the other person in the Lord's hands. Yet there's such safety and comfort in knowing you're responsible for your responses and not anyone else's. You can pray for the other person; Lord willing, you may even be able to talk to him or her about "the issue." Whether he or she responds well or not, whether he or she changes or not, you are not accountable for the other person's response. If the person belongs to the Lord, He will work in them, just as He is working in you. Your goal is to *give God glory in everything you do,* trusting that the other person will do the same.

As Paul gave instructions for Euodia and Syntyche in Philippians 4:2–3, he didn't take sides in the argument. This in and of itself lends weight to my theory that the conflict between these two women most likely stemmed from unmet expectations, and the hurt and misunderstanding that results. Paul enlisted the help of the church and its leaders to guide these women back to reconciliation and harmony. The point wasn't to dredge up all the details of "I said and then she said," but to cover a multitude of sins, forgive, and move forward to the glory of God. Choosing to restore harmony shows a love for the Lord Jesus and a desire to obey His commands.

Two Simple Ways to Maintain Harmony in our Relationships

To get started, let's look at two practical ways to maintain harmony in our relationships. First, *we're to love one another.* Paul wrote to the Colossians,

"Beyond all these things *put on love, which is the perfect bond of unity.* Let the peace of Christ rule in your hearts, to which indeed you were called in one body; and be thankful" (3:14–15, emphasis added).

God knows our propensity to turn away from one another, rather than pursue peace. Yet the Scriptures teach us that our love provides the glue for the stick-to-it kind of unity God desires. The "perfect bond of unity" kind of love is made up of tougher stuff than the sticky, ooey-gooey, heart-emoji love we tend to rely upon. The love we need to show toward one another is patient, kind, not provoked, and refuses to take into account a wrong suffered, among other things (1 Cor. 13:4–7). It's the kind of love that doesn't give up. Peter summarized it well when he wrote, "Above all, *keep fervent in your love for one another*, because love covers a multitude of sins" (1 Peter 4:8, emphasis added). If we're actively engaged in extending patient, unprovoked love toward one another, it makes it much easier to allow irksome idiosyncrasies to slide by.

Biblical unity lives in an atmosphere of persistent love, as Christ's peace rules in our hearts. The word "rule" in Colossians 3:15 means *to hold sway, to arbitrate, to umpire over*. What a picture! As we seek to love one another, we're to let peace arbitrate or call the shots in any conflict we may have with another person.

Another way to practically maintain harmony in our relationships is simply to think the best of others. This is huge because we often assume the worst! Have you ever had one of those imaginary conversations with someone while you're standing in front of the mirror in the morning? As you look at yourself, you create a whole conversation of rebuttal and defense with a zinger or two thrown in for good measure. Have you ever done that? Oh goodness! Perhaps I'm the only one.

When I find myself in imaginary debate mode, there are two key passages I go to. They show me my sin and help me change my response. God's Word helps me change when I remember, "But refuse foolish and ignorant speculations, knowing that they produce quarrels. The Lord's bond-servant must not be quarrelsome, but be kind to all, able to teach, patient when wronged" (2 Tim. 2:23–24). Quarreling with someone is nothing more than engaging in "foolish and ignorant speculations," leading to conflict, even if the quarrel remains locked in my head. That kind of mental sword-fighting is foolish and ignorant simply because it is speculation. Until I *actually* talk to the person and hear what he or she *actually* says, it's just conjecture on my part.

The other text that helps me to think well of others is found in James. This passage is a bit scarier and reminds me how truly serious it is to God that I think rightly and well of others. James 5:9 reads, "Do not complain, brethren, against one another, so that you yourselves may not be judged;

behold, the Judge is standing right at the door." It certainly makes me pause and think when I picture God listening *as a judge*, while I harangue another of His dear ones in my heart. God takes note of my speech and listens to and judges my thoughts.

Seeking harmony in our relationships demands that we think well of one another. "Let the words of my mouth and the meditation of my heart be acceptable in Your sight, O LORD, my rock and my Redeemer" (Ps. 19:14).

It Can Happen to Anyone

Sometimes, a situation doesn't get resolved right away or at all. Paul was no stranger to unresolved conflict, as we read in Acts 15:39: "And there occurred such a sharp disagreement that they separated from one another, and Barnabas took Mark with him and sailed away to Cyprus." The episode described in that one sentence dripped a stain upon Paul's ministry, and he knew it. It's no wonder Paul writes so eloquently and lovingly about the conflict between Euodia and Syntyche. He understood how easily believers can find themselves in a similar mess. Knowing what trouble unresolved conflict can create, Paul urged the Philippians, and Euodia and Syntyche, to deal with it so it wouldn't fester any longer.

In his commentary on Philippians, John MacArthur states, "The tragic conflict between Euodia and Syntyche reveals that even the most mature, faithful, and committed people can become so selfish as to be embroiled in controversy if they are not diligent to maintain unity."[75] The best among us can get drawn into silly disagreements, affronts, and grudges, so that, before we realize it, we've dug in our heels and refused to give grace, show love, and forgive. Understanding how susceptible people can be to these kinds of conflicts, Paul enlists the help of the whole church to get these two women back on track.

Bringing in a Third Party to Maintain Unity

Conflict, especially unresolved conflict among believers, doesn't bring God glory, plain and simple. Yet, sometimes two people need the help of other believers to gain a more objective, heavenly perspective in order to resolve their issues. In his letter to the Philippians, Paul enlists the aid of another brother in the church to mediate the conflict and bring an end to the feud. It was time for a little biblical pressure to be applied in love. The tiff between these two women had gone on long enough. It was

75   John F. MacArthur Jr., *Philippians, MacArthur New Testament Commentary* (Chicago: Moody Press, 2001), 273.

polarizing the church as more people were brought into the conflict. As is often the case with people in the middle of a conflict, Euodia and Syntyche weren't asking for help. Pride blinds us to the steps necessary to restore unity.

What if Paul came to you with this request? He may say, "Indeed, true sister, my yoke fellow, my fellow worker in the faith, I ask you to help these women." Your first reaction may be, "Oh no, Paul, you've got the wrong gal! I'm not a good mediator. Besides, these women are my friends. If I start getting in the middle of this, I might lose both friendships." But, if you are living for Jesus and love Him more than you love yourself, you will seek His will, which may mean jumping into the middle of a scuffle so the peace of Christ can rule.

When conflict gets to the stage where names are read before the church, the whole church grieves. *However, the Scriptures tell us that it's a privilege to be part of the restoration process.* James 5:19–20 says, "My brethren, if any among you strays from the truth and one turns him back, let him know that he who turns a sinner from the error of his way will save his soul from death and will cover a multitude of sins."

A Step-by-Step Guide to Restoring Unity

- *Pray*–Pray for them; pray for yourself as you mediate; pray for the body; pray for the glory of God to be manifested; pray all the way through the process of restoring unity.
- *Examine your heart for sinful responses* as we are exhorted in Galatians 6:1: "Brethren, even if anyone is caught in any trespass, you who are spiritual, restore such a one in a spirit of gentleness; each one looking to yourself, so that you too will not be tempted."
- *Remember that there are two sides to every story*, so don't rush to make judgments. Proverbs 18:17 wisely counsels, "The first to plead his case seems right, until another comes and examines him." If you're going to proceed wisely, you must give fair consideration to both sides. Sometimes, discerning the "right" side isn't as simple as you think.
- As you listen to each side, listen well, but *don't allow either side to "vent" in an ungodly manner.* Encourage both sides to speak carefully, truthfully, and with self-control.
- *Gain wisdom* from Philippians 4:2–3 and put it into practice.
- *Appeal to their shared past history.* In Philippians 4:3, Paul wanted Euodia and Syntyche to remember how they had labored together to start the church and to use this as a way to encourage reconciliation

between them. Look for ways they had labored and served together.
- *Appeal to their common future.* At the end of Philippians 4:3, Paul reminded these quarreling ladies of their future together in heaven. Again, this was a means of persuading them to repent of their quarreling.
- *Appeal to their love for other believers.* Paul also reminded Euodia and Syntyche how their conflict was affecting the church in Philippians 4:3.
- And finally, if necessary, *bring prideful and ungodly responses out in the open,* as Paul did in Philippians 4:2.
- Once you've put the steps in place, *stand firm.* Paul began with the admonition to "stand firm" because dealing with conflict can make us weak-kneed, small of faith, and susceptible to ungodly partiality. Out of love for the Lord Jesus and for the glory of God's name, we must stand firm once we wade into the murky waters of another's controversy.

When You're the One in a Scuffle

What if you are embroiled in a quarrel with someone? How should you respond if you are approached with an offer of help to resolve your conflict? We may be tempted to respond in any number of ways that are not so nice. If you truly love the Lord, you must pause and listen to the wisdom of the wise.

Six Steps to Responding Well When Someone Wants to Help You

- *Be humble.* James 4:6 reminds us that God is opposed to the proud, but gives grace to the humble. So, if another person speaks to you about some sin, or sins, in your life, you must humble yourself and listen. Don't give into stubborn pride. Humble yourself and listen.
- *Remember your sin is not hidden.* No matter how artfully you think you've managed to keep it under wraps, Galatians 5:19 tells us that "the deeds of the flesh are evident." Other people can see your sinful responses. They might not know what's behind it all, but the sin does show up.
- *Admit you are in sin.* Holding onto grudges or choosing to stay offended is sinful. 1 John 1:9 tells us that "if we confess our sins, He is faithful and righteous to forgive us our sins and to cleanse us from all unrighteousness." In 1 John 8 and 10, we're told that if we lie about our sin, we deceive ourselves and make God out to be a liar.
- *Admit and repent of your part in the conflict.* Ephesians 4:25 forthright-

ly counsels us to "[lay] aside falsehood, speak truth each one of you with his neighbor, for we are members of one another." Repent and tell the truth about your role in the conflict.

- *Do what's necessary to fix or heal the conflict, if possible.* Matthew 5:23 gives us some practical steps toward reconciliation: "Therefore if you are presenting your offering at the altar, and there remember that your brother has something against you, leave your offering there before the altar and go; first be reconciled to your brother, and then come and present your offering." Our worship of God is impeded by our conflicts. So, we're called to do what we can to bring reconciliation, as quickly as possible.

- *Submit to the healing process.* If your church leaders have lovingly pre-scribed steps for reconciliation and healing, then strive to humbly submit to their guidance. Hebrews 13:17 tells us, "Obey your leaders and submit to them, for they keep watch over your souls as those who will give an account. Let them do this with joy and not with grief, for this would be unprofitable for you."

Why Bother?

Why work so hard to reestablish harmony? Paul provides the reason when he implores his coworker in the Philippian church to "help these women who have shared my struggle in the cause of the gospel, together with Clement also and the rest of my fellow workers, whose names are in the book of life" (4:3). *We will be together in heaven.* Because fellow believers' names are in the book of life, we are called to seek peace to the best of our ability (Rom. 14:19).

It's helpful to remember that the Lord is working in the other person's life, just as He is in yours. He sees the motives of that person's heart just as He sees yours. God is perfecting us until the day of Christ Jesus (Phil. 1:6). You are nearer heaven today than you were yesterday, so do as Thomas Brooks wisely counsels, "Labor mightily for a healing spirit. Put away anything that may hinder the applying of balm to heal your wounds.... Discord and division are not becoming to any Christian. For wolves to distress the lambs is no wonder, but for one of the lambs to trouble another lamb, this is unnatural and monstrous."[76]

---

76 Thomas Brooks, *A Puritan Golden Treasury,* ed. I.D.E. Thomas (Edinburgh: The Banner of Truth Trust, 1989), 304.

Preparing for Peace in the Midst of Unmet Expectations

The truth is, we are going to disappoint one another. We'll often fail to meet expectations others may have of us. That's a given. *But, even when things feel less than heavenly, we can still deal with ourselves biblically.* We can learn to think rightly within ourselves and about our circumstances. We can respond to one another in a biblical manner, so that godly unity reigns within our churches and our relationships with other believers.

Let us put into practice Paul's encouragement to the Philippians from chapter 2 verses 1–4. Here it is with some paraphrasing on my part: "Dear pioneer girls, if you have enjoyed encouragement from Jesus Christ, if you have known the consoling and comforting power of His love, and have experienced the sweet fellowship of His Spirit, then bring joy to us all by living in harmony and pursuing the goal of knowing God and giving Him glory. Even if you've experienced unmet expectations, hurt, or betrayal, do nothing from selfishness or pride. The Lord will help you humbly regard others as more important than yourselves, not merely looking out for your own personal interests, but also for the interests of others."

Let me close with this prayer from John MacDuff, a Scottish pastor who lived during the 1800s, "Lord, unite Your own people more and more. Why should we be guilty of such sad estrangements, crossing and recrossing one another on life's highway with alien and jealous looks, when professing to be sprinkled with the same blood, to bear the same name, and be heirs of the same inheritance? Let me live near to Jesus and then I shall live near all His people, looking forward to that blessed time when we shall see eye to eye and heart to heart—no jarring or discordant note to mar the everlasting ascription of 'blessing, and honor, and glory and power, to Him who sits upon the throne, and to the Lamb, forever and ever.' Amen."[77]

---

77   John R. MacDuff, *The Morning Watches and the Night Watches,* a reprint of the original, (Memphis, TN: Bottom of the Hill Publishing, 2012), 44.

QUESTIONS for REFLECTION

Chapter 10: Stories from the Choir Loft

I would particularly advise those that have adhered to me in the late controversy to watch over your spirits and avoid all bitterness towards others. However wrong you may think others have been, maintain with great diligence and watchfulness a Christian meekness and gentleness of spirit; and labour, in this respect, to excel those who are of a contrary part.[78]
Jonathan Edwards

1. Read Philippians 1:15–18. What attitudes did Paul display when he faced those who were trying to undermine his ministry? How are those attitudes an example to follow for maintaining godly unity?

2. Read Philippians 1:27–30 and list the components necessary to maintain unity against a common enemy.

3. In Philippians 2:1–4 Paul digs deeper into the issues of the Philippians' disunity. According to verses 1–4, what qualities were lacking in the way people in the church were treating one another?

4. How would striving for *one* goal and *one* purpose protect you from disunity? (Phil. 2:2). How would not being selfish, proud, or not grumbly be a protection against conflict? Why would rejoicing be an antidote against disunity?

5. Read Philippians 2:14–15. What two actions help maintain unity in the body of Christ? What is the goal? Why is this important to Paul according to verse 16?

6. What things keep *you* from dealing with discord in the body, be it discord between you and another person, or in helping others to overcome a dispute?

7. Name at least one way you can help maintain godly unity in the body of your local church.

78 Jonathan Edwards, "Farewell Sermon," *Works*, 1:ccvi-ccvii quoted in *Voices from the Past*, vol. 1, 7.

For Further Reflection

1. If Paul were writing his letter to your church today, would you be in danger of having your name included in the letter like Euodia and Syntyche?

2. What are the steps you must take to overcome breaches in your relationships?

3. If you have a quarrel with someone, do you need someone else to help you in the process of reconciliation? What's at stake if you don't get help? What is the goal for getting help?

11

What if You Were Married to Nabal?

Faith comes to God through His Word and pleads His promises.[79]
Richard Sibbes

79 Richard Sibbes quoted in *Voices from the Past: Puritan Devotional Readings, vol. 2,* ed. Richard Rushing (Edinburgh: The Banner of Truth Trust, 2016), 135.

"I, take you to be my husband; and I do promise and covenant; before God and these witnesses; to be your loving and faithful wife; in plenty and in want; in joy and in sorrow; in sickness and in health; for as long as we both shall live."

I made that promise to my darling husband on a sweltering August day in 1984, while he made its counterpart to me. All these years later, we're still living out those promises. By God's ever present and sustaining grace, we've enjoyed a magnificent marriage. We've had times of plenty and times of want. We've most certainly had joy, more joy than sorrow during our years together. Up to this point, we haven't endured much sickness, though I expect that's on the horizon, since we're not getting any younger. We've also experienced unmet expectations, ones Jack had for me and ones I had for him. Some of the things we've expected of each other have been silly and rather laughable, while others felt vitally important. Frivolous expectations easily fade into the background, but the deeper ones take more biblical thought, prayer, and help from the Lord to work through.

It's safe to say no relationship suffers more under the weight of unmet expectations than marriage. Even the best of husbands can fail to meet a wife's expectations and vice versa. It's for that reason that we want to take a special look at the marriage relationship and the role unmet expectations can play within it. Since we can only work on our own hearts, we're going to examine in detail how to apply God's admonition in Ephesians 5:33. It tells a wife to "[respect] her husband," *especially* when expectations within marriage may remain unmet. Armed with God's promises, the Holy Spirit, and prayer, wives can lovingly honor their husbands "for better or for worse, in sickness and in health, in joy and in sorrow."

The Challenge of Marriage

Every marriage has moments or seasons of time that are challenging, when circumstances turn out differently than expected. When a season of unmet expectations stretches into months, and possibly years, hope for change dwindles. God never intended His children to endure in a life of hopelessness. But, pursuing hope does leave us with a choice: *Will the disappointment, frustration, or regret from unmet expectations in marriage so enslave us that breaking free of those expectations seems impossible? Or will those same feelings of disappointment, frustration, or regret propel us to seek the Lord in prayer, to study the Scriptures, and accept our circumstances as part of God's plan to produce spiritual growth in us?* Every married person confronts this choice sooner or later. In fact, the unfulfilled areas in any relationship offer opportunities for spiritual growth.

Gaining a Better Picture

If you only looked at social media, you might be tempted to think you're the only one in all the world who experiences the challenges of unmet expectations in married life. Yet the pictures of happy couples with their amazing declarations of love and devotion don't paint the full picture. Marriage is a work in progress, not a snapshot of happiness.

Even our interactions and observations of other people's marriages within the confines of the church foyer must be viewed with a wide-angle lens. It's easy to look at other couples and be tempted to envy their easy camaraderie and loving looks, to the point that our romanticized version of their marriages lures us into discontent with our own. *All* married couples experience misunderstanding, disappointment, and hurt at times. *Every* marriage has pleasant travel routes and "no fly zones," where, like the Bermuda Triangle, it seems best to steer clear. The certainty of difficulties explains *why* we promise in our marriage vows to keep loving in both the hard times and the easy.

Though we're addressing marriage in this chapter, which is a two-party gig, the truths, counsel, and encouragement we'll gain apply only to one person—you. This chapter isn't about how you can fix your spouse. That's the Holy Spirit's work. Instead, we want to assess and examine our own hearts to see where change might need to take place. It's the responsibility of every believer to seek the Lord and to do what's right according to His Word. For our purposes, that means dealing head on with the havoc unmet expectations and sinful reactions produce. Thankfully, the Lord has kindly preserved the stories of real women in real marriage situations to help us as we think through how to respond when the flight plan of our marriage takes a sharp turn into the Bermuda Triangle.

Learning from Abigail, a Real-Life, Bible Woman

One real-life woman from the Bible was married to a foolish man who went out of his way to disrespect the future king of Israel. First Samuel 25 tells us that Abigail's husband was "harsh and evil in his dealings" (v. 3). Abigail herself reveals in verse 25 that her husband's name, Nabal, means "fool." Regrettably, for all who knew him, Nabal lived up to his name. When we enter into Abigail's story, David is running from King Saul and living in the wilderness with his army. When David asks for Nabal's hospitality on behalf of his men (which wasn't out of line for David to do), Nabal not only refuses, but heaps insults upon him! Heartily displeased by this treatment, David contemplates killing Nabal and plundering his possessions. When news reaches Abigail about her husband's latest she-nanigans, she immediately takes action to remedy the situation.

Through her wisdom and quick thinking, her household is rescued from destruction. Later, when Nabal finds out how close he was to being wiped out, the Bible says, "his heart died within him so that he became as a stone" (1 Sam. 25:37). To say that Nabal was a challenging man to live with is an understatement. It's difficult to respond well to a husband who seems determined to make the world, and everyone in it, his enemy. Thinking well of a husband like that would have been a constant battle.

Learning from Sarah, another Real-Life Bible Woman

Sarah, another real-life woman from the Bible, was married to Abraham, a very godly man, whose exemplary faith led the author of Hebrews to include him twice as an example for believers to follow (Heb. 11:8–10, 17–19). Abraham, however, was far from perfect. He was a sinner like all husbands are. Twice, in unbelief, fearing for his life and thinking only of himself, Abraham asked Sarah to say that she was his sister. On a technicality, this was true—she was his half-sister. As a result, Sarah was taken into the harems of two pagan rulers! (Gen. 12:10–20; 20:1–18). Can you imagine it? Thankfully, the Lord graciously intervened both times, protecting Sarah from their advances. My! It would have been so difficult to pick up the pieces of her shattered trust and move on after such betrayal and lack of concern from Abraham.

Today, women may not find themselves in circumstances like those of Abigail and Sarah. Yet, any time a woman feels insecure, unprotected, or unloved by her husband, she can find it difficult to show him the respect the Lord requires. Ephesians 5:33 instructs us, *"The wife must see to it that she respects her husband"* (emphasis added).

When Unmet Expectations are Added to the Marriage Mix

God doesn't provide us with additional step-by-step instruction concerning His command to wives to respect their husbands. As we study Ephesians 5:33 and other texts directed toward women, we gain remarkable insight into the nuts and bolts of *how* to respect our husbands. Some women may find respecting their husband easy to put into practice, while others may find it downright difficult. Whether a command is easy for us to obey or not, we know that, if God has given it in His Word, He intends us to obey it. Thankfully, God gives abundant grace to help His children to obey.

Relationships come with built-in expectations, and marriage is no exception. We'd be here all day if we tried to make a comprehensive list of reasons why some women struggle to respect their husbands. Statements like, "I thought he would. . ." or "I never could have predicted that he would. . ." or "It hurts that he. . ." or "I haven't been able to see him the same way since. . ." are the rumblings of unmet expectations. However, the Bible teaches us that, even if a woman is married to an unbeliever, or a man who is disobedient to the Word, or one who is prone to making foolish decisions in leading his family, or a spouse who never seems to gain victory over his sin, the command remains. What if one of those scenarios is true of you? *Now what*? If you have the desire to give God glory in all that you do, then "now what" takes on massive implications as to how you will live and respond to your husband.

Even if Your Husband is Just Like Jesus

Have you ever considered that, even if your husband were a paragon of perfection, you may *still* struggle to show him respect, simply *because of your own sin and weaknesses*? Your husband may be a truly godly, gracious man, but your own desires for control in the home may tempt you to respond disdainfully and rebel against the Lord's clear command. It is important to remember that people found fault with Jesus, who was perfect! This teaches us that contentment and true happiness don't come from having everything or everyone "just so." Proverbs 27:20 tells us that the heart is never satisfied, which means that your poor, imperfect, though perfectly wonderful hubby doesn't stand a chance against all your expectations.

David was a godly man whose heart was tender toward the Lord. Yet his evident desire to please the Lord wasn't enough for Michal, his wife. 2 Samuel 6:16 tells us, "Then it happened as the ark of the LORD came into the city of David that Michal the daughter of Saul looked out of the window and saw King David leaping and dancing before the LORD; and she despised him in her heart." She didn't like the way he was acting, so she willfully chose not to love and respect her husband. Though her bitter attitudes toward David were hidden away in the dark recesses of her heart, the Lord saw, and closed her womb as a consequence (2 Sam. 6:23).

As we've learned earlier, bitterness, anger, depression, disappointment, or selfishness aren't God's will for us. Thankfully, God *always* helps His children walk in righteousness when they turn to Him for help. The transformation from an ungodly response to one that gives God glory lies in trusting the Lord's wisdom and sovereignty over *every detail* of our lives.

Discovering God's Calling for Your Marriage

In Ephesians 5, beginning at verse 22, we find specific encouragement and commands for husbands and wives. In verse 22, wives are called to submit to their husbands, as to the Lord. The Bible is so wonderfully succinct! In just a few words, we see the parameters of submission. We learn that a woman isn't to submit to all men, just her man—her husband. We also learn that a woman's submission is rendered *as to the Lord*.[80] "As to the Lord" means the submission we give to our husbands must model our submission to the Lord Himself. If a husband asks his wife to rob a bank or look at pornography or lie, then she should not submit to those commands because they wouldn't be things the Lord would want her to do.

Following the command for wives to submit to their husbands in Ephesians 5:22 are ten verses inspired by the Holy Spirit which instruct husbands how to love their wives. Spelled out in detail, God's commands can be easily summarized as, "Husband, loving your wife is easy to understand! Just love her in the same sacrificial way that Christ loves His bride, the church." Paul summarizes his statements on a God-honoring marriage with these words: "Nevertheless, each individual among you also is to love his own wife even as himself, and the wife must see to it that she respects her husband" (Eph. 5:33).

Four words in verse 33 lead us to an unmistakable truth, a truth God doesn't want us to miss. The phrase "must see to it" means *pay attention to, heed*. It's a sanctified, "Yoo-hoo! This is important! Don't miss this verse!" No matter what the rest of verse 33 says, we know that if wives "must see to it," then whatever else is tucked into the verse is a big deal. *Wives, respect your hubbies.* There's no hiding from God's clear call for wives to respect their husbands.

Wait! What if You Aren't Married?

Just because this chapter addresses marriage doesn't mean the Lord has nothing to teach you if you aren't married. If you quit reading, you'll miss out on some important truths God wants *everyone* to understand. Remember "*All* Scripture is inspired by God and profitable for teaching, for reproof, for correction, for training in righteousness" (2 Tim. 3:16, emphasis added).

Being single gives you the opportunity to study these truths now. If, at some time in the future, the Lord brings someone to you to share life with

---

80 This substitutionary obedience is referenced by the Lord in Matthew 25:40, "Truly I say to you, to the extent that you did it to one of these brothers of Mine, even the least of them, you did it to Me." John 14:15 reminds us, "If you love Me, you will keep My commandments."

you, you can move into marriage undergirded and prepared by His Word. Once you are married, there isn't any wiggle room on this command. So, studying God's will for marriage is crucial to having a God-glorifying one. You *must* respect your hubby, for this is God's will for you.

For those of you who have been married before and are now single, you can speak with wisdom and insight about how to have a God-glorifying marriage. You may have faithfully obeyed God's commands in your marriage or fought them tooth and nail. Yet now, with a clear understanding of God's will for wives, you can be His instrument to strengthen a discouraged, married friend by speaking truth to her from the Scriptures.

Getting a Handle on Respect

You've read the verse; you know God desires you to apply it; but how to practice the art of respecting your husband can seem a bit nebulous. What is respect? One dictionary defined respect this way: It means to "admire (someone or something) deeply, as a result of their abilities, qualities, or achievements."[81] I find this definition inadequate for this reason: what happens if your husband's so-called "admirable qualities" disappear or were never really there to begin with? Does that mean a wife is off the hook and doesn't have to respect her husband? That's exactly what the world says. But God views it differently. God expects wives to respect their husbands, no matter how many admirable qualities they do or don't have.

In the book *Anna Karenina* by Leo Tolstoy, the main character, Anna, devalues respect with these words: "Respect was invented to cover the empty place where love should be."[82] My! What a shockingly pessimistic view of respect! Surely that's not what God is saying in Ephesians 5:33 that respect is a lesser emotion used as a filler when love is lacking. That's an awful idea! But it's useful to consider it in helping to examine what God is asking of wives. The opposite of *respect* is *contempt,* which means disrespect, disdain, scorn, or to consider worthless or beneath oneself. Another dictionary pointed out that "Respect shouldn't be confused with tolerance."[83] This definition raises a great point and something for us to consider. When it comes to marriage, *tolerating someone isn't the same as respecting them.*

81 "Respect," English Oxford Living Dictionaries, https://en.oxforddictionaries.com/definition/respect.

82 Leo Tolstoy, *Anna Karenina*, Goodreads, https://www.goodreads.com/quotes/74807-respect-was-invented-to-cover-the-empty-place-where-love.

83 "Respect," Project Gutenberg Self-Publishing Press, http://self.gutenberg.org/articles/eng/Respect.

Spelling Out R-E-S-P-E-C-T

Not surprisingly, one of the best definitions of respect comes from the Bible. Ephesians 5:33 is explained this way in the Amplified Bible: "and let the wife see that she respects and reverences her husband—that she notices him, regards him, honors him, prefers him, venerates and esteems him; and that she defers to him, praises him, and loves and admires him exceedingly."[84] Wow! What a great definition! The Amplified Bible's translation of respect does away with a fairly common excuse women make when it comes to respecting their husbands. The excuse goes like this: "I'll respect his role, but I don't have to respect him." Yet, if we're *noticing* and *regarding* our husbands, if we're *honoring* and *preferring* them, *venerating* and *esteeming* them, *deferring, praising, loving* and *admiring* them, then there's just no way we can reduce the command to "I'll just respect his role."

For further protection against minimizing God's command to respect our husbands, the Bible reminds us in Titus 2:4 that wives are to love their husbands. The Greek word for love in this verse is not the more common word employed by Paul, but the word "phileo," which means "to like" or "take delight in." This goes beyond a wooden, duty-laden expression of love. Instead, we see that it is God's desire that wives enjoy spending time with their husbands, delighting in them and their little idiosyncrasies. It's really about wives loving their husbands with their whole hearts. It's about wives working at the relationship and continuing to make their husbands a priority in the way they did in the early days of their courtship and marriage.

Along with respecting and liking their husbands, wives are told to submit to their husbands. Peter wrote, "Wives, be submissive to your own husbands so that even if any of them are disobedient to the word, they may be won without a word by the behavior of their wives, as they observe your chaste and respectful behavior" (1 Peter 3:1–2).

To submit means that a wife follows her husband, arranges herself under him, and yields to him as he leads the family. Peter even links submission to respect when he says that God can use a wife's voluntary submission to win a disobedient husband to the Lord, as he "observe[s] [his wife's] chaste and respectful behavior."

The triad of the three commands to wives to respect, like, and submit to their husbands reveals how they are to respect their husbands. There's no place for merely tolerating him or "doing her duty." The three commands together reveal that God wants wives to be fully engaged and committed to their husbands and the health of their marriages.

---

84 *The Amplified New Testament* (La Habra, CA: Zondervan; The Lockman Foundation, 1987), Eph 5:33.

I knew one young wife who adored her husband. They were perfectly suited to each other in every way until he was involved in a serious car accident. When he came out of his coma, his personality had changed due to the brain injury he had sustained. And from her perspective, the personality change wasn't for the better. She found it difficult to like her "new" husband. Yet she knew God had called her to something higher—*for better, for worse, for richer, for poorer, in sickness and in health*. By faith, she committed herself to her husband, put her trust in the Lord, and began to build into her "new" husband and marriage.

When Respect Seems Nigh Impossible

I just can't.
You don't know what he's done.
I can't trust him.
I'm better at this than he is. Why should I respect him?
I'm afraid.
I don't want to.

What should you do to respect your husband when it feels like an impossible task? How do you obey the Lord when real-life issues loom large? You may find it difficult to respect your husband if he has let you down or betrayed your trust. You may find respecting your husband a challenge because of the way his weaknesses, failures, or sins have hurt you. You may struggle to respect your husband simply because you've been married f-o-r-e-v-e-r and developed sinful habits of not respecting him. Possibly you've allowed bitterness and unforgiveness to grow toward him, suppressing respect or tenderness. Yet there is no criterion given by God that a husband must meet in order to earn your respect. You must realize that the problem lies more in your own heart than it does with anything your husband has or hasn't done. *Whatever the reason*, you know deep down, that you are struggling to respect your husband.

What do you do? Is there hope? Is respect for him even possible?

Nothing is Impossible with God!

Don't give up! God's grace is sufficient to help you (2 Cor. 12:9). The Word of God gives you the encouragement and impetus you need to respect your husband—even in times of difficulty, even when you don't want to, even when you feel as though he isn't "worthy" of your respect. If you know Jesus Christ as your Savior, *you can* respect your husband. If pleasing the

Lord and desiring to give Him glory is your goal, then the motivation for respecting your husband isn't predicated on his behavior.

If you've been fighting against the command to respect your husband, you will be frustrated and discouraged. You can't please the Lord while harboring sin in your heart. Yet moving from a place of unbelief and disobedience can change in a moment. *Your rescue begins with your repentance, just as it does with any other sin you commit.* When wives choose not to respect their husbands, they are sinning, simple as that. God says that the "one who knows the right thing to do and does not do it, to him it is sin" (James 4:17). But there is hope!

Every sin is forgiven in Christ and, by His grace, can be overcome (2 Cor. 5:21; Titus 2:14; 2 Peter 1:4)![85] If the Lord Jesus is your Savior, then His death on the cross broke the power of sin in your life. You don't have to stay in a cycle of sin, discouragement, and hopelessness. Remember the first step to overcoming *any* sin must start with repentance—a turning away from sinful rebellion and turning to God for help and grace. And yes, that is one step. Turning to the Lord, of necessity, requires turning away from sin. Be encouraged! No sin is too big or too entrenched for the Lord to overcome in your heart. Listen to the hope found in Romans 6:17–18: "But thanks be to God that though you were slaves of sin, you became obedient from the heart to that form of teaching to which you were committed, and having been freed from sin, you became slaves of righteousness."

God Provides the Help You Need to Obey

First, understand this truth and take it to heart: it is possible to show respect to your husband in a God-glorifying way. *Whenever God gives us a command, He always provides the resources and the ability to obey.* Ultimately, it comes down to trusting the Lord. Will you trust that He has your best interests in view and believe that His commands to you are the expression of His wisdom? Hebrews 11:6 says that "without faith it is impossible to please Him." When you respect your husband, you are exercising faith that is pleasing to God. Hebrews 11:6 goes on to say that when you apply faith in obeying God's Word, you're trusting what you know of God's character and that He sees you seeking Him. It's such an encouragement to know that God sees our efforts to seek Him, even when those efforts are sporadic and tainted with sin.

85 2 Corinthians 5:21: "He made Him who knew no sin to be sin on our behalf, so that we might become the righteousness of God in Him." Titus 2:14: "who gave Himself for us to redeem us from every lawless deed, and to purify for Himself a people for His own possession, zealous for good deeds." 2 Peter 1:4: "For by these He has granted to us His precious and magnificent promises, so that by them you may become partakers of the divine nature, having escaped the corruption that is in the world by lust."

Second, God never intends His commands to crush us under their weight, which is why John tells us, "For this is the love of God, that we keep His commandments; and His commandments are not burdensome" (1 John 5:3). For a believer, obedience is a privilege, not a burden. The path of obedience may not be easy, but our way is directed by a loving God who desires our good. Respecting husbands is meant to be a blessing to wives, not a prison sentence. And when wives obey the command to respect their husbands, they will grow in grace, wisdom, and fellowship with the Lord. Obedience always leads to intimacy with the Lord, while sin makes God seem far away.

Third, no one, and I mean no one, is exempt from God's all-powerful, heart-searching, life-transforming Word—not you, not me, and certainly not even the most stubborn or rascally of husbands. The Word of God is powerful to save, convict, encourage, and grow. It is a sword that pierces to the deepest parts of the soul (Heb. 4:12–13). God's Word is a mirror that reveals our sin so we can grow in godliness (James 1:23–24). The Word of God is seed that bears fruit in the good soil of every believer's life (Matt. 13:23; 1 Peter 1:23). It is milk, providing sustenance and nourishment for the soul (1 Peter 2:2). God's Word is a lamp that guides us in paths of righteousness (Ps. 119:105). The Word of God is a fire to burn away sin, and a hammer that breaks through the hardest of hearts (Jer. 23:29). Even if your husband is an unbeliever and doesn't attend church with you, don't despair. God is more than able to soften his heart. Your responsibility is to trust in God's mighty Word to deliver you, to change you, and to help you obey.

Fourth, even with the Lord's help, there will be times when you'll find it a challenge to respect your husband. It won't always be hearts and flowers. For some marriages, there have been far too few hearts and no flowers. Yet, even in a drought of romance, the blossoms of respect can bloom. Choose to respect your husband because you love Jesus. Leave your husband's performance out of it. Your husband may be more like Nabal than Ruth's charming Boaz, but it's still possible to respect your husband. God never commands us to do anything without giving us the grace to obey.

What Sarah's Example Means for You

Not only does God provide us with the help we need to obey, but He also gives us Sarah, Abraham's wife, as an example. Her real-life story teaches us that it's possible to show respect to our husbands, even in challenging circumstances. We draw valuable lessons from Sarah's life in 1 Peter

3:1–6. In order to get there, a few introductory comments are necessary.

In 1 Peter 3:1–2 we read, "In the same way. . ." The phrase "In the same way" refers to 1 Peter 2:21–24, which details Christ's example of submitting to the Father in difficult circumstances. Peter points to Jesus as an example for all wives when he says in 1 Peter 3:1, "In the same way, you wives, *be submissive to your own husbands so that even if any of them are disobedient to the word*, they may be won without a word by the behavior of their wives, *as they observe your chaste and respectful behavior*" (emphasis added). In 1 Peter 3:1–2, God encourages wives to let their "chaste and respectful behavior" be the God-appointed means of witnessing to their disobedient husbands.

Then, wives are encouraged with these words, "Your adornment must not be merely external—braiding the hair, and wearing gold jewelry, or putting on dresses; but *let it be the hidden person of the heart*, with the imperishable quality of a gentle and quiet spirit, which is precious in the sight of God" (1 Peter 3:3–4, emphasis added). God wants wives to focus more on their hearts than on their appearance.

Next, we get to Sarah and how she's every wife's example. We read in 1 Peter 3:5–6, "For in this way in former times the holy women also, *who hoped in God*, used to *adorn themselves, being submissive to their own husbands*; just as Sarah obeyed Abraham, calling him lord, and you have become her children if you do what is right without being frightened by any fear" (emphasis added). We see in those two verses that the godly women of olden times, of which Sarah is the star, made themselves even more lovely by submitting to their husbands. Peter even says that wives will be known as her daughters if they follow in her footsteps and do what is right by entrusting themselves to God, as they submit to their husbands.

Did you notice Peter's carefully chosen words in 1 Peter 3:6? He writes, you have become Sarah's daughters "if you do what is right without being frightened by any fear," which suggests that Sarah found herself in a frightening situation. She chose to submit to her husband after putting her trust in the Lord. *What was happening in her life that produced such anxiety?* The Scriptures provide us with two vignettes from Sarah's life where Abraham asks her to lie about their relationship because he feared the pagan kings would kill him in order to take beautiful Sarah as a wife. Surely, with great trepidation, Sarah obeyed Abraham in order to preserve his life. And, thankfully, God protected her. This incident is recorded for us in Genesis 12.

Later, Sarah again had to submit to something similar in Genesis 20. In this case, Abraham and Sarah were traveling through the Negev and, as before, Abraham feared for his life. A second time, Sarah submitted to the same foolish deception. Again, God rescued her from her disobedient husband.

Sarah is our example because she trusted the Lord in dire circumstances. She submitted in an extreme situation. Amazingly, her submission isn't Peter's primary focus. Peter wants wives to see how Sarah entrusted herself to the Lord. First Peter 3:5 reminds us that the godly women of old kept their eyes on the Lord, which made their submission all the more precious to Him. Submission was the means that God used to put their lovely trust in the Him on display. And God intends that same hope and trust to shine in our lives as well.

A Couple of Comments on Sarah's Submission

Peter puts the spotlight on Sarah as an example of submission because she submitted to her disobedient husband, entrusting herself to the Lord for deliverance. Abraham's selfish plans left her without protection, feeling vulnerable, defenseless, and fearful. Yet the Scriptures record that she trusted God to rescue her.

When it comes to understanding the value of Sarah's submission, it's helpful to remember that she didn't have the Bible. She did the best she could with what she had been taught about God. She didn't have the wealth of instruction that we do about God's will for wives.

We may wonder if Sarah is supposed to be an example of unconditional submission. We can rest assured she is not. That's not why Peter shines the light on her. Sarah is preeminent as an example of faith—a woman who, in perilous circumstances, put her trust in the Lord. Remember she didn't have the Bible. We do. Sarah had no special instruction about the extent of submission. We do. But Peter does want us to take note of how she entrusted herself to the Lord in difficult circumstances, in much the same way that Jesus submitted Himself to the unkind and unjust dealings of men (1 Peter 2:21–25).

Five Takeaways from Sarah's Submission

There are five simple, yet profound, takeaways from 1 Peter 3:1–6 that shine light on how we, too, can follow in Sarah's footsteps.

- First, we see Sarah focused on her *heart*, rather than on Abraham's behavior. All wives are told to do this in 1 Peter 3:2–4.[86]
- Second, we see from 1 Peter 3:5 that her submission was a *practical way* in which she showed respect to Abraham.

86 1 Peter 3:2-4, "as they observe your chaste and respectful behavior. Your adornment must not be merely external—braiding the hair, and wearing gold jewelry, or putting on dresses; but let it be the hidden person of the heart, with the imperishable quality of a gentle and quiet spirit, which is precious in the sight of God."

- Third, we see Sarah's trust was primarily in the *Lord,* not in her husband. She sought to trust the Lord when she found herself in fearful circumstances (1 Peter 3:6).
- Fourth, she is an *example* of submitting in extreme circumstances. If Sarah was able to continue showing respect to Abraham even after two respect-denting events, then we can follow her example and show respect to our "Abrahams."
- Fifth, a practical *picture* of a wife's submission can be found in 1 Peter 3:2, where wives are told to conduct themselves in a chaste and respectful way toward their husbands.

Further on in Peter's first letter, as he continues to address the issue of persevering through unjust suffering, he writes, "Therefore, those also who suffer according to the will of God shall *entrust* their souls to a faithful Creator in doing what is right" (4:19, emphasis added). This was Sarah's secret. She was able to show respect to Abraham because *she entrusted herself to the Lord.* She trusted God's power, wisdom, care, and faithfulness to protect her in every circumstance. Her trust in the Lord allowed her to "do what is right without being frightened by any fear (1 Peter 3:6)." *Sarah's real-life example encourages us to believe that nothing is impossible with God.*

The Holy Spirit Provides the Help You Need to Obey

Not only does God give us Sarah as an example in His Word and His faithful promise to provide for us, but we also have His Holy Spirit indwelling us. The Holy Spirit makes it possible for us not only to *do* the Father's will, but also to *desire* to do it. Paul, in his prayer for the Ephesian believers, helps us understand how the Holy Spirit assists us. He prayed that the Ephesians would be "strengthened with power through His Spirit in the inner man" (3:16). The Holy Spirit helps believers obey God by giving them His strength. Paul also knew that the power available to believers is commensurate with the riches of God's glory (Eph. 3:16a). This means that the power to help believers is mighty indeed! In Romans 8:26, we learn that the Holy Spirit helps us in our weaknesses, especially when it comes to prayer. *The Lord knows how difficult we find it to submit, even wives who are devoted to the Lord. So, He provides us with the great Helper—His Holy Spirit.* How kind He is!

Jesus Himself Provides the Help You Need to Obey

It's possible for wives to show respect to their husbands because Jesus Himself comes alongside to help them. As the author of Hebrews reminds them: "He gives *help* to the descendant of Abraham" (2:16, emphasis added). And two verses later he states that Jesus "is able to *come to the aid* of those who are tempted" (2:18, emphasis added). Jesus assists us because He Himself knows how intensely our flesh can tempt us to do what is wrong. *Jesus helps us show respect to our husbands.* As we have seen in the paragraphs above, we have the help of the Triune God, Father, Son, and Holy Spirit, in our responsibility to submit and show respect to our husbands. We should pause and reflect on this profound reality. The Triune God Himself promises to give us the help we need to obey His commands!

The Scriptures Provide the Help You Need to Obey

The command to respect our husbands is not too out of reach because God always gives us all we need to obey Him. We've seen how He provides Sarah as an example for us, how the Holy Spirit empowers us, how Jesus aids us in obeying the Lord. Now we come to our next help, God's Word. Wives can look to the Scriptures to help and guide them, which means that the next time they might be tempted to grouse about their hubbies or chafe at showing him respect, remembering God's promises will help them persevere.

We read in 1 Corinthians 10:13 for "No temptation has overtaken you but such as is common to man; and *God is faithful, who will not allow you to be tempted beyond what you are able,* but with the temptation *will provide the way of escape also, so that you will be able to endure it*" (emphasis added). The promises given in this verse stand at the ready to help and strengthen you the next time you're struggling with unmet expectations in your marriage.

Think for a moment of that thing your husband does, or that thing he says, or the way that he says it that gets your back up or hurts your feelings. At that point, you will probably feel *tempted* to lash out at him, to pout, grow bitter, shut down, or give into any number of ungodly responses. But consider the soul-sustaining promises found in 1 Corinthians 10:13.

Though you may *feel* tempted, there is still a way for you to obey. God is faithful to help His children. The Lord will sustain you if you ask Him for help to love and respect your husband. In 1 Corinthians 10:13, God promises a way of escape when you're tempted to give in to sin. That doesn't necessarily mean that He gives you a way of escape from your circumstances. But it does mean that there is a way of escape from the temptation to haul off and spew venom, harbor grudges, or think the worst.

We're also told in 1 Corinthians 10:13 that *God provides the way of escape* from temptation, so that we're able to endure in trying circumstances. Comments like "I just can't hack it anymore. I just can't do it. I'm through with our marriage and I'm through with you." have no place in our conversations. There's a way back to love and respect toward your husband *because* God is faithful. Your husband may never change. Yet there is hope for you! God will help you obey His instructions to you as a wife. His promises will provide you with strength and needed encouragement. God will help you live for His glory, even if your marriage expectations remain unmet.

All this talk of escaping temptation and enduring might sound dreadfully dismal, but it truly isn't, for our God is an amazing God. God's plan always produces the most happiness and joy. Read how Jeremiah, who was constantly persecuted, exults in the Lord: "Ah Lord GOD! Behold, You have made the heavens and the earth by Your great power and by Your outstretched arm! Nothing is too difficult for You" (32:17). God, who made the heavens and earth, comes to our aid when we call out to Him for help. There is no heart, no situation, no person too big, too hopeless, or too stubborn for God. He will support those who are His. How? I have no idea. God doesn't provide us with the particulars. We do know that when we cast ourselves on Him, He has committed Himself to fulfilling His promises and delivering us. The human heart may be out of our reach to change or direct, but it certainly isn't outside of God's transforming influence. Jesus reminded His disciples of this very truth when they realized the difficulty involved in effecting change in a person's heart. Jesus encouraged them with these words: ". . . with God all things are possible" (Matt. 19:26).

The life of a believer is a life of faith. The author of Hebrews explains: "Now faith is the assurance of things hoped for, the conviction of things not seen" (11:1). You may not see how God can change your current circumstances or even change the bitterness you may have in your heart toward your husband, but seeking the Lord in faith means trusting Him, in spite of what you "see." No matter what your situation, whether you are married to foolish Nabal or Prince Charming, God is able to give you grace to obey and respect your husband. God is faithful!

Issues for You to Consider

We all know of women in dangerous marriages—you may be in one your-self. So, I want to clarify further what the Bible teaches in order to give you wisdom to navigate threats to your life. *I'm not saying* that, if you are in a physically abusive marriage, you should stay there in order to show respect. Never submit to physical abuse. Get help! Talk to your pastor, the police, your Bible study leader, a family member, a friend, and get to a place of safety. Physical abuse is a crime that must be reported to the police by you or those you confide in—for your protection. The details for navigating your specific situation can be worked out at a later time. The priority is to protect your life.

The Bible teaches us how to prioritize when two difficult decisions are in view such as preserving your life or preserving an "institution," i.e., marriage. In fact, we see examples in the Scriptures of recognizing the priority of life over institutions. In 1 Samuel 21:3–6, we read of David feeding his hungry men the showbread, which was normally reserved only for the priests. Jesus cites the example of David as He explains why He allowed His disciples to pluck grain from a field on the Sabbath, which was technically classified as "doing work" (Matt. 12:1–8). If you are in danger, first get to safety, ask others for help, then later, you can work out how to preserve your marriage.

Beyond life-threatening situations, *I'm also not saying* that you should never talk to your husband about the issues or expectations that hurt or hinder your relationship. *I am saying* that God provides the help and hope you need as you wait for Him to work in your heart and in your husband's heart.

I'm also not advocating living with a false smile plastered over your face. *I am saying* that as you put your trust in the Lord, you can show love and respect to your husband, even if things are less than perfect, simply because the respect you show to your husband is first offered up to the Lord as a means of worshiping Him. If you desire to live for God, then every circumstance, every difficulty, every unmet expectation becomes an opportunity for you to give Him glory through it.

Let me summarize by saying that in every circumstance of your life, you can give God glory by exercising your faith and by trusting in Him. Be comforted knowing that the Lord sees your circumstances and hears your prayers. Though your circumstances may be different than you expected, take courage knowing you can be a shining example of love, faith, and respect that gives glory to God.

Respecting Your Husband in the Day-to-Day of Life

Gaining a clear picture of what respecting your husband looks like can be difficult. So, to get you started, here are seven snapshots of how to show loving respect. First, respect for your husband begins with love, which may seem like a no-brainer. But ponder for a moment what 1 Peter 4:8 says, "Above all, *keep fervent in your love for one another*, because love covers a multitude of sins" (emphasis added). First Corinthians 13:4–7 provides a beautiful, concrete picture of what love acts like in the day-to-day. So, let's take Peter's instruction to fervently love one another and combine it with the way love acts from 1 Corinthians 13:4–7. Together those verses teach us that "love is *wholeheartedly* patient when dealing with someone who is frustrating. Love is *dedicated* to kindness in the face of grouchiness. Love is *committed* to acting in a becoming manner, *passionate* in seeking the good of others, *zealous* in remaining unprovoked, even when others are being difficult. Love *ardently* works not to take into account a wrong suffered; love *fervently* bears all things, *intensely* believes all things, *eagerly* hopes all things, *devotes* itself to enduring all things" (my paraphrase). If you actively, enthusiastically commit to loving your husband in the way described in 1 Peter 4:8 and 1 Corinthians 13:4–7, then respect will most certainly follow.

Second, respecting your husband means that you treat him like a husband, not like a puppy. All too easily women fall into the trap of treating their husbands like lovable golden retriever puppies who need lots of training to become "housebroken." The whole "treating hubby like a puppy" mentality reveals itself when wives subtly lead their husbands and relegate them to the role of second place in the home. You can show respect to your husband by respecting him as the leader of your home.

Third, respecting your husband means that you do his things first. The simple act of making him a priority in your heart and in your actions tangibly reveals your commitment to give God glory. Show your husband you respect and love him by making sure that the phone call he asks you to make gets done *first thing*. Show him what a high place he has in your heart by taking care of anything he asks you to do *before* you tackle your own list. Often, those simple choices reveal the true landscape of your heart. If you have children, know that they are watching and listening. And if you have a daughter, your discipleship in this area provides the framework for her own future marriage. Hayley DiMarco, in her excellent book, *The Fruitful Wife*, writes, "Loving your husband isn't about being in love with him but about serving him. You aren't your husband's servant; you are God's servant. And you serve God through your service to others."[87]

Fourth, respecting your husband means giving God time to work on him. Oh my, but we can be excited to fix our husbands! Instead, rest in the promise of Philippians 1:6: "He who began a good work in you [or your

---

87 Hayley DiMarco, *The Fruitful Wife* (Wheaton, IL: Crossway, 2012), 36.

husband] will perfect it until the day of Christ Jesus." If your dear one belongs to the Lord, then the Lord will keep working in him, just as He continues to work in you. Trust the Lord's timing for the heart-work and life transformation He intends to accomplish in your husband's life.

Fifth, respecting your husband means watching and guarding your thoughts about him. Both Proverbs 10:12 and 1 Peter 4:8 state that love covers a multitude of sins. In essence, these verses tell you that you should not dwell on another person's sins and weaknesses. In other words, you are to be forbearing with your husband. Outward patience begins with inward thoughts. So, a gracious spirit toward your hubby begins with how you think about him, especially during the times when your love needs to spread a blanket over his foibles and weaknesses that irritate or hurt you.

Sixth, respecting your husband means forgiving him, especially if you're feeling grumbly in your heart toward him. The counsel of Colossians 3:13 applies here: "bearing with one another, and forgiving each other, whoever has a complaint against anyone; just as the Lord forgave you, so also should you." Would the Lord ever have cause to "complain" about some way you have wronged Him (if it were possible for God to complain)? Absolutely, He would! Yet the infinitely holy God has forgiven you, which is why He tells you to forgive your husband when he's driving you crazy, and you're finding him difficult to get along with. Colossians 3:12 tells us that bearing with others gets much easier once we've put on a "heart of compassion, kindness, humility, gentleness and patience."

And, finally, respecting your husband is revealed in how you pray for him. If you're struggling, pray. If you're still struggling, pray more. And then pray even more for both yourself and your husband. Pray for him the way you would want him to pray for you. The Lord answers the prayers of those who continually seek Him for help (Heb. 4:16, James 4:8).

You Can't Do This on Your Own

The wife must see to it that she respects her husband. Putting this command into practice in our hearts and lives requires that we rely on the Lord. There are just no ifs, ands, or buts about it. We may try to muscle our way through, applying these truths in our own strength, but we'll end up frustrated ourselves and frustrating to everyone around us. God never intended that we live the Christian life without His help. It's not a matter of making personal commitments to try harder, but to trust the Lord more consistently. Proverbs 3:5–6 gives us such practical wisdom for learning how to rely on the Lord: "Trust in the LORD with all your heart and do not lean on your own understanding. In all your ways acknowledge Him, and

He will make your paths straight." We're dependent upon the Lord's help, grace, and strength for every aspect of our lives. Foolishly, naively, without even realizing we're doing it, we engage in the details of life without seeking the Lord and relying on Him.

Encouragingly, Peter wrote in his letter: "Whoever speaks, is to do so as one who is speaking the utterances of God; whoever serves is to do so as one who is serving by the strength which God supplies" (1 Peter 4:11). We know that *whoever respects her husband is to do so through the resources and support the Lord has given* so that "in all things God may be glorified through Jesus Christ, to whom belongs the glory and dominion forever and ever" (1 Peter 4:11b). There it is, our great calling—*so that in all things God may be glorified.* We've spent time looking at how to respond rightly when faced with unmet expectations because the ultimate motivation for us, as believers, is to give God glory in our lives. Giving God glory is all the reason we need for putting the command to respect our husbands into practice, no matter what our circumstances, and no matter how many unmet expectations we have.

> *"...and let the wife see that she respects and reverences her husband—that she notices him, regards him, honors him, prefers him, venerates and esteems him; and that she defers to him, praises him, and loves and admires him exceedingly" (Eph. 5:33, The Amplified Bible).*

As I close this chapter on unmet expectations in marriage, I hope you will gain fresh courage to live fully for the Lord's pleasure, knowing He gives you the help you need. "Now the God of peace, who brought up from the dead the great Shepherd of the sheep through the blood of the eternal covenant, even Jesus our Lord, *equip you in every good thing to do His will, working in us that which is pleasing in His sight, through Jesus Christ, to whom be the glory forever and ever.* Amen" (Heb. 13:20–21, emphasis added).

QUESTIONS for REFLECTION

Chapter 11: What if You Were Married to Nabal?

1. What are the specific commands for women found in Ephesians 5:33, Titus 2:4, and 1 Peter 3:1–2?

2. When taken as a whole, what do the commands in Ephesians 5:33, Titus 2:4, and 1 Peter 3:1–2 make clear about God's will for wives? How do they fully refute the idea of "just doing my duty" toward husbands?

3. Titus 2:4 tells us that women are to *love their husbands*. As we have seen, the Greek word translated love is *phileo* and is generally understood to be the love of friendship. Yet, if we leave it at that elementary level, we're really missing what God wants us to understand. To *phileo love* our husbands means to delight in them, to *like* them, and to place them above all others in our thoughts, emotions, and actions. If you're married, what are some specific ways you can apply this command? Even if you're not married, what are some of the ways you can think of applying this command in the future or in encouraging your married friends?

4. In 1 Peter 3:1–2, we're told to be submissive to our husbands. As we have seen, submission means to arrange oneself under, to be in subjection to, to yield oneself to another. One commentator perceptively remarked, "The moment we divorce the thought of subjection from that of affection, we have lost its God-given significance."[88] What role is *love* intended to play in *submission*?

5. Peter's first letter isn't the only place where a wife's submission is mentioned. Look up the following verses and summarize what you learn from them about submission: Ephesians 5:22–24; Colossians 3:18; Titus 2:3–5.

6. According to 1 Peter 3:1–4, where should a woman focus her energies, rather than "talking" her husband into obeying the Lord? What do you discover?

7. What are some specific ways *you* can show respect to *your* husband? If you're not married, think of someone you can honor

---

88   Tom Westwood, quoted by D. Edmund Hiebert, *1 Peter* (Winona Lake, IN: BMH Books, 1992),195.

by showing respect to that person. What are some specific ways you can show respect to him or her?

8. How can the following verses be an encouragement in showing respect to your husband? Jeremiah 32:17; Romans 8:26; Philippians 1:6; Colossians 3:13–14; 1 Peter 4:8

12

Math is More Fun *after* You Pass the Class

This life was not intended to be the place of our perfection, but the preparation for it. As the fruit is far from ripeness in the first appearance, or the flower while it is but in the husk or bud; or the oak when it is but an acorn; or any plant when it is but in the seed; no more is the very nature of man on earth. As the infant is not perfect in the womb, nor the chicken in the shell, no more are our natures perfect in this world.

Richard Baxter[89]

89   William Orme, *The Practical Works of the Reverend Richard Baxter,* vol. XI (London: James Duncan Publisher, 1830), 254.

Most people know the story about Peter, one of Jesus' disciples, who denied any affiliation with Jesus when He had been brought before Herod on false charges. Do you remember how shocked Peter was when he realized he had taken the coward's way out, rather than standing courageously with the Lord? (Luke 22:33–34, 54–62). Peter never expected to fall prey to cowardice. He was plenty used to falling into sin, but he never expected to respond in such a spectacularly fainthearted and self-preserving way. The depth of his own weakness, sinfulness, and selfishness shocked Peter. *He never expected to give way to that kind of sin.*

Just like Peter, I'm quite used to sinning with my "normal" sins. I'm so well acquainted with them that they are almost like neighbors who pop in on a regular basis for a chat and an afternoon "cuppa." My "regularly engaged in" sins and I are on such friendly terms that I'm not surprised when I am anxious or fearful, when I struggle with doubt or despair, or when my thoughts spiral out of control. Though I confess and repent of them, I don't necessarily feel shaken when I commit them.

Yet there have been times when, just like Peter, I've been shocked at committing "that" sin—the one I never thought I'd even find tempting and, therefore, the one I foolishly never guarded against. And just like Peter, sinning in unexpected ways causes me to see the depth of my weakness and depravity. It's uncomfortable and humbling to be reminded once again how easily I am able to sin, and sin boldly and wickedly, though the pattern of my life has been to walk faithfully with the Lord. The painful look at my sinful heart often reveals subtle and unbiblical expectations I have for my walk with the Lord.

In the three previous chapters, we've delved into ways our expectations toward others can hinder and harm our relationships. Now, we're going to take a look at some ways the expectations we have of ourselves can hinder our progress in Christ. Whether we're aware of it or not, we all have ideas about the kind of person we should be or hope to be, how we should live, and how we think we should respond. While we may find unmet expectations of others challenging, we can find the unmet expectations we have of ourselves just as difficult to overcome. Thankfully, God's Word helps us assess whether our expectations are biblical or not and, if not, how to align our thinking with the Scriptures.

I Expected to Get Past My Sinfulness

I've run into the wall of my own expectations many a time. In talking with women over the years, I've discovered common areas of frustration when it comes to expectations of ourselves. One expectation that has tripped me up a few times is thinking I will get to a point where I won't struggle with sin, wrong attitudes, or discontentment anymore. *Somehow this unbiblical thinking gets rooted in my heart, even though I know better.* To think that, at some point, I'll be so godly that I'll sail past my disappointments and struggles is ludicrous.

Suffice it to say, this expectation is entirely *un*biblical. I will *never* reach a state of sinless perfection this side of heaven. The Scriptures never tell us that we will. But somehow this expectation wriggles and niggles its way into my thoughts and I begin to expect that someday I'll be so godly that sin won't have a hold on me. Of course, I would probably be very old by the time this happens or would have experienced some kind of spiritual nirvana to achieve the obliteration of indwelling sin. Obviously, this isn't even close to being possible, and the Bible certainly doesn't teach it. But my heart longs for it just the same. Does yours?

Had anyone been able to overcome sin and reach a sort of spiritual pinnacle, it would have been the Apostle Paul. Interestingly, he admitted to continually battling the flesh. Read some of the language he used to describe wrestling with sin and temptation in Romans 7:

> "Nothing good dwells in me, that is, in my flesh" (v. 18).
> "The good that I want, I do not do, but I practice the very evil that I do not want" (v. 19).
> "Sin . . . dwells in me" (v. 20).
> "Evil is present in me, the one who wants to do good" (v. 21).
> "Waging war" (v. 23).
> "Making me a prisoner" (v. 23).
> "Wretched man that I am! Who will set me free from the body of this death?" (v. 24)

Even Paul found the battle relentless, continual, and unabated. If this was true for Paul, who was discipled personally by the Lord Jesus, then an ongoing battle to conquer sin is certainly true of us. If we *expect* to someday "arrive," only to discover how elusive "someday" is, we may grow despairing, faithless, even bitter or angry by our false hope. We will never completely conquer sin this side of heaven. Yet we can grow strong in the Lord, using the resources of the Word to break sin's grip. Recognizing the ongoing battle in our hearts between the flesh and the Spirit drives us to the Lord, with the result that we grow increasingly dependent upon Him. The author of Hebrews speaks to this when he says, "For we do not have a high priest who cannot sympathize with our weaknesses, but One who has been tempted in all things as we are, yet without sin. Therefore let us draw near with confidence to the throne of grace, so that we may receive mercy and find grace to help in time of need" (4:15–16). We may grow in spiritual maturity and biblical wisdom, but we will always be sinners in need of a Savior.

Why It Matters That You Get These Truths Right

To think we'll someday grow out of our need for a Savior is not only bad theology but also very dishonoring to the Lord Jesus. Not only do we need Jesus' perfect righteousness applied to us for the *beginning* of our salvation, but we also need the Spirit's *ongoing* sanctifying work in us for the whole of our earthly lives. To expect that we will "grow out of" our sinfulness and arrive at a state of perfection strikes at the very heart of God's plan of redemption. It devalues Jesus' all sufficient and complete sacrifice for sin. This wrong thinking also places a harmful and deceptively wicked temptation before us to rely on our efforts at being righteous rather than trusting in Jesus' sinlessness to accomplish salvation for us. *Forgetting our need of the Lord's redemptive work on our behalf and our need of sanctification every day of our earthly life cause us to stand on a foolish and dangerous mental footing.*

Thinking we've "arrived" leads to self-righteousness. Self-righteousness feels sorry for those *other* people who still struggle with their sin like the Pharisee who proclaimed, "I thank You that I am not like other people" (Luke 18:10–12). Self-righteousness doesn't need any help battling sin because it denies there's even a battle. This creates an inflexible, unteachable, and unreachable spirit in us. Self-righteousness means we're no longer seeing our sin rightly, or at all. The devil loves it when we're self-righteous because it keeps us from seeing our need of a Savior. And if our souls already belong to Jesus, then Satan will do what he can to snatch away our devotion and steal glory from God. Self-righteous satisfaction slithers into the den of unguarded hearts, deceiving us into thinking that we don't need Christ or daily cleansing from sin. *Thinking we'll someday be little Mary Poppins wannabes, "practically perfect in every way," diminishes the incredible, saving work of Jesus and our constant need of Him.*

We can replace our unbiblical expectation that we'll somehow overcome our sinfulness by remembering that God is holy and we are not (Ps. 77:13). God is so holy that we can never attain His holiness in this life. Though we may grow more like Him, we will never be rid of our sin nature until our perishable body is transformed into an imperishable one (1 Cor. 15:42–44). While we wait for our earthly tent to be clothed with immortality (2 Cor. 5:1–4), we can expect to struggle against sin. Even then, all things work together for good to those who love Him (Rom. 8:28). Amazingly, God uses our ongoing struggle against sin to our good and His glory when we rely on His help, cling to His promises, and live by faith.

I Expected to Get Past the Need for Trials

Somewhat similar to the expectation discussed above is the common, but unbiblical, thought, "As I grow in maturity, I won't really need disappointments or trials to strengthen my faith." If this is your expectation, you are deluding yourself. It is a fact that when you finally get to the place where you think you are spiritually mature, you will discover that struggles, afflictions, and unmet expectations continue unabated.

Underlying our unbiblical expectation that we only go through troubles when we are young in the Lord and *need* them is often the thinking that, if we grow in spiritual maturity, we won't need the sanctifying influence of trials. Thankfully, we're given solid truths in the Scriptures to counter this expectation, which is a misconception that can trip us up. God intends so much more for us than ease and happiness. He is more concerned with our holiness (1 Peter 1:15–16) and our living by faith (James 1:2–4), neither of which happens apart from the testing, training, and reshaping influences of trials and difficulties. We experience unmet expectations because denied prospects and thwarted plans produce spiritual growth in us. If we were given everything we expected or planned, we would become peevish, self-reliant, self-sufficient, and proud.

At the core of the "I'm not going to *need* trials if I'm living faithfully" expectation is our belief about how *God should deal with us*. We're told that Jesus Himself "learned obedience from the things which He suffered" (Heb. 5:8). The Scriptures teach us that Jesus' sufferings taught Him more about obeying God. He was *already* obedient, but the afflictions trained Him to obey in greater and more difficult circumstances. God intends our trials to work in a similar way in our lives, so that, like Jesus, we'll learn increasingly greater degrees of obedience.

We *need* trials and sorrows to wean our hearts off this world and to remind us that we are temporary residents here. We *need* difficulties to drive us to the Lord. We *need* weakness and frailty to teach us to lean on the never-failing, always faithful God. My fellow pioneer girls, we *need* unmet expectations to produce a harvest of righteousness in us (Heb. 12:11).

I Expected to Grow Faster Than I Am

Have you ever expected to grow faster in spiritual maturity than you're experiencing? Oh my, this expectation has popped up in my life more times than I'd like to admit! So many of my *short*cuts to godliness ended up as *long* detours simply because I was impatient with waiting. As a child, it seemed like my mom was often warning me, "Haste makes waste." I easily default to the expectation that I should be farther along in my Christian walk.

Of course, there are theological problems with this expectation too, such as when I think my timetable is better than God's, when I think I have what it takes to gauge my spiritual progress, when I think I can somehow speed up God's "before the foundation of the world was formed" plan for my spiritual growth, and when I think that I alone, of all the people on earth, have found *the* shortcut to spiritual maturity. Expectations, like the ones in this chapter, often remain unmet simply because they are unbiblical to begin with. *God grows each of us in His time, in His way, and through His means.*

John Newton constantly reminded his congregation that "grace matures slowly."[90] He wisely observed, "God works powerfully, but for the most part gently and gradually." "He does not teach all at once, but by degrees." "A Christian is not of hasty growth, like a mushroom, but rather like the oak, the progress of which is hardly perceptible, but in time becomes a great deep-rooted tree."[91] God is in charge of our spiritual growth, bringing us to maturity. Though the Lord works from His own timetable for our transformation, He will finish the job He began, as we're promised in Philippians 1:6: "He who began a good work in you will perfect it."

When we come to Christ, we're newborn babies, whom the Lord faithfully cares for, teaching and training us. Unlike human parents, whose parenting comes to an end, our faithful God *continues* His work in bringing us to *full* spiritual maturity. We need to learn to wait upon His timing in our lives for the perfecting of our faith. Thinking we can somehow speed up God's work foolishly pits us against the Lord. *God is at work.* We can trust Him to transform us into Jesus' likeness at His pace, in His way, until the work is done.

---

90 Quoted in Iain Murray, *Heroes,* (Edinburgh: The Banner of Truth Trust, 2009), 99.
91 Ibid.

I Expected the Tests Would Get Easier, Not Harder

Math was difficult for me, especially long division in the third grade. I remember moaning about it to my dad. I didn't think I would ever understand it. And then came fractions. Oh, they were hard! But not as challenging as decimals. And don't even get me started on geometry. Yet I made it through all my math requirements, graduated high school, only to discover more math awaited me in college. Those math milestones were tough. Later, as a mommy, I have to admit I thoroughly enjoyed restudying division when our kids got to it in school. It's amazing how easy something is once you understand it. *Ahem*. Oh yes, math is way more fun when you've already passed the test.

We have math classes in the spiritual sense too. We begin the Christian life in the "first grade" of our spiritual walk, where we learn the basics. Our faith is proved by simple problems geared toward young believers. To a first-grade believer those tests are hard. A third-grade believer may scoff at their ease, compared with their more difficult third-grade level tests. The testing continues throughout our lives as we grow in the Lord. Eighth-grade tests remain difficult for eighth-grade believers; tenth-grade tests still pose a challenge to those of tenth-grade spiritual maturity. Even when we arrive in twelfth grade, near the end of our spiritual journey, we still have to undergo testing.

Just as it is in school, growing in knowledge, understanding, and application of the truth can be challenging, whether you're in second grade or tenth. Each test challenges us in unique ways. From these tests, the Lord purposes to form in us greater love, greater faith, hope, trust, and holiness. God doesn't give third-grade tests to twelfth-grade believers, though we may prefer it that way. At least, I would. Then I could skate through my trials and afflictions with ease and be really, really godly. God's wisdom, however, dictates that the testing of our faith produce endurance, which will result in a perfect and complete faith, lacking in nothing (James 1:3–4). In God's perfect wisdom, the tests keep coming to each of His children, prodding them to rely on Him for all-sufficient grace.

Before our kids were born, I taught seventh-grade English. As a newbie teacher, I quickly discovered the need to produce good tests to gauge my students' *understanding* of the material and not merely their knowledge of the facts. Gaining a picture of my students' learning generally meant creating tests with essay or short-answer questions, rather than fill-in-the-blank, multiple choice, or true and false questions. My students' short paragraphs revealed their understanding of the material. Similarly, God wants to see how we apply our Bible knowledge to real-life, faith-building opportunities, which means He's looking for more than knowledge of the correct answers. As our beliefs affect how we live, God tests us to produce a holy and healthy trust in Him.

Expecting the trials and difficulties we face in life to get easier as we grow in the Lord only sets us up for despair, guilt, shame, and we "didn't do it right" feelings of failure or frustration. Remembering that God gives unmet expectations, troubles, and afflictions to all His children throughout their lives enables us to respond with graceful submission, and even joy, for the fact that God is continuing His faithful work in us.

I Expect God's Disapproval

One woman told me, "I feel guilty all the time. I must be such a disappointment to God. I figure I'm disappointed in me, so God must be too." She's not alone. Many women feel this way.

Often, when we focus on ourselves and not enough on Christ, we end up with this "God is disappointed with me" expectation. Our focus is on looking at and examining our sins, defects of character, weaknesses, and failures, instead of turning our eyes *upon Jesus*. Self-focus is a dangerous place to linger because it minimizes the justifying and sanctifying work of Jesus. *Dwelling on ourselves for too long always results in wrong thinking.*

Not all introspection is bad. We're told to examine ourselves to see if we are in the faith (2 Cor. 13:5). Jeremiah urges us in Lamentations 3:39–40 to "examine and probe our ways," looking for waywardness and sin. Considering where we've failed or sinned and then turning to the Lord in confession and repentance is far different than looking so long and so hard at our own hearts that we lose sight of the Lord. Without the Word of God to constantly keep us thinking biblically, we quickly grow petulant and sickly. Proverbs 2:6 reminds us: "For the LORD gives wisdom; from His mouth come knowledge and understanding."

Continually living under the dark cloud that we are a disappointment to our loving Father is the ultimate picture of unbelief. We refuse to believe God's declarations of unconditional love, perfect forgiveness, or indwelling presence by His Spirit to help us. Often, this stems from not understanding God correctly because we're not studying the Bible to know Him as He truly is.

Dismantling our upside-down thinking begins when we hang our expectations on the God-revealing Word. For example, we're told in 2 Corinthians 5:21: "He made Him who knew no sin to be sin on our behalf, so that *we might become the righteousness of God in Him*" (emphasis added.) Jesus' substitutionary death means that "When I sin, God feels no wrath in His heart against me."[92] We often fear that God will be disappointed in us because of our sin or failure. Yet Jesus' applied righteousness means that "there is now no condemnation for those who are in Christ Jesus" (Rom. 8:1).

Gaining Balance and Grace

The Lord wisely gives us trials and dashes our expectations to pieces because trials help us grow more and more like Jesus. We can look ahead to difficulties and trials as long as we are on this earth. God gets the glory when we put our trust and hope in Him, especially when things are far different than we expected. It's helpful to remember no event in our lives ever happens outside of God's control. In fact, He powerfully wields every detail to work for our good. Perseverance in any time of waiting and testing is possible when we remember:

> I am a sinner. Yet the Lord has mercifully withheld the consequences of my sin that are due to me.
> My trials are still fewer than the sins I've committed.
> If I am experiencing unmet expectations, it's because God has considered them good for me.
> The Lord will never disappoint me, when I put my trust in Him.

When we travel across the United States, we encounter all kinds of terrain—deserts, mountains, hills, prairies, valleys, twisting roads and wide highways—yet all are part of the journey. So, too, with our trek toward heaven. Unmet expectations, failures, and difficulties are part of the landscape we must travel as God leads us Home. But the Lord is near to the broken hearted (Ps. 34:18), is our help and deliverer (Ps. 40:17) and equips us to do His will (Heb. 13:21). We may bump and bumble along, but God is blessed by our obedience when we strive to give Him glory.

Replacing our unbiblical expectations with right thinking about God, His ways, and His purposes helps us trust the Lord with joyful submission. When we see how skillfully God uses unmet expectations for our good, we are more willing to patiently trust that He is working His righteousness in us.

---

92 Milton Vincent, *A Gospel Primer for Christians: Learning to See the Glories of God's Love* (Bemidji, MN: Focus Publishing, 2008), 63.

If Thou seest in me any wrong thing encouraged, any evil desire cherished, any delight that is not Thy delight, any habit that grieves Thee, any nest of sin in my heart, then grant me the kiss of Thy forgiveness, and teach my feet to walk the way of Thy commandments.[93]

---

93 *The Valley of Vision*, 103.

QUESTIONS for REFLECTION

Chapter 12: Math is More Fun *After* You Pass the Class

1. Facing up to unmet expectations can be a painful business! "I shoulda. . .I coulda. . .I didn't. . .I can't. . .I won't. . .I wouldn't. . .I'm not" clutter our thoughts and keep us from trusting the Lord. Thankfully, the Lord has provided many promises and encouragements in His Word to help us. One such passage is 2 Peter 1:2–4. Where does Peter tell us more grace and more peace come from according to verse 2?

2. Look up John 17:3; 2 Peter 1:8; 2:20; 3:18. Summarize what you discover from those verses as they relate to 2 Peter 1:2 and the multiplied grace and peace we gain from knowing God.

3. According to 2 Peter 1:3, what has the power of God granted us? To round out your understanding of 2 Peter 1:3, look up Psalm 84:11; Romans 8:32; 2 Corinthians 12:9; Ephesians 3:16–20. From these verses, summarize what you learn about the power of God that is available to us.

4. Second Peter 1:3 says everything we *need* is rooted in what? See also Ephesians 4:11–16; Philippians 3:8–11; 1 John 2:3 to discover what effect that "understanding" should have upon our lives.

5. What else has been granted to us? See 2 Peter 1:4.

6. What are those promises supposed to do for us according to 2 Peter 1:4? See also 2 Corinthians 7:1; Titus 2:11–14.

7. Consider the implications of what you learned in 2 Peter 1:4 when it comes to overcoming sin and growing in godliness. Try to identify at least three ways that your life should be impacted.

8. Though you may have unmet expectations galore, what encouragement to give God the glory He deserves can you gain from 2 Peter 1:2–4?

[The Word of God] is the compass by which the rudder of our will is to be steered.[94]
Thomas Watson

The Bible applied to the heart by the Holy Spirit, is "the chief means by which men are built up and strengthened in the faith," after their conversion. It is able to make them pure, to sanctify them, to train them in righteousness, and to thoroughly equip them for every good work. (Psalm 119:9; John 17:17; 2 Timothy 3:16–17). The Spirit ordinarily does these things by the written Word; sometimes by the Word read, and sometimes by the Word preached, but seldom, if ever, without the Word.[95]
J. C. Ryle

Growth in Christian grace is closely related to our growth in theological knowledge. If our progress in doctrine is poor, either because we hear poor preaching or do not care to read books on Christian doctrine, we shall hardly advance in a true knowledge of God and of His thoughts. Doctrine, after all, is just a word for God and for his works and ways as these are divinely revealed to us in holy Scripture.[96]
Maurice Roberts

---

94 Thomas Watson quoted in *Voices from the Past, vol. 2*, 180.
95 J. C. Ryle, (2010-08-06). *Practical Religion* (Kindle Locations 1774-1777). Kindle Edition.
96 Maurice Roberts, *The Christian's High Calling*, (Edinburgh: The Banner of Truth Trust, 2000), 32.

13

Get Back
on the Horse

It is hard to prescribe a just measure of humiliation. It is the same in the new birth as in the natural. Some give birth with more pangs, and some with fewer. But would you like to know when you are bruised enough? When your spirit is so troubled that you are willing to let go those lusts which brought in the greatest income of pleasure and delight. When not only is sin discarded but you are disgusted with it, then you have been bruised enough. The medicine is strong enough when it has purged out the disease. The soul is bruised enough when the love of sin is purged out.
Thomas Watson[97]

Let us not be discouraged by any humiliating discoveries we may make of the evils of our hearts. God knows them all, and has provided the blood of Jesus Christ His Son to cleanse us from all sin.
R. C. Chapman[98]

97   Thomas Watson, *The Godly Man's Picture* (Edinburgh: The Banner of Truth, 1991), 227.
98   Chapman, *Choice Sayings*, 9-10.

Maurice Roberts, in his wonderful book *The Thought of God*, has a chapter titled, "When Good Men Fall." Roberts' use of the term "good men" refers to believers—and specifically, believers who stumble and fall into sin. He perceptively comments on the devastation a believer can feel *after* falling into sin, even while understanding that Christ's forgiveness completely cleanses from sin. Roberts writes, "There is nothing half so bitter to a good man as the realization that he has brought disgrace on the Name of the Lord. That is truly the wormwood of the soul. It is as near as the believer will ever come to the miseries of hell. When a good man falls and he becomes conscious of his fall, he does not need to be scourged with the tongues of men. His own conscience will heap coals of fire on his head."[99] The Apostle Peter was one such man. For him, the searing pain of shame in his own conscience was punishment enough to remove independence and pride.

As Jesus and His disciples celebrated the Passover the night before His crucifixion, Jesus was trying to communicate His last thoughts and encouragements to His disciples, knowing they would need those strengthening words in the days to come. As was usually the case, His disciples weren't quite tuning in to what He was saying. What a group they were! Only moments before, Jesus had explained the details of His death and taught them how to celebrate His special memorial supper. He had also revealed that there was a betrayer lurking among them. This significant news was soon overlooked, and they began arguing about who was going to be the greatest among them in the kingdom.

Not to be deterred by their denseness, Jesus continued preparing them for the events soon to unfold, predicting how they would all fall away from Him (Mark 14:27). For Peter, this was unthinkable, so much so that he blurted out, "'Even though all may fall away, yet I will not.' And Jesus said to him, 'Truly I say to you, that this very night, before a rooster crows twice, you yourself will deny Me three times.' But Peter kept saying insistently, 'Even if I have to die with You, I will not deny You!' And they all were saying the same thing also" (Mark 14:29–31). None of the disciples thought they would lack the courage to stand with Christ, even in the face of death. It was inconceivable to them—certainly not a temptation they imagined they would ever succumb to.

Of course, you probably know what happened next in Peter's story. Luke 22:54–62 recounts the painfully uncomfortable event:

> Having arrested Him, they led Him away and brought Him to the house of the high priest; *but Peter was following at a distance.* After

---

99 Roberts, *The Thought of God*, 168.

they had kindled a fire in the middle of the courtyard and had sat down together, Peter was sitting among them. And a servant-girl, seeing him as he sat in the firelight and looking intently at him, said, "This man was with Him too." *But he denied it*, saying, "Woman, I do not know Him." A little later, another saw him and said, "You are one of them too!" But Peter said, "Man, I am not!" After about an hour had passed, another man began to insist, saying, "Certainly this man also was with Him, for he is a Galilean too." But Peter said, "Man, I do not know what you are talking about." Immediately, while he was still speaking, a rooster crowed. *The Lord turned and looked at Peter.* And Peter remembered the word of the Lord, how He had told him, 'Before a rooster crows today, you will deny Me three times. *And he went out and wept bitterly* (emphasis added).

Peter's defection makes us cringe. Reading his story, we feel his shame, humiliation, reproach, and guilt for turning his back on Christ. *How could Peter look anyone in the eyes ever again?* We can well understand why the Bible says Peter went out and wept bitterly. He failed Jesus. He completely and utterly blew it, giving in to fear, pride, and doubt. Never in his life would he ever have thought he would cower like that and deny Christ. Peter never expected to be "that guy."

When You're Surprised by Your Sin

Yet, if we're honest, the possibility of responding similarly looms very close to all of us. Looking into our own hearts makes us shrink from examining Peter's story too closely. We read it quickly because it's too painful, too embarrassing, and hits too close to home. Peter's failure makes us wonder, "If I had been there, would I have done the same?" I know that my own cowardice, fear of man, self-preservation, and desire for acceptance make me all too prone to the same temptations.

Without a doubt, the events of that day were unprecedented and terrifying. *All* the disciples abandoned Christ in His hour of need. To his credit, Peter didn't run as far away or hide like the rest of the disciples, which is why he was noticed in the first place. Yet, after coming under scrutiny because of his affiliation with Jesus, Peter responded far differently than he ever would have expected.

Whether you've sinned out of fear and cowardice like Peter or engaged in a host of other sins, most likely you know what it is to be bitterly disappointed with yourself. Almost certainly you've experienced the crippling sense of failure from responding sinfully and falling below your self-made standards. Failing to meet up to your own expectations can become a huge stumbling block as hopelessness and despair invade your soul. *You can quietly wonder, "I never thought I would sin in this way. What happened? I never thought I would respond this way. I'm not even close to the person I thought I was. How did I end up here?"*

You can grow heartsore when you realize that you don't even meet your own expectations of who you imagined yourself to be. A variety of situations can give rise to the feeling of not measuring up to your own expectations. It can be things like discouragement over losing your temper with your kids *again*, despair at ever gaining the right kind of self-control to conquer bad eating habits, feeling frozen in overcoming different fears, feeling powerless to conquer your anxiety, struggling with bitterness and unforgiveness, ashamed to the depths of your being because you were unfaithful to your husband or stole from your employer or engaged in pornography. When pierced through the heart with the sharp spear of your own failures, what is the biblical response?

How You Respond Next is Crucial

No matter what struggle or sin you've engaged in that has you convicted to the core, *how you respond next is critical.* As already mentioned, some spiritual probing is good, but too much can cause you to wallow in your woefulness without remembering the forgiveness of Jesus Christ. Your disappointment with yourself can cause you to spiral down, so that you feel you will *never* get past the shame of your sin. If you have experienced chastening from the Lord and painful consequences for your sin, you may wonder if there will ever be a time when you're not haunted by the ghosts of your past transgressions. Maurice Roberts commented:

> Good men who have defiled their garments in public are their own tormentors and they commonly do that work as thoroughly as the Inquisition ever went about it with thumb-screw or burning faggot [a bundle of sticks used for fuel]. They cannot see their own face in the mirror without self-loathing. They cry by night and sigh by day. Their only motto now is the forlorn: *If only.* If only time could be recalled, or events effaced from one's past life forever! If only the clock could be put back or the sun made to return to that moment before the scandalous sin was committed![100]

Maurice Roberts is right. Sustained grieving over our failures and sins,

---

100 Ibid., 168-69.

our trips, tumbles, and falls can lock us into a prison of our own making, where we torture ourselves on the rack of "if only." *We can become so demoralized by our past sins and failures that we feel unable to break free, even though God has granted us full pardon and freedom in Jesus Christ.* When we allow the memory of former sins to maintain its grip on us, we can find it difficult to view our circumstances in a biblical framework and believe that God's promises apply to us. We imagine that our past failures dictate our present identity.

Yet for those who are in Christ, there is hope! By trusting in Christ alone for salvation and relying on the Lord for strength, we can live in the present completely forgiven with new hearts, new identities, new purposes—new lives. It's as though we've entered the Witness Protection Program where old things have passed away, and new things have begun! (2 Cor. 5:17).

Be Encouraged, Even Great Saints Stumbled and Fell

Within the pages of Scripture, we have the examples of prominent saints who were able to pick up and move past their hurts, failures, discouragement, and shame to find peace, usefulness, and joy once again. Romans 15:4 reminds us that the failures of God's people have been preserved for our help and encouragement today: "For whatever was written in earlier times was written for our instruction, so that through perseverance and the encouragement of the Scriptures we might have hope." We know that we will sin, but, from their stories, we learn that we can also ask God to help us get back up after falling.

Moses Stumbled Close to the Finish Line

Besides Peter's crash and burn story, we have others of note as well. There is Moses in the book of Numbers, for example. Moses' flame-out story happened during the fortieth year of the wilderness wanderings of the nation of Israel. God decreed that Israel would wander in the desert region for forty years because they had refused to believe Joshua and Caleb's reports about the incredible land God had promised to give them. Yet, even as the nation waited until their "time-out" was completed, God cared for them in amazing ways. Daily, God provided water in a desert region for roughly three million people plus livestock for forty years! He provided food in the form of manna every morning, shaded them during the day with a cloud and comforted, warmed, and gave them light from a pillar of fire during the night. This served as a warming night-light during their long, wilderness sojourn. Not only that, their clothing and shoes never wore out as they dwelt in tents for forty years. Every aspect of their time in the wilderness was intended to teach them to trust the Lord and live in humble dependence upon Him.

Although God cared for them, there were times when His provision wasn't immediate or easy. One such episode occurred during the last year of their sojourning. They needed water. God knew it. Yet He purposely delayed in providing water to test them. Rather than trusting the Lord, who had so faithfully been caring for them for thirty-nine years, the people grumbled. Their discontent fomented to such a degree that a crowd formed and blamed Moses for everything they could conjure up. Appalled, Moses and Aaron quickly ran to the Lord for help. The Lord told Moses to *speak* to the rock and water would come out to quench the thirst of all the people.

Numbers 20:10 records the moment everything changed for Moses, the moment he gave into the temptation to vent and gain a little glory for himself. The Bible tells us that Moses gathered the people and said, "'Listen now, you rebels; shall *we* bring forth water for you out of this rock?' Then Moses lifted up his hand and *struck the rock twice* with his rod; and water came forth abundantly, and the congregation and their beasts drank. But the LORD said to Moses and Aaron, 'Because you have not believed Me, to treat Me as holy in the sight of the sons of Israel, therefore you shall not bring this assembly into the land which I have given them'" (Num. 20:10–12, emphasis added). Those verses are painful to read! For thirty-nine years, Moses patiently dealt with grumbling, distrusting people. And yet, at the very end of his life, in a moment of weakness, Moses stumbled, giving in to impatience and pride.

And Then There's David and Hezekiah

King David stumbled and fell when he looked at and lusted after Bathsheba, committed adultery with her, and sought to cover up her pregnancy by ordering her husband Uriah's death (2 Sam. 12:9–14). Later in David's life, pride and self-sufficiency led him to sin by relying on the size of his army, rather than trusting in the Lord (1 Chron. 21:1–17).

King Hezekiah's story, recorded in both Isaiah 38 and 2 Chronicles 32, is another example of how ingratitude can leave an indelible stain upon an otherwise exemplary life. *David, Hezekiah, Moses, and Peter join the ranks of other men and women who were characterized by faithfulness to the Lord, yet, in an unguarded moment, foolishly, stubbornly, or carelessly did something that led to sin and disgrace in their lives.* Suffice it to say, failure and the subsequent shame over falling into sin is nothing new, not even for exemplary saints in the Bible.

God tells us through Paul's pen in 1 Corinthians 10:6: "Now these things happened as examples for us, so that we would not crave evil things as they also craved." God preserved the failures of His people *for our sake*, so we would learn from their trials and not fall into sin ourselves. Only a few verses later, Paul adds, "Now these things happened to them as an example, and they were written for our instruction, upon whom the ends of the ages have come. Therefore let him who thinks he stands take heed that he does not fall" (1 Cor. 10:11–12). God wants us to learn from those who've gone before us. As we study the stalwarts of the faith and their sins, we learn what *not* to do, so we won't stumble and fall.

Knocking on Heaven's Door

Of course, none of us wants to stumble and fall in the spectacular way some of our Bible friends have. Yet to think we will arrive at heaven's gate without going to battle with our sins and temptations is a false hope. It is far better to arrive in heaven wearing broken-in, broken-down, battle-tested armor that attests to the skirmishes we've waged in overcoming sin and parrying the fiery darts of temptation.

The way to heaven is long and hard. We will stumble at times, dirtying our face in the mud. Yet we'll also rise again, ready to fight against the flesh, so as not to hand Satan a too-easy victory. Proverbs 24:16 reminds us: "For a righteous man falls seven times, and rises again, but the wicked stumble in time of calamity." The way isn't perfect, but all believers get back up and keep slogging on. Though weary and wounded from the battles, the thought of seeing Jesus face to face spurs us on.

The Lord Won't Let You Go

Along with the rather humbling truth that we can expect to sin, sometimes grievously, we discover in God's Word an equally important expectation that provides valuable balance in our thinking. This steadying truth is seen in Psalm 94:18, where the psalmist reflects, "If I should say, 'My foot has slipped,' Your lovingkindness, O LORD, will hold me up." The Lord keeps a firm grip upon His children *when they fall*. Do you see the wonder of that truth? We might expect God to turn His back on us when we trip and plunge into sin. We might fear He will be so disappointed with our "performance" that He will want nothing to do with us. Yet those are false and God-dishonoring expectations. *The Scriptures teach the opposite.*

When we sin, our wise and loving Father holds onto us to protect, guide, support, and comfort.

Within the pages of the Bible, we see again and again the Lord's mercy and patience with His erring children. We read of another instance in Luke 22:31–32. This one concerns Peter. Jesus said, "Simon, Simon, behold, Satan has demanded permission to sift you like wheat; *but I have prayed for you, that your faith may not fail; and you, when once you have turned again,* strengthen your brothers" (emphasis added).

It would make me quake in my boots if Jesus spoke those words to me. "Lisa, Satan has demanded permission to sift you like wheat." Can you imagine? Satan requested to try Peter and God approved it. Even in the testing, the Lord lovingly provided for Peter. Jesus told him, *"I have prayed for you, that your faith may not fail; and you, when once you have turned again, strengthen your brothers"* (Luke 22:32, emphasis added). Jesus prayed that Peter's faith wouldn't falter, though He was fully aware that Peter would soon deny being acquainted with Him. Notice that the Lord didn't cut ties with Peter after his cowardly betrayal. He held onto Peter with His sustaining grace even after the denial. He didn't want Peter to be consumed with anguish over his sin and never recover. *The Lord intended to use Peter on the other side of his humbling failure.* If ever there was a hopeful, helpful example, Peter is it!

We continue to see the Lord's compassion on Peter. In Mark 16, we read that Jesus had risen from the dead. An angel waited at the garden tomb with a message for the women, who were soon to arrive to prepare Jesus' body for burial. God wanted them to "Go, tell His disciples and Peter, 'He is going ahead of you to Galilee; there you will see Him, just as He told you'" (v. 7). *"Go, tell His disciples and Peter"* (emphasis added). All the disciples needed encouragement after they had abandoned the Lord in the hours of His suffering. But Peter is singled out. Jesus wanted Peter to know there was hope on the other side of his failure.

Our Father Parents Us Well

The Lord never loosened His grip on Peter, and He doesn't loosen His grip on us either. When we sin against Him, we may experience His chastise-ment—*and rightly so*, for He is the perfect Father, who knows exactly how to discipline His children. Yet, even while we experience the consequenc-es of our sin, the Lord still shows mercy. In fact, the consequences them-selves are a mercy the Lord uses to mold us into Christ's image.

Our sin cannot separate us from the love of God (Rom. 8:38–39). God's providential use of all things for our good is especially helpful to remember when we feel low and dejected because of our sins and failures, or when we're discouraged because we haven't matched up to the ideals or expectations we had for ourselves. We may be tempted to believe God will reject us because of our failure. *Yet the truth of God's Word keeps us and bolsters us.*

First John 1:9 staunchly reminds us that "If we confess our sins, He is faithful and righteous to forgive us our sins and to cleanse us from all unrighteousness." We will experience consequences as a result of our sin, but repentance restores our communion with Him. Our sin doesn't diminish God's love or care for us, though it does hinder our fellowship with Him. God is always near His children. Yet when we sin, we turn our backs on Him. Think of it, each time we sin, we turn away from the Lord. But, when we confess and repent of our sins, we turn away from sin and face the Lord again in faith, hope, and trust. This gives us all the more reason to turn from our sin quickly, so less time is spent with our backs toward Jesus.

God Is Committed to Training Us

We wouldn't learn and grow if there were never consequences for the sins that we commit. Moses experienced consequences for his sin when he didn't treat God as holy before the people. This resulted in his not being able to enter the Promised Land with the people. Moses was understandably grieved over not receiving what he had labored for forty years to accomplish. Yet knowing the Lord's lovingkindness and compassion, he hoped God would relent. Apparently, Moses repeatedly asked the Lord to change His mind for Deuteronomy 3:26 tells us the Lord replied to him, "Enough! Speak to Me no more of this matter." Moses had to humbly accept the consequences of his sin and learn to fear the Lord. Our unchanging God is unswerving in His commitment to teach us His ways in order that we may share in His holiness (Heb. 12:10).

God's Training Is Framed in Compassion

Even while the Lord was training and teaching Moses, He was still kind and compassionate to him. Moses wasn't allowed to enter the Promised Land, but the Lord allowed him to see it before he died. Deuteronomy 34:1–4 recounts: "Now Moses went up from the plains of Moab to Mount Nebo, to the top of Pisgah, which is opposite Jericho. And the LORD showed him all the land. . . . 'I have let you see it with your eyes, but you shall not go over there.'" God corrects, then in great compassion, warmly comforts His sorrowful child. When we repent of our sin, we can look for the tender ways in which the Lord will comfort us in the aftermath.

God's Training Is Never Vindictive

Because David left us his journal record in the Psalms, we know he was encouraged and strengthened by the Lord even *after* committing heinous, public sins. Though the consequences of his sins remained, David knew the Lord *still* intended good toward him. He rejoiced in the Lord's forgiveness, knowing it was undeserved. As a case in point, take a look at Psalm 32 and Psalm 51. Both were written *after* David sinned with Bathsheba. Consider David's wonder as he reviewed the Lord's mercy:

> How blessed is he whose transgression is forgiven, whose sin is covered! How blessed is the man to whom the LORD does not impute iniquity, and in whose spirit there is no deceit! When I kept silent about my sin, my body wasted away through my groaning all day long. For day and night Your hand was heavy upon me; my vitality was drained away as with the fever heat of summer. I acknowledged my sin to You, and my iniquity I did not hide; I said, 'I will confess my transgressions to the LORD'; and You forgave the guilt of my sin. (Ps. 32:1–5)

David knew he possessed God's complete and total forgiveness, although he experienced fallout from his acts of presumption and rebellion for the rest of his life. When we turn from our sin, God forgives us fully and freely, though the consequences of our disobedience may remain.

God's Training is For Our Blessing

Isaiah 38:9–20 is King Hezekiah's commentary on the Lord's discipline. Hezekiah wrote, "Behold, it was for my welfare that I had great bitterness; but in love You have delivered my life from the pit of destruction, for You have cast all my sins behind Your back" (Isa. 38:17, ESV). Hezekiah acknowledged the goodness of God's forgiveness and His wisdom in humbling him. *"The bitterness I experienced was actually for my own good."* Pastor R. C. Chapman said, "To quarrel with the instruments of God used for our correction is to quarrel with God Himself. It is, in fact, to say to Him, 'I do not approve of Thy government, and I could order matters better if they were left to me.' What is this but to aim at casting down God from His throne, and setting ourselves thereon?"[101] Ahhh, that gets to the heart of it, doesn't it? Often, we don't like the means God uses to sanctify our hearts. We have a better idea, which is, as Chapman points out, simply usurping God's place as rightful King. We want to rule and dispense our own brand of justice, order, and wisdom because in pride we think we

---

101 Chapman, *Choice Sayings*, 71.

know better than God!

Learning to respond well, with tender humility and quick-hearted recognition of God's faithful work in our lives, is what we're looking for here. Let us learn to respond like Hezekiah: "Behold, it was for my welfare that I had great bitterness; but in love You have delivered my life from the pit of destruction, for You have cast all my sins behind Your back."

How Do You Get Back Up After Getting Bucked Off?

During my elementary school years, we lived in the country and had horses. When my dad was teaching me to ride, one of the things he told me was, "If you get bucked off, make sure you get back on the horse. Lots of people who get bucked off never get back on a horse because they are afraid, and they never ride again."

Anyone who's ridden a fair bit has probably been bucked off at least once. There's a surprising jolt, a flailing ride through the air, a hard, painful landing with a subsequent whoosh, as the breath gets knocked out of you, a quick roll away from the horse's hooves, then a lying still on the ground until air returns to your lungs and the sky stops spinning. Finally, there's a shaky return to standing upright. *But merely getting upright isn't the goal; getting back on the horse is.*

My dad also taught me not to let a horse know that I was afraid. This meant that when I was bucked off, I had to master my shaking hands, trembling knees, and quavering voice as I reached for the saddle horn, put my foot in the stirrup, and eased back into the saddle. Invariably, I rode differently after being bucked off—with a bit more caution, respect, and wisdom. I also learned the value of getting back in the saddle and conquering my fears.

Life, trials, hurts, and traumas can knock the wind out of us, to the point that the thought of getting back up and moving on is daunting, to say the least. Yet God never intends our trials to incapacitate us, harm us, or keep us from "getting back on the horse again." It is critical to understand how we should think and respond *after* we fall into sin. It's not overstating it to say that *our present response determines what our spiritual walk will look like in the years to come.*

Just as my dad prepared me for the day I would get bucked off, so we need to be prepared for the day when we find ourselves in the dust because of sin. The best plan to overcoming the sorrow, shame, and degradation we may feel in the face of our sin begins by regulating our thinking according to the Word of God.

Just like Peter, there may come a day when you will sin in some way that completely takes you by surprise. And just like Peter, you will feel ashamed and sorrowful about it. Hopefully, you will quickly confess your sin to the Lord and humbly repent of it. Then what? How will you proceed from there? *In your head,* because you've confessed and repented of your sin, you know all is right between you and God (1 John 1:9). But you may still feel as though the wind has been knocked out of you. You will wonder if you'll ever be able to stand upright again. *Revising unrealistic expectations takes some work.* It certainly takes right thinking that has to be founded on the Word of God itself. If you don't take the time to order your thoughts according to the Word of God, you may continue to wallow in the dust of your own sinfulness and never get in the saddle again.

Expect to Eat Dust

Just as my dad taught me that I would *eventually* get bucked off, you need to know you will stumble and sin. And it will happen again—and again. In fact, it's good to remember what one pastor often reminds himself of as he counsels people, "We are all just a moment away from committing great evil." It's foolish to think we won't stumble and fall into sin. In fact, God tell us, "There is not a righteous man on earth who continually does good and who never sins (Eccl. 7:20)."

Our expectations can trip us up if we're not prepared for the sinfulness of sin! Even though we know we are sinners—and even expect to sin—it's often the *way* we sin or the *degree* to which we sin that can throw us from our horse. We need to remind ourselves of this simple truth: *believers sin.* Believers can engage in high-handed rebellion against the Lord. They can fall into sins that they never expected to commit.

Maurice Roberts has said, "Christians cannot fall away; but they can fall far."[102] What he means is that no sin can endanger our salvation; all are safe who have trusted in Jesus (John 10:27–29). In our earthly experience, however, we can certainly fall into sin. We can compound our sin by stubbornly refusing to repent and engaging in more sin, which only serves to lead us further from the Lord. We need to remember that though we are redeemed, rescued, made into a new creature, and given the Holy Spirit, the Word of God, and the fellowship of the saints as resources, we will still sin *because we still live in a sin-cursed body.* One day, when our earthly body is exchanged for that which is eternal, we will be freed from the presence of sin as it resides in us. For now, today, in this life, we remain weak and easily tempted to sin.

However, we are not left without comfort. Proverbs 24:16 tells us, "For a

---

102   Ibid., 167.

righteous man falls seven times, and rises again, but the wicked stumble in time of calamity." Often, when seven is used in the Scriptures, it describes completeness or something all-encompassing. Here, in Proverbs 24:16, seven simply means that the righteous man will fall a lot! But notice the encouragement in that verse too. The righteous, that is, believers, will rise again. They dust themselves off in confession and repentance and get back in the saddle of living for God.

Psalm 145:14 explains how it's possible for sinners to get back up again. We read, "The LORD sustains all who fall and raises up all who are bowed down." Notice who is doing the work in that verse. When we fall because of sin and weakness, the Lord Himself picks us up. A corollary truth is found in Psalm 37:24 where we learn, "When he falls, he will not be hurled headlong, because the LORD is the One who holds his hand." This perfectly pictures a loving parent walking with a little one, holding the child's hand while he or she toddles and teeters along. The parent protects that little bit of sweetness from getting seriously hurt because he or she has a firm grip on the child. Believers may fall into seriously ugly sin, but never a soul-damning sin. Our Lord's grip on us keeps us from destruction, though we may get a bit bruised or skinned up while pursuing our own way.

The psalmist wrote, "When my heart was embittered and I was pierced within, then I was senseless and ignorant; I was like a beast before You. *Nevertheless I am continually with You; You have taken hold of my right hand. With Your counsel You will guide me, and afterward receive me to glory* (Ps. 73:21–24, emphasis added). Even when we act in a beastly manner, the Lord never relaxes His grip, which makes a mundane word like "nevertheless" grow in beauty and significance. We are weak, frail creatures sustained and upheld by our loving Savior for future glory.

Eating Dust Teaches Us Good Lessons for Life

John Bunyan said, "He that is down need fear no fall."[103] Because God is opposed to the proud and gives grace to the humble (1 Peter 5:5), Bunyan notes that "men thrive in the Valley of Humiliation."[104] There's a certain sweetness in a humbled spirit, and Bunyan tells us to take advantage of it. After repenting of sin, continue to learn from the trial by keeping your head and heart humble before the Lord. Jeremiah echoes Bunyan when he writes in Lamentations 3:27–30, "It is good for a man that he bear the yoke in his youth. Let him sit alone in silence when it is laid on him; let

---

103 John Bunyan, *The Pilgrim's Progress* (London: Pickering & Inglis Ltd, no publication date), 263.
104 Ibid.

him put his mouth in the dust—there may yet be hope; let him give his cheek to the one who strikes, and let him be filled with insults" (ESV).

The Lord uses trials, unmet expectations, and failures to teach us humility. Maurice Roberts writes: "It follows that the best and the safest course is to study humility. There ought to be nothing flashy or cocksure in the Christian. . . . The man of God, however, ought to see that humility is the spirit of heaven itself and the mind of Christ."[105] By keeping our hearts humbled, we'll gain the blessings that come on the other side of our sin. Our hearts can grow to love the place where self is continually emptied because there's nothing left to lose. My husband has said, "Humility is the place where our arrogance gets knocked out of us." It almost sounds like a train stop along our journey to heaven. "Ladies and Gentlemen, our next stop is Humility. This is our final stop for the evening so all passengers will need to disembark at the station." Come to think of it, we'll make many such stops at Humility Junction on the way to Heaven.

Keep Your Eyes Glued to the Lord Only

One time Jack left his sunglasses in a restaurant, so I ran back in to get them. On the way in, I tripped over the door jam, not a silent little hop, but one of those arm flailing, feet stumbling ones where everyone looks up to see what has happened. Those times can be tremendously embarrassing; I speak from multiplied experience. Usually, the best option is just not to look around to see who noticed and go about your business. That is definitely true when it comes to standing up after a fall. It can be tempting to look around and see who has noticed the spiritual crash and burn. While doing so, you tumble into a deeper hole by worrying about what others are thinking. Focusing on what others think of us only compounds the trauma of failure and falling into sin. An "I wonder what they are thinking about me" kind of response isn't helpful, and only leads to more discouragement for an already discouraged soul.

As we learned earlier, keeping your head down and heart low before the Lord helps you learn the lessons God desires to teach you. Don't focus on what others may think or say. This was part of Peter's training after his colossal failure. The Lord wanted Peter to keep his eyes on Him and not worry about His interactions with the other disciples. John 21:20–22 records, "Peter turned and saw the disciple whom Jesus loved following them. . . . When Peter saw him, he said to Jesus, 'Lord, what about this man?' Jesus said to him, 'If it is my will that he remain until I come, what is that to you? You follow me!'" The lessons of humility can be summed up

---

105   Roberts, *The Thought of God*, 172.

in Jesus' words: *"What is that to you? You follow Me"* (ESV).

When it's all said and done, it really doesn't matter what other people think of us. The Lord wants us to prize what He thinks. Whenever we humble our hearts before Him and keep our eyes on Him, we are exactly where we need to be. It is wise to heed the counsel of Jeremiah found in Lamentations 3:26: "It is good that he waits silently for the salvation of the LORD." With a humbled heart and our eyes on the Lord alone, we're ready to heed the call, "You, follow Me."

Truths That Keep You Walking

Jerry Bridges in his book, *Trusting God*, said, "Does failure on our part to act prudently frustrate the sovereign plan of God? The Scriptures never indicate that God is frustrated to any degree by our failure to act as we should. In His infinite wisdom, God's sovereign plan includes our failures and even our sins."[106] Isn't it good to know that our sins don't derail the sovereign plan of God which He put into place before the worlds were formed? God will get us where He wants us, using our sins, failures, weaknesses, and, yes, even our unmet expectations to teach us more about Him and make us more like Jesus. When we're hurting over the sins we've committed, kicking ourselves because of our failures, it's important that we remind ourselves of biblical truth. *God's Word heals our wounded hearts.*

Comfort from the Scriptures

- First Corinthians 10:11–13 will help heal our hearts if we remember, "Now these things happened to them as an example, and they were *written for our instruction, upon whom the ends of the ages have* come. Therefore let him who thinks he stands take heed that he does not fall. No temptation has overtaken you but such as is common to man; and God is faithful, who will not allow you to be tempted beyond what you are able, but *with the temptation will provide the way of escape also, so that you will be able to endure it.*" (emphasis added). What a balm to know that even the failures of those who've gone before provide wisdom and encouragement for our walk. It's so helpful to read their stories and heed their lessons. It's also a good reminder that not paying attention to their lessons can result in falling into sin. What a wonder that with every temptation we face, God *always* provides a way to escape. He will come to our aid, if we sincerely ask Him.

106 Bridges, *Trusting God*, 114-15.

- Psalm 103:3 can bring great relief if we remember, "[The LORD] *Who pardons all your iniquities,* who heals all your diseases." The text says every last one of your sins is pardoned—every one of them. You can't commit a sin too big or too awful for God to forgive because Jesus' sacrifice was perfect! God always forgives and cleanses us from all unrighteousness, when we repent of our sin (1 John 1:9). Reminding ourselves of God's unending and complete forgiveness will help us move forward.
- Psalm 30:5 brings comfort when we remember, "For His anger is but for a moment, His favor is for a lifetime; *weeping may last for the night, but a shout of joy comes in the morning"* (emphasis added). The sorrow over sin and the consequences of it won't last forever. Night always gives way to day. We may have to weep during our appointed "night," but God always brings the morning—and with it comes joy.
- Romans 8:1 alleviates shame and guilt when we remember, "Therefore there is *now no condemnation* for those who are in Christ Jesus." (emphasis added). There are no frowning looks; there is no reproach, no condemnation for those whose souls have been washed clean by the blood of Jesus.
- Romans 8:33–35 strengthens our hearts when we remember, "Who will bring a charge against God's elect? God is the one who justifies; who is the one who condemns? Christ Jesus is He who died, yes, rather who was raised, who is at the right hand of God, who also intercedes for us. *Who will separate us from the love of Christ?* Will tribulation, or distress, or persecution, or famine, or nakedness, or peril, or sword?" (emphasis added). Sin cannot put a barrier between us and Christ when He's *already* forgiven all our sin. The Scriptures are clear; we have nothing to fear. Will we believe it and keep walking, trusting that God will use us on the other side of our sin?
- First John 2:1 brings reassurance when we remember, "My little children, I am writing these things to you so that you may not sin. *And if anyone sins, we have an Advocate with the Father, Jesus Christ the righteous"* (emphasis added). To know that we have sinned and to have Jesus stand up for us and be the One to argue our case because we belong to Him is beyond marvelous!
- Romans 8:28 comforts us when we remember, "And we know that *God causes all things to work together for good* to those who love God, to those who are called according to His purpose" (emphasis added). The unequivocal scope of God's working all things for our good should draw us near to the Lord when we're feeling forlorn and forsaken after falling into sin. Knowing that *all,* even our rebellion and

sin, will be worked together for good can greatly minister to bruised hearts, bringing healing and hope.

Even in our failure, when we are fearful of rejection, God's Word urges us to come again into the Lord's presence. What a blessing to know the Lord will use everything for His glory—our sin, failures, and subsequent repentance. God intends our lives to be a means of strengthening and encouragement to other believers too. It can be a bitter pill to consider that the memory of our sin may be used to keep others from sinning or to encourage them after they have sinned. Just the thought of it can tempt us to wail, "Oh, woe is me! If only I hadn't done that thing! If only I hadn't given into sin!" Yet trusting the Lord to do whatever He thinks is best with our lives helps us to move forward. John Newton said, "We serve a gracious Master who knows how to overrule even our mistakes to His glory and our own advantage."[107]

Charles Spurgeon echoed these truths in his words: "If we have lived in any sin and the Spirit leads us to purge ourselves of it, we may count on the blessing of the Lord. His smile, His Spirit, His grace, and His fuller revelation of His truth will prove an enlarged blessing."[108] Now that's certainly a different response than we might expect from God! Yet it's perfectly in keeping with the Lord's generous nature.

Trust God to Use You on the Other Side of Failure

God loves it when His children turn to Him in faith—anytime, anywhere and under any circumstances. If you have stumbled in sin, and repented, will you trust Him to redeem your failures and use them for good? Are you willing to relinquish any unbiblical expectations you may have created that keep you from moving forward? Will you trust Him to be the God He says He is, the One ever ready to receive you with open arms? If Peter could write words of hope and forgiveness on the other side of his sin, then take heart, you too can press on. Abandon the constraints that unbiblical expectations impose and entrust yourself to the Lord's transforming, redeeming grace. "He Himself bore our sins in His body on the cross, so that we might die to sin and live to righteousness; *for by His wounds you were healed*. For you were continually straying like sheep, *but now you have returned* to the Shepherd and Guardian of your souls" (1 Peter 2:24–25, emphasis added).

---

107 John Newton, *The Amazing Works of John Newton: Words of Grace and Encouragement From the Famous Hymn Writer*, ed. Harold Chadwick (Alachua, FL: Bridge-Logos, 2009), 337.
108 Spurgeon, *The Cheque Book of the Bank of Faith*, 324.

QUESTIONS for REFLECTION

Chapter 13: Get Back on the Horse

1. Read Psalm 30. Remember that, when David wrote this psalm, it was on the heels of his sin in numbering the people. (Read the details of this event in 1 Chronicles 21:1–17 and 2 Samuel 24:1–17.) When he wrote this psalm, David had confessed, repented, and been restored in his relationship with the Lord, but he still experienced consequences for his sin. What truths does David focus on in Psalm 30:1–3 that were an encouragement to him? What truths do you find particularly encouraging?

2. If we fall into sin, what truths can we count on to help ease the pain of our hurting souls? See Psalms 41:4; 147:3; Isaiah 53:5; 1 Peter 2:24.

3. Look back at Psalm 30:4–5. What things do you notice in verse 5 about the Lord and the way He works in the lives of His children?

4. How would the truths from Psalm 30:5 help you to apply the truths in verse 4?

5. Psalm 30:6 talks about prosperity—times of spiritual satisfaction or "fatness" when it's difficult to imagine stumbling or falling. Yet, *when* we do fall or struggle spiritually, what can we count on according to verse 7? See also Psalms 37:24; 38:17; 73:21–24; 145:14; Proverbs 24:16.

6. Why would God "hide His face," as it says in Psalm 30:7? See also Isaiah 59:2.

7. What causes the "smile" to return to God's face? See Isaiah 38:17; Micah 7:18–19; and Psalm 32:5.

8. Review Psalm 30:8–10. What encouragement can we find in these verses if we are trying to recover from the consequences of sin or failure?

It has been thought by some that as long as Peter lived, the fountain of his tears began to flow whenever he remembered his denying his Lord. It is not unlikely that it was so, for his sin was very great, and grace in him had afterwards a perfect work. This same experience is common to all the redeemed family according to the degree in which the Spirit of God has removed the natural heart of stone.

We, like Peter, remember our boastful promise: "Though all men shall forsake thee, yet will not I." We eat our own words with the bitter herbs of repentance. When we think of what we vowed we would be, and of what we have been, we may weep whole showers of grief.

He thought on his denying his Lord. The place in which he did it, the little cause which led him into such heinous sin, the oaths and blasphemies with which he sought to confirm his falsehood, and the dreadful hardness of heart which drove him to do so again and yet again. Can we, when we are reminded of our sins, and their exceeding sinfulness, remain stolid and stubborn? Will we not make our house a Bochim, and cry unto the Lord for renewed assurances of pardoning love? May we never take a dry-eyed look at sin, lest ere long we have a tongue parched in the flames of hell.

Peter also thought upon his Master's look of love. The Lord followed up the cock's warning voice with an admonitory look of sorrow, pity, and love. That glance was never out of Peter's mind so long as he lived. It was far more effectual than ten thousand sermons would have been without the Spirit.

The penitent apostle would be sure to weep when he recollected the Savior's full forgiveness, which restored him to his former place. To think that we have offended so kind and good a Lord is more than sufficient reason for being constant weepers. Lord, smite our rocky hearts, and make the waters flow.
Charles Spurgeon[109]

---

109   Charles Spurgeon, *Morning and Evening,* revised and updated by Alistair Begg (Wheaton, IL: Crossway, 2003), July 30, Morning.

14

Wonky Thinking and God's Good Will

He sometimes will leave us to ourselves to reveal the weakness of our own hearts.
Thomas Manton[110]

We sometimes think that we have strong faith when our faith is weak. How are we to know if it is weak or strong until it is tried? If you were to lie in bed week after week and perhaps get the idea that you were strong, you would certainly be mistaken. Only when you do work that requires muscular strength will you discover how strong or how weak you are. God would not have us form a wrong estimate of ourselves. He does not want us to say that we are rich and increased in goods and have need of nothing when just the opposite is true. Therefore, He sends trials to test the genuineness of our faith (1 Peter 1:7), that we may understand how strong or weak we are.
Charles Spurgeon[111]

---

110 Thomas Manton, *Works*, I:145-147 quoted in *Voices from the Past*, vol. 1, 73.
111 Charles Spurgeon, *Beside Still Waters*, ed. Roy H. Clarke (Nashville: Thomas Nelson, 1999), 338.

During every believer's lifetime, there will be seasons of testing when it seems that the God we thought we knew and understood becomes inscrutable. We simply won't understand what He is doing. To us, His ways will seem beyond reason or even unreasonable. Try as we might, we won't be able to figure out how He can bring good out of the chaos and disruptions He has ordained for us. When we endeavor to make sense of it all, we may be tempted to judge God. Like Job, we want God to give an account of His ways (Job 31:35). We are inclined to think that, if we had the opportunity to explain our wonderful plan for our life, God would see our wisdom, instantly remove the trials and say, "Sorry, I couldn't have planned it better. We'll do it your way!" We are tempted to think that, if we could only reason with Him,[112] then God would deviate from His plan for our lives and enact our plans instead.

All kinds of wrong thoughts come into our minds when we're trying to make sense out of life, such as wondering if God really cares about us when He doesn't heal a sick child, or whether He is really good when the long-prayed-for spouse dies without knowing Christ. When God's reasons, ways, and plans seem so far beyond the scope of how *we* would do things, unbiblical thinking leaves us wondering whether God is really sovereign or whether He truly cares for us. Knowing that God has the power to rescue us or remove the pressure, and yet allows it to remain, can tempt us to think wrongly about the Lord.

Expecting God to Do Things Our Way

When a much-desired change in our circumstances never occurs, we may default to thinking that God doesn't really love us. Nothing could be further from the truth! Yet, how do we counter our unbiblical "I wish God would do it my way" response? *How can we learn to think rightly when our hearts are hurting and confused?*

Our daughter suffered with a chronic headache for eight long years. During the first year of this trial, I was trying desperately to make sense of God's good plan for our family. I had been crying out to Him in prayer, asking Him to heal her or relieve her of the constant pain. While praying, I read through Psalm 33 with verse 6 catching my attention. It proclaims, "By the word of the LORD the heavens were made, and by the breath of His mouth all their host." As I read about David rejoicing in God's power and might in creation, I reasoned that, if God could speak worlds into existence, He was powerful enough to relieve our daughter's pain. I

---

112 Job desired to reason with God too. He felt sure that if God had all the facts, then God would remove the trials (Job 23:1-7).

remember praying, "Lord, You can do anything. Your Word tells us that You made the heavens with a word, from the breath of your mouth you made all the host of heaven. Lord, nothing is too difficult for You."

As I prayed about that verse, my eyes strayed back up the page to verse 4, which says, "For the word of the LORD is upright, and all His work is done in faithfulness. He loves righteousness and justice; the earth is full of the lovingkindness of the LORD." And so, I began to pray through those verses also, considering what was true of God and how His attributes underscored our family's circumstances. *His work is done in faithfulness. He loves righteousness and justice.* All of this meant that the trials we were experiencing were tailor-made for us by God's faithful, righteous, and just nature. God would never do anything wrong or unjust because of the love He has for righteousness and justice.

I realized my inward battle with my circumstances revealed a deeper and far more serious problem. *I was judging God.* I didn't think it was *right* or *just* of God to allow our daughter to suffer with pain. Right then and there, clear as day, I realized how wrong my thinking had been—and would continue to be—until my heart's thoughts matched what God said about Himself in His Word.

Learning to Reorient Our Thinking Through the Word

All too easily, we trust *our* judgment of things. The problem is our perceptions are sin-based, man-centered, and me-centered—all the more reason to reorient our thinking to line up with the Scriptures. God's Word says that He never does anything wrong, tainted, or in any way worthy of blame. Psalm 33:4–5 reminds us that God so loves righteousness that He only does what is right. He is always faithful and always acts in line with His character. In fact, Psalm 33:5 tells us that the earth is *full* of His lovingkindness. *As God Himself is full of love and kindness, His actions are too.* This means that when life's circumstances are different than *we* think they should be, *we* must adjust our thinking to line up with the Scriptures. We are not in charge. God is. *We don't get to decide whether God's ways are right or not. He has already declared that they are perfect, righteous, and just.*

To further cement our thinking on this subject, verse 10 of Psalm 33 says, "The LORD nullifies the counsel of the nations; He frustrates the plans of the peoples." What a picture of a sovereign, active God! Have you had your day planned before your feet even touched the floor in the morning, only to find, barely an hour later, that your well-ordered plans have fallen by the wayside? Psalm 33:10 explains why this is so. It is because *God is at work.* The verse tells us that He frustrates our plans. But why? We're given the answer to that question too: "The counsel of the LORD stands forever, the plans of His heart from generation to generation" (Ps. 33:11). Similarly, Isaiah 25:1 says, "O Lord, You are my God; I will exalt You, I will give thanks to Your name; for You have worked wonders, plans formed long ago, with perfect faithfulness." Both passages tell us that God thwarts and changes *our plans* because *He has better ones.* In fact, *His* plans were formed long ago—way, way, way, way before we were born. God's plans are perfect and can't be improved upon.

We think our way makes the most sense. *We think* our plans are God-glorifying. *We think* our ideas are brilliantly inspired. But *we don't know* the things God knows. *We don't understand* the needs of our hearts the way God does. *We don't have* the perfect knowledge and wisdom that God has. The Lord speaks to us through Isaiah proclaiming, "For My thoughts are not your thoughts, nor are your ways My ways" (55:8).

God Knows All Things

So, when God doesn't answer your prayers in the way you thought He would or, if circumstances in your life are far different than you ever would have orchestrated for your life, it should tell you that God's plan, formed long ages ago, is far better for you than anything you could dream up in your fifteen minutes before getting out of bed. God's ways are the best ways. He has considered everything from the beginning to the end (Isa. 46:10). He examined every scenario—and judged your present circumstances in perfect wisdom as the absolute best way to produce godly maturity in you.

Oh, pause and let these thoughts about God sink in. *There are no mistakes with God.* You are not powerful enough to derail God's "determined long-ago plan" for your life, nor can someone else's wickedness or plain, old stubbornness shuttle you off into a place God never intended you to be. Your job is to trust Him, to trust and wait and watch the unfolding of His perfectly planned, wise, and loving works for your life. *Trust Him* while He uses the *unthinkable* for your good. *Trust Him* while He uses the *uncomfortable* to refine you. *Trust Him* while He uses the *unfathomable* to strengthen your faith.

Lest you think your case is somehow different and you got lost in the details of His plans for the world, remember Psalm 33:13 which explains, "[The Lord] . . . sees *all* the sons of men" (emphasis added). *He sees you.* You are not hidden. He knows your present circumstances. *Yet you experience unmet expectations because He lovingly, righteously, perfectly planned your days for your good and for His glory.*

Your Expectations about God Must Line Up with the Scriptures

Let's take some time to examine some all-too-common expectations that can play havoc with our hearts and minds, if we're not careful to correct them. Below are some expectations I've had to face during the course of His heart training in my life. Even though I'm using myself as a guinea pig, I hope you'll see how some of these expectations could show up in your life as well.

- *I expect God to think like I do.* Of course, that statement has lots behind it. It really means that if God thinks as I do, then I can figure Him out, and predict what He'll do in the details of my life. This expectation shows the depths of my pride. I pridefully think I have God figured out and can understand how He will proceed. Goodness! My considerations have been woefully obtuse and dishonoring to the Lord at times. But I've still found myself getting bogged down by this expectation. Paul declares: "Oh, the depth of the riches both of the wisdom and knowledge of God! How unsearchable are His judgments and unfathomable His ways! For who has known the mind of the Lord, or who became His counselor?" (Rom. 11:33–34). *God doesn't think like we do.*
- *I expect God to think that my plans are good and go along with them.* This little snippet of flawed thinking goes wrong on a number of levels. First, it's just out and out prideful to think that I can lead the all-powerful God. Second, it's even more prideful to think that my plans are better for my soul's training than God's. "'For My thoughts are not your thoughts, nor are your ways My ways,' declares the LORD (Isa. 55:8)." *God's plans are best. End of story.*
- *I expect I will somehow outgrow my need for training and discipline.* Maybe I'm the only one who has tripped over this particularly thickheaded thought-nugget. It subtly positions itself in my heart, causing me to stumble when God faithfully *continues* His gracious work of sanctification in my life. The truth is that no one, *not one of us,* will outgrow the need for soul-strengthening and faith building. This side of heaven, we need the refining work of the Holy Spirit, as James 1:2-4 so lovingly reminds us: "Consider it all joy, my brethren, when you encounter various trials, knowing that the testing of your faith produces endurance. And let endurance have its perfect result, so that you may be perfect and complete, lacking in nothing." *God continues to sanctify us.*
- *I expect that if I do everything "right," I won't need trials.* This expec-

tation, like the previous ones, again assumes that we know what is best for our souls. It also looks at sanctification in the wrong way. It harkens back to the thinking of our school days when, if we do really well on Test A and also on Test B, then we won't have to take Test C. That is not how God deals with us. Every believer takes all the tests God designs exclusively for him or her. There aren't any "opt outs" for us in the Christian life. We have the example of Abraham who, even after many trials, underwent one of the greatest tests of his faith when God told him to offer up Isaac. Abraham believed God (Test A), and he kept hoping in Him (Test B), but there was no exemption for Abraham. God continued to prove the genuineness of Abraham's faith with Test C. "Now it came about after these things, that God tested Abraham" (Gen. 22:1). *God tests and strengthens our faith with trials and unmet expectations.*

- *I expect to fulfill my quota of trials and then I'll be done.* This unbiblical idea is similar to the one above in that it expects some sort of accounting for how many trials, difficulties, or dashed hopes I might experience within a given length of time, whether a week, year, or lifetime. As with the previous expectation, this one assumes that I know what is best for my soul. It also has a sort of "timecard" feel about it. It carries with it the attitude that states, "I've experienced more than my fair share of trials, so I should now be exempt from further inconveniences upon my soul." I confess that my heart has grown petulant and bitter when I've undergone *more* unmet expectations and trials than *I thought* I should have had to bear. The truth is that God knows the exact number of trials and unmet expectations I need to produce Christlikeness in me, *far better than I do.* May God give me the grace to respond like Job: "Though He slay me, I will hope in Him" (Job 13:15). *God gives us the exact number of trials and difficulties we need for our spiritual growth.*

- *I expect that if I do what is right, I will experience a blessing.* This A+B=C mentality wrongly supposes that blessing *doesn't include* trials, difficulties, or suffering. Yet, even the most faithful and obedient of saints experience affliction, as Job, Abraham, David, and Paul prove. This expectation also tries to escape God's good and perfect means of sanctification, supposing that unmet expectations and the soul-testing they introduce is "bad." Psalm 119:71 teaches, "It is good for me that I was afflicted, that I may learn Your statutes." Trials aren't an indication of God's disfavor. In fact, they reveal how much God loves us (Heb. 12:7–8). *God blesses His children "in prosperity" and "in need"* (Phil. 4:11–13).

- *I expect God to be easier on me.* We can be tempted to think that He is being too hard on us, to the point that we begin to think bitter thoughts of Him. Nothing could be further from the truth, which is why we need to remember Hebrews 12:5–6: "My son, do not regard lightly the discipline of the LORD, nor faint when you are reproved by Him; for those whom the LORD loves He disciplines, and He scourges every son whom He receives." Did you catch the all-important truth tucked away in those two verses? Don't think *too lightly* of the work God is doing in your soul. *Don't faint* under it like a little four-year-old at the end of a long day at Disneyland. We need to remember trials are His *modus operandi* for all His children. In fact, our unmet expectations and difficulties reveal the depth of His love for us. Lamentations 3:33 says that God doesn't "afflict willingly," which means He doesn't have a desire to hurt us with trials, suffering, and unmet expectations. He does what is necessary to produce holiness in us. We see from Hebrews 12:5–6 and Lamentations 3:33 that God applies principles from the story of Goldilocks and the Three Bears when it comes to our spiritual growth. He doesn't use anything "too hard," nor does He use anything "too soft." He always uses the means that are "just right" to get the job done. *God's methods are "just right" in bringing about our sanctification.*

Still Lugging Around Our Survival-Mode Backpack

Every unbiblical thought or ungodly response can and must be corrected by the Word of God. When bewildered by distress and sorrow, what bottom-line thinking do we need to pull out of our survival-mode backpack? Do you remember what they are? I am a sinner and haven't received what I deserve. My trials are fewer than my sins. If I am experiencing unmet expectations, it is because God has deemed them good for me. And finally, the Lord will never disappoint me.

Our bottom-line thinking is true *for every believer*. Believers don't receive what they deserve because they have placed their hope in Jesus Christ for salvation. Believers have confidence that God will use their trials and unmet expectations for good and, one day, all sorrow and trouble will be taken away. If you are an unbeliever and you've never turned to Jesus Christ in repentance and faith, you can't claim those comforts for yourself. Instead, you will receive what you deserve for your sins: death, judgment, and separation from God forever. Yet the forgiveness and mercy of God can be yours *today*, if you will turn to Jesus Christ right now in faith, acknowledging:

"Lord, I am a sinner. I do deserve to die right now, according to your righteous judgment. But You, in Your kindness and patience, have allowed me to live. I no longer want to presume upon Your patience. I also fully acknowledge and see how You have blessed me again and again, though I have not sought You nor loved You. I'm missing out! I realize I don't have a relationship with You as a daughter to her loving and ever faithful Heavenly Father. Right now, the only relationship I am experiencing with You is one of a guilty sinner before a righteous Judge. If You were to require my soul at this very moment, I would die and live eternally separated from You in hell, tormented forever, with no hope of rescue or redemption. I realize that You sent Your own Son, the Lord Jesus Christ, to die on the cross *for me,* to take away *my* sins, so that I might have eternal life, be forgiven and be made clean by the blood of Jesus. I long to experience true fellowship with You. I no longer want to live for myself or by my own standards. Lord, may today, by Your grace, be the day of my salvation. Today, I place my hope in Jesus and ask that His blood would cleanse me from all my sins. I repent of my sin and prideful independence. I long to live for You today and always."

Saying that prayer, or any special prayer, won't save you. Only Jesus can save you, but I've included that prayer so you can see how to talk to God about your need of salvation and your desire to accept the gracious gift of His Son, Jesus Christ. You can be saved when you turn away from your sin and turn to the Lord in faith, receiving His offered gift of salvation in Jesus (John 1:12). I can guarantee you will never be disappointed by placing your hope in Jesus as your Lord and Savior.

For those of you who do know the Lord as your Savior and King, remember every unmet expectation is an opportunity for you to turn to the Lord in faith and cling to Him. The Lord doesn't always give us the things we think we need, but He always gives us what is best for us. The author of Hebrews lovingly reminds us: "For [our earthly fathers] disciplined us for a short time as seemed best to them, but He disciplines us for our good, so that we may share His holiness. All discipline for the moment seems not to be joyful, but sorrowful; yet to those who have been trained by it, afterwards it yields the peaceful fruit of righteousness" (12:10–11).

There's such sweetness in knowing that God never misses His mark. When He intends to do something, He does it. And He intends our good through the delays, difficulties, and growth associated with unmet expectations. The words from the hymn, "Day by Day," remind us that we can trust God—no matter what we're experiencing in our lives.

Day by day, and with each passing moment,
Strength I find, to meet my trials here;
Trusting in my Father's wise bestowment,
I've no cause for worry or for fear.

He Whose heart is kind beyond all measure
Gives unto each day what He deems best—
Lovingly, its part of pain and pleasure,
Mingling toil with peace and rest[113].

113 Lina Sandell, "Day by Day," *Hymns for the Family of God* (Nashville: Paragon Associates, 1976), 102.

QUESTIONS for REFLECTION

Chapter 14: Wonky Thinking and God's Good Will

1. A right understanding of God is crucial to responding well when life turns out differently than we expected. Only a biblically accurate view of God will help us when our hearts are hurting. In Psalm 145, David rejoices in the character and nature of God. Because David meditated on these truths about God's character, he was able to respond well amidst the many pressures and pains of his life. According to Psalm 145:1–7, what are some of the things about God that David purposefully recalled to mind?

2. What four attributes of God should we consider from Psalm 145:8? Describe how those qualities are at work in God's dealings with you right now.

3. Notice the use of the word "all" in Psalm 145:9. Think about how God's goodness and mercy surrounds *every* circumstance in your life. Does the word *all,* as it is used in verse 9, change your perception of your unmet expectations in any way?

4. When we reflect on the Lord's character, what should be our automatic response? See Psalm 145:10–13.

5. Psalm 145:14–16 provides us with a most tender portrait to gaze upon when we are hurting. What do you notice about *how* the Lord ministers to His children? While the Lord is doing that for us, what should be our response according to verse 15?

6. More all-encompassing language is seen in Psalm 145:17. What do you learn about the Lord in this verse? If you're struggling with any unmet expectations, filter your thoughts and feelings through the truths found here. How does relying on God's character as revealed here strengthen you, even when life is difficult?

7. What do you learn about the Lord in Psalm 145:18–20? What is required of you? How are you taking advantage of the privilege mentioned, especially when it comes to unmet expectations?

8. How should we respond to God, who is kind, personal, powerful, holy, and generous? See Psalm 145:21. What are some of the ways you can put into practice today what Psalm 145 teaches you about God?

Dear refuge of my weary soul, on Thee, when sorrows rise,
On Thee, when waves of trouble roll, my fainting hope relies.
To Thee I tell each rising grief, for Thou alone canst heal;
Thy Word can bring a sweet relief for every pain I feel.

But oh! When gloomy doubts prevail, I fear to call Thee mine;
The springs of comfort seem to fail, and all my hopes decline.
Yet gracious God, where shall I flee? Thou art my only trust;
And still my soul would cleave to Thee, though prostrate in the dust.

Hast Thou not bid me seek Thy face, and shall I seek in vain?
And can the ear of sov'reign grace be deaf when I complain?
No, still the ear of sov'reign grace attends the mourner's prayer;
O may I ever find access to breathe my sorrows there.

Thy mercy seat is open still, here let my soul retreat;
With humble hope attend Thy will, and wait beneath Thy feet.
Thy mercy seat is open still, here let my soul retreat;
With humble hope attend Thy will, and wait beneath Thy feet.[114]

---

114 Anne Steele, "Dear Refuge of My Weary Soul," public domain.

15

Lessons from the Waiting Room

Surely He does no wrong to make you pray, and that long, for a mercy which
you do not deserve when it comes at last.[115]
William Gurnall

Missionary Ann Judson's husband, Adoniram, hadn't been heard from in
seven months. He had sailed away to another part of Burma on mission
business, expecting to be home within a month. Seven long, weary months,
without any news of her dear husband's condition, tested Ann's faith. She
wrote these words to her parents in 1818 when he had been gone six months:

"I am still, my dear parents, in the same lonely situation as when I last
wrote, full of anxiety and suspense. I know not what conclusion to draw
from the circumstance of receiving no intelligence from Mr. Judson. It is
now six months since he left me, and not a single line has ever been received
relative to the ship. . .I am trying to bear this state of uncertainty as a heavy
affliction, a painful chastisement, from my heavenly Father, inflicted, no
doubt, for wise and gracious purposes. Perhaps it is only a prelude to greater
afflictions. Perhaps this is the school in which I am to be taught the rudiments
of suffering, and to prepare for those heavy trials, which without these first
few lessons, crush as soon as inflicted. I feel, however, a dreadful conflict;
sometimes inclined to complain of these dark dispensations of Providence, at
others endeavoring to make this language my own: 'Though He slay me, yet I
will trust Him.'"[116]
Ann Judson

115   William Gurnall, *The Christian in Complete Armour,* quoted in *Voices from the Past,* vol. 2, 261.
116   Sharon James, *My Heart in His Hands: Ann Judson of Burma* (Durham, England: Evangelical Press, 1998), 95-96.

God skillfully uses the tools of waiting, silence, and His *apparent* indifference or rejection to build our faith. The means or methods He uses may vary, but His purposes do not change. Always, always, *His purpose is our good*. While we may heartily acknowledge that all things work for good in our lives, the *means* He uses often leave us perplexed as we try to make sense of what He is doing. It's another example of our expecting one thing and God working in a new and different way. Just as in every other area we've discussed so far, we want to consider our responses when God works in unexpected ways. When we stand at that "response crossroad," it's an opportunity to offer up *our* hopes and willingly accept *His* dealings as good. We bring praise, honor, and glory to God when we give up *our* expectations and submit to *His* wiser ways.

God Tests Every One of His Children

The testing of our faith is God's personalized sanctification process to make us more like Christ. Not only do the tests He sends our way purify, transform, and fortify our faith, but also they reveal the current strength and depth of our faith in Him. This, too, is necessary, and an encouragement in times of training and ongoing unmet expectations.

In Exodus 16:4, we learn how *God uses testing to see if we'll obey Him or not*. "Then the LORD said to Moses, 'Behold, I will rain bread from heaven for you; and the people shall go out and gather a day's portion every day, that I may test them, whether or not they will walk in My instruction.'" Earthly parents test their children's obedience, and our heavenly Father is no different.

God uses testing to shape our character. Deuteronomy 8:16 tells us, "In the wilderness He fed you manna which your fathers did not know, that He might humble you and that He might test you, to do good for you in the end." We might not think we need that special kind of testing, but God knows better! Every test has a divine design and purpose built into it.

God uses testing to reveal our love for Him. Deuteronomy 13:3 says, "You shall not listen to the words of that prophet or that dreamer of dreams; for the LORD your God is testing you to find out if you love the LORD your God with all your heart and with all your soul." Our obedience and willingness to follow the Lord reveals our love for Him.

There's no getting around it. *God will test us*. An exam for each one of us will be prepared both to strengthen our faith and reveal its current state. And, in case you haven't guessed it by now, unmet expectations, trials, and difficulties are some of the means God uses to cause us to grow spiritually.

Hezekiah's Expectations Unmasked

You and I both know that the Lord intends every circumstance in our lives to produce spiritual growth and steadfastness in us. He knows just what we need and exactly where our thinking is off-kilter. God orchestrates and uses the events in our lives to reveal how much we've been hoping for some desired outcome or how much we've been relying upon a certain event to come to pass. We can really be knocked for a loop when our expectations are not met. At least, that's what happened to King Hezekiah. In this chapter, we'll mine treasures from Hezekiah's life as God worked in him during a dark and difficult time. Hezekiah's story gives us the wisdom we need for those times when things turn out differently than expected.

When we meet Hezekiah in 2 Chronicles 32, it's on the heels of God's miraculous rescue of the Israelites from an attempted invasion by the Assyrians. Hezekiah's steadfast faith in that long and trying siege was exemplary. Yet, shortly after his faith-victory, Hezekiah got sick, really sick, and was told by God that he would soon die.

Devastated by the news of his impending death, Hezekiah begged the Lord to spare his life. The Lord graciously granted his request. Sadly, rather than responding humbly and gratefully for the Lord's mercy, Hezekiah reacted with pride to the Lord's kindness. Second Chronicles 32:25 says, "But Hezekiah *gave no return for the benefit he received*, because his heart was proud" (emphasis added).

Thankfully, Hezekiah eventually understood his sin and repented of his ingratitude and pride. His story holds special interest for us in our study of unmet expectations. In the aftermath of the feared invasion and Hezekiah's near-death experience, the Bible rather cryptically inserts these words at the end of 2 Chronicles 32:31: "God left him alone only to test him, that He might know all that was in his heart." Ahh. . .there it is! That is the purpose of the trials God sent to Hezekiah. God used afflictions and sickness to reveal Hezekiah's expectations and to bring to light where he was placing his hope.

When God Tests Our Faith

As we have seen, the text says, "God left Hezekiah alone only to test him, that He might know all that was in his heart" (2 Chron. 32:31). There will be times when the Lord is at work in our lives, but we will feel utterly alone and abandoned by Him.

Proverbs 17:3 says, "The refining pot is for silver and the furnace for gold, but the LORD tests hearts." God tests hearts to see all that is in them.

How interesting! God is omniscient. He already knows everything. If God wanted to know what was in King Hezekiah's heart, all He needed to do was look there and He would see everything. In fact, God doesn't even need to peer into the recesses of our heart, He already knows what's going on in there. *So why the test?*

Then Jesus went up on the mountain, and there He sat down with His disciples. Now the Passover, the feast of the Jews, was near. Therefore Jesus, lifting up His eyes and seeing that a large crowd was coming to Him, said to Philip,

> Where are we to buy bread, so that these may eat?" *This He was saying to test him, for He Himself knew what He was intending to do*. Philip answered Him, "Two hundred denarii worth of bread is not sufficient for them, for everyone to receive a little." One of His disciples, Andrew, Simon Peter's brother, said to Him, "There is a lad here who has five barley loaves and two fish, but what are these for so many people? (John 6:3–9, emphasis added)

The disciples needed to be taught and trained. The tests Jesus gave them showed them the condition of their hearts and where their faith was lacking. And that's *why* God tests us. The Lord tests *us* to reveal to *us* what's going on in our hearts—whether our faith is firmly grounded in the Lord or whether we are hoping in something else to rescue us.

We May Feel Forsaken

Not only did God intend to test and strengthen Hezekiah's faith, but we also see from 2 Chronicles 32:31 that God used Hezekiah's feelings of abandonment and loneliness to do it. The text says, "[He] *left him alone* only to test him" (emphasis added). This God-given method of increasing faith can be tremendously stressful, painful, confusing, and discouraging. *Why would God allow His child to feel alone?* It's helpful to remember that even the best of earthly parents test a child's maturity by leaving them home alone. When a child is old enough, having received enough training, and having exhibited a certain level of wisdom and maturity, the parent will leave the child by himself or herself. No matter the reason, the point is that for a period of time, the parent, with wisdom and purpose, leaves the child alone.

It's always with a bit of trepidation that we, as parents, leave our children alone for a time. But there's nothing quite like it for revealing our children's hearts. Will they obey? Will they follow through? Will they be responsible? The "leaving them home alone" test is a wise and necessary one for every parent for it reveals what the child has taken to heart and learned, and those areas still to be mastered.

Not Abandoned, Not Forsaken

When we read in 2 Chronicles 32:31 that the Lord left Hezekiah alone, we understand that God did it to test and train Hezekiah's heart. When God "leaves us alone," what does that mean? We know it can't mean abandoned, for Jesus Himself taught, "I will never desert you, nor will I ever forsake you" (Heb. 13:5). We know from Romans 8:38–39 that nothing, not death, life, sin, circumstances, or any created thing can separate us from the love of God. Nothing can break the bonds of commitment and care God has for His children. Proverbs 5:21 states: "For the ways of a man are before the eyes of the LORD, and He watches all his paths." God is never so distracted that He doesn't see what is happening in our lives. He watches over us with diligence and commitment.

With those promises from God firmly lodged in our hearts, and when we read that "God left Hezekiah alone," we understand that Hezekiah *felt* abandoned. Though Hezekiah had been faithfully trying to honor and obey the Lord, he was still blind to the misplaced trust and selfish ambition residing in his heart. But God saw it and, in His perfect wisdom, sovereignly orchestrated events in Hezekiah's life to bring his sins to light.

God did this for Hezekiah because He loved him. And because God loves you, He will lovingly test your heart. Like Hezekiah, you may be trying to live by faith, seeking to trust the Lord, and fulfill His Word daily. And like Hezekiah, you may not be aware of the worldly hopes, rebellious desires, or selfish temptations lurking in the recesses of your heart. But God is. The author of Hebrews explains: "And there is no creature hidden from His sight, but all things are open and laid bare to the eyes of Him with whom we have to do" (4:13). You may *feel* forsaken and alone while God tests and trains you. But take courage. The Lord is at work in you both to will and to work for His good pleasure (Phil. 2:13).

Applying Faith in the Face of Our Feelings

As God works good for us, it's crucial to remember that the Bible says God will *never* forsake us—and never means *never* when God says it (Pss. 9:10; 37:25). It's important that we call to mind the Scriptures that tell us He is near to the brokenhearted (Ps. 34:18)—*whether we feel His nearness or not.* We must not forget that the Word of God instructs us to live by faith, not by sight—which most certainly means, not by our emotions (2 Cor. 5:7).

Jesus Felt Forsaken

When the Lord "leaves us alone," for whatever length of time He thinks best, it may well be one of the most difficult tests we endure. It certainly was for Jesus. When He was dying upon the cross, the greatest part of His agony came when the Father hid His face from Jesus. It was at that point that Jesus cried out, "My God, My God, why have You forsaken Me?" This aspect of Jesus' trial pressed the limits of His suffering.

Job Felt Forsaken

Job went through much of his trial feeling very alone, without a sense of the comfort of the Lord. Job 23:8–10 gives us some insight into what this was like for Job. He said, "Behold, I go forward but He is not there, and backward, but I cannot perceive Him; when He acts on the left, I cannot behold Him; He turns on the right, I cannot see Him. But He knows the way I take; when He has tried me, I shall come forth as gold." Job's assurance of faith in God's character and His unchanging nature helped him stand firm *though he felt alone.*

Job went on to declare in Job 23:11–17:

> My foot has held fast to His path; I have kept His way and not turned aside. I have not departed from the command of His lips; I have treasured the words of His mouth more than my necessary food. But He is unique and who can turn Him? And what His soul desires, that He does. For He performs what is appointed for me, and many such decrees are with Him. Therefore, I would be dismayed at His presence; when I consider, I am terrified of Him. It is God who has made my heart faint, and the Almighty who has dismayed me, but I am not silenced by the darkness, nor deep gloom which covers me.

Job persevered in faith and trusted in the Lord, even in the midst of great spiritual and emotional darkness and gloom. Job understood that though he *felt* abandoned by the Lord, by faith he knew he wasn't abandoned. Oh, what a lesson for us to learn! *Just because we feel something to be true doesn't mean it is true.* Our feelings and thoughts must always be sifted, sorted, and measured by the Word of God, for only then can we respond with God-honoring faith and trust.

We Might Feel Forsaken Too

If those mighty ones who've gone before us were "left alone" for the testing and trying of their faith, then we can rest assured that our faith will be tested in a similar way. Jesus reminded His disciples of this very principle when He said, "A pupil is not above his teacher; but everyone, after he has been fully trained, will be like his teacher" (Luke 6:40). Jesus endured all manner of trials and temptations, so that we would not grow weary or lose heart (Heb. 12:3). He was the first to walk this path and, therefore, He helps us follow in His footsteps. This gives us all the more reason to prepare our hearts for the inevitable times of waiting, testing, and feeling left alone. Remembering the Lord's compassion toward us will also enable us to respond like Job did: "Though He slay me, I will hope in Him" (13:15).

Each time God tests our faith, He intends for us to learn more about Him. Our doctrinal understanding of God shapes our response, which is why it's necessary that we grow in our love and understanding of the Scriptures—which is where God reveals Himself to us. *What we believe about God, whether rightly or wrongly, determines how we will cope with waiting and feeling alone.*

Wait for the Lord to Do His Work

As God works all things for our good, we must often wait for God to bring the time of testing to an end. We cannot rescue ourselves or shorten the trial's duration. *We must wait.*

The school of waiting hands out special diplomas for all who have walked its hallowed halls. Charles Spurgeon said this about the instruction gained from waiting:

> Possibly the hard suspicion that Jesus does not care for you takes another form. "I do not ask the Lord to work a miracle, but I do ask him to cheer my heart. I want him to apply the promises to my soul. I want his Spirit to visit me, as I know he does for some people, so that my pain may be forgotten in the delight of the Lord's presence. I want to feel such a full assurance of the Saviour's presence that the present trial shall, as it were, be swallowed up in a far more exceeding weight of joy. But, alas, the Lord hides his face from me, and this makes my trial all the heavier." Beloved, can you not believe in a silent God? Do you always want tokens from God? Must you be petted like a spoiled child? Is your God of such a character that you don't trust Him when His face is veiled? Can you trust him no further than you can see him?[117]

117 Spurgeon, *Beside Still Waters* (Nashville: Thomas Nelson, 1999), 116.

Lessons We Learn from the School of Waiting

There are times in the lives of all believers, when the Lord lovingly enrolls them in His special School of Waiting. It's our Lord's intention that we would learn the faith-building lessons that only patient endurance can teach us.

Waiting teaches us that the Lord is the only answer for our heart's need of comfort. Peter said it well in John 6:68: "Lord, to whom shall we go? You have words of eternal life." The Psalmist said the same thing in Psalm 73:25: "Whom have I in heaven but You? And besides You, I desire nothing on earth." The delays, and even God's withholding of the thing much longed for, drive us to the Him, so we will learn to find our comfort and heart's joy in Him and not in what He gives us.

Waiting teaches us patience. James 5:7–8 says, "Therefore be patient, brethren, until the coming of the Lord. The farmer waits for the precious produce of the soil, being patient about it, until it gets the early and late rains. You too be patient; strengthen your hearts, for the coming of the Lord is near." A farmer soon learns that he cannot rush the growth of his crops. He must wait and let the sun, the rain, and time to do their work. Yet he knows that eventually the crop will reach maturity. James teaches us that spiritual growth cannot be rushed. God will bring us to maturity and, at the right time, the trial will come to an end. Until then, we are to be patient, and strengthen our hearts. James goes on to explain that those who learn patience in waiting are blessed (James 5:11). An enduring faith gains the compassion and mercy of the Lord.

Waiting teaches us courage. It takes courage, often *great* courage, to wait with a quieted, trusting heart for the Lord's rescue. David said it so well in Psalm 27:13–14: "I would have despaired unless I had believed that I would see the goodness of the LORD in the land of the living. Wait for the LORD; be strong and let your heart take courage; yes, wait for the LORD." Consider the language David uses in those verses—*wait, be strong, take courage, wait.* How do we gain that strong, courageous spirit? While waiting, we trust in the Lord's goodness. Remembering God's character strengthens us to wait well.

Waiting teaches us hope. Psalm 130:5–6 teaches us where to place our waiting hope. The psalmist writes, "I wait for the LORD, my soul does wait, and in His word do I hope. My soul waits for the Lord more than the watchmen for the morning; indeed, more than the watchmen for the morning." Waiting teaches us the folly of looking to a person or earthly possessions or a change in circumstances for our rescue. The deliverance our souls need can only come from the Lord. I love the picture of the watchman looking eagerly for the morning light. He wasn't distracted while he waited for morning. He looked with perseverance for God's eventual rescue. Waiting teaches us to hope well.

Waiting teaches us faith. We grow to trust the Lord *more*, not less, during times of waiting so that we learn to say just like Job, "Though He slay me, I will hope in Him" (Job 13:15). Waiting builds in us gritty determination to trust God to the very end. It's the "I. Will. Not. Let. Go." resolve all God's children display when He stretches their faith.

Truths to Tell Ourselves as We Wait

When we find ourselves taking courses at "The School of Waiting," we can supply ourselves with the Teacher's Guide to pass our classes with honor. Our Wise and Loving Instructor wants us to remember:

- *All waiting eventually comes to an end.* Psalm 30:5 proclaims this bedrock truth: "For His anger is but for a moment, His favor is for a lifetime; weeping may last for the night, but a shout of joy comes in the morning." Morning always comes. The night of waiting may be long, but eventually night turns to day, and with it comes joy and an end to every trial.
- *Waiting is good for us.* That is what Lamentations 3:25–26 tells us, "The LORD is good to those who wait for Him, to the person who seeks Him. It is good that he waits silently for the salvation of the LORD." Waiting keeps our hearts humbled. Waiting on the Lord provides us with time to examine our motives and desires, to see if we're thinking wrongly about Him and to expose areas where we need to repent. By remembering that God intends to do us good through the time of waiting helps us more easily endure it. And, oh, how the Lord loves to see His children waiting on Him!
- *Waiting teaches us to think on God's character and His attributes.* When I need to keep my thoughts right and centered on the Lord alone, I turn to Psalm 145:17. It says, "The LORD is righteous in all His ways and kind in all His deeds." The very act of remembering and praying about God's righteous ways and kind deeds gives Him glory and encourages us to trust Him. "Lord, You are righteous in *all* Your ways. There isn't any part of Your plan that doesn't reflect that. I cannot impugn Your motives with any shadow of unrighteousness for You always do what is right. You are also kind in *all* Your deeds. No part of my circumstances is outside of Your kind purposes for me. Your plan for me is bathed in Your kindness."

- *Waiting reminds us of the preciousness of access.* Those who have placed their faith in Jesus Christ alone to save them have constant and continual access to their heavenly Father through Christ. They may have to wait for the Lord to bring an end to a trial, but they never have to wait to enter into His presence. As children of the King, they have access to the throne room. Ephesians 3:11–12 says, "This was in accordance with the eternal purpose which He carried out in Christ Jesus our Lord, in whom we have boldness and confident access through faith in Him." Isn't that a precious truth?
- *Waiting teaches us to live with our eyes fixed on Jesus.* Waiting has a way of whittling down our expectations, so that we long for the Lord above all else. Waiting builds in us the same spirit as Paul, so that we proclaim with him, "For to me, to live is Christ and to die is gain" (Phil. 1:21). The precious lessons David learned become ours as well, "My soul waits in silence for God only; from Him is my salvation. He only is my rock and my salvation, my stronghold; I shall not be greatly shaken" (Ps. 62:1–2).

God may test your faith by "hiding" His face from you as He says in Isaiah 54:7, "For a brief moment I forsook you, but with great compassion I will gather you." You may *feel* forsaken in your circumstances, but God desires that you learn to trust Him by faith, believing in the soul-strengthening promises of His Word. *Choose to live by faith, rather than living by your feelings.* He will never forsake you. Be assured, the School of Waiting has a purpose. Keep trusting in the Lord. Remember His goodness. Call His Word to mind. Give Him glory by your hopeful faith, even when it *feels* as though He has utterly forsaken you.

Matthew Henry insightfully noted that "God left Hezekiah to himself, that, by this trial and his weakness in it, what was in his heart might be known; that he was not so perfect in grace as he thought he was. It is good for us to know ourselves, and our own weakness and sinfulness, that we may not be conceited, or self-confident, but may always live in dependence upon Divine grace. We know not the corruption of our own hearts, nor what we shall do if God leaves us to ourselves."[118] Ah, there it is. God's purpose put on display once again. Until we actually go "take the test," we have no way of knowing how we will really respond. Our hearts are difficult to know and discern, so God uses trials, pressures, and unmet expectations to reveal what is in them and to bring about change.

---

118 Matthew Henry and Thomas Scott, *Matthew Henry's Concise Commentary* (Oak Harbor, WA: Logos Research Systems, 1997), 2 Ch 32:24.

Testing Builds a Determination in Us to Love God Better

Understanding our weaknesses builds determination in us to be faithful and to live wholly for the Lord. So, we say with the psalmist in Psalm 17:3: "You have tried my heart; You have visited me by night; You have tested me and You find nothing; I have purposed that my mouth will not transgress." True faith always desires to be found faithful. True faith desires to live more like Christ did, to respond well, and to live more completely for the glory of God. True faith is the reason why David prayed what he did in Psalm 139:23–24: "Search me, O God, and know my heart; try me and know my anxious thoughts; and see if there be any hurtful way in me, and lead me in the everlasting way."

Even when our testing reveals in our hearts a lack of faith and trust, we have this promise in 2 Timothy 2:13: "If we are faithless, He remains faithful, for He cannot deny Himself." Though we may fail to keep our focus on God, He will never let us go.

> When I fear my faith will fail, Christ will hold me fast;
> When the tempter would prevail, He will hold me fast.
> I could never keep my hold through life's fearful path;
> For my love is often cold; He must hold me fast.[119]

There's purpose in all we experience in our lives. *Nothing is arbitrary.* Consider the assurance God gives us in two texts. The first is James 1:2–4: "Consider it all joy, my brethren, when you encounter various trials, knowing that the testing of your faith produces endurance. And let endurance have its perfect result, so that you may be perfect and complete, lacking in nothing." Any test we undergo at the hand of the Lord has endurance as its goal, that is, a strengthened, patient, and devoted faith. If we humble ourselves in the training, a mature and strong faith will be the result.

The second text is 1 Peter 1:6–7. Peter says the same thing as James: "In this you greatly rejoice, even though now for a little while, if necessary, you have been distressed by various trials, so that the proof of your faith, being more precious than gold which is perishable, even though tested by fire, may be found to result in praise and glory and honor at the revelation of Jesus Christ." God ensures that our tested faith brings Him glory.

---

119   Ada Habershon, "He Will Hold Me Fast," *Hymns of Grace* (Los Angeles: The Master's Seminary Press, 2015), 388.

What to Expect When Our Expectations are Tested

Let me tell you a story. There was once a young boy, who was very sick. After a time, he began to get well, but was still far too weak and sick to leave his little room. His mother, who had been in constant attendance upon him during his illness, was absent from the sickroom one day. She left everything he would need for most of the day, along with a loving note explaining that she would be absent for a while. He was perfectly cared for and looked in on by the cook, although his mother was not there.

At first, the boy was distracted by the book and small toy his mother had left on the breakfast tray. But, after a time, he began to wonder at her absence. When the cook brought his lunch tray up and still there was no mother to be seen, he began to complain to himself, "I'm lonely. Doesn't my mother care about me anymore? Where is she?" He began to feel unloved and, in the space of a few hours, grew suspicious and hard-hearted toward his mother.

After a long time, or so it seemed to him, his mother appeared in the sickroom ready to entertain her poor, sick boy for the afternoon. She had seen him growing more restless as he began to get better, so she had made plans to bring joy and refreshment to his little heart. Her morning had been filled gathering surprises to bless her much-loved son.

She arrived in the sickroom with joy and anticipation in her heart, only to find a fretful, grumpy, and ungrateful child, who wasn't ready for the sweet time she had planned for him. "Mother," he grumbled, "where were you? I've been all alone all day!"

"Well, my darling," the mother replied, "it wasn't *all* day. Although I admit, I was gone for a few hours but, you weren't really alone. I asked Cook to check in on you. I'm sorry to see you've grown so fretful in my absence. I have been preparing some surprises and cooking up some treats to help ease your restlessness and to cheer you up. I left you alone, but only so I could bless you."

At that news, the little invalid gave a small cry of repentance, *"Oh mother! If only I had known what you were doing! I would have borne the time alone more bravely. I wouldn't have complained at all. Please forgive me."*

"But, darling," said the wise mother, "if you had known what I was doing, it wouldn't have been a surprise, now would it? I thought you would have trusted me enough to know that, if I wasn't there with you, it was for a good reason."

Sometimes, we grow just as suspicious and hard-hearted toward the Lord as the little boy did toward his mother. We forget the Lord's goodness, and instead, rehearse in our hearts ways in which we think He has misused us. We grow grumpy, self-focused, and cry out, "Lord, why have you left me alone?" The Lord's response to us is like the one He gave to the children of Israel in Deuteronomy 8:16: "In the wilderness He fed you manna which your fathers did not know, that He might humble you and that He might test you, to do good for you in the end." *Testing...all for our good.*

God also shared His training plan for the nation of Israel with Hosea, His prophet: "I will go away and return to My place until they acknowledge their guilt and seek My face; in their affliction they will earnestly seek Me" (Hosea 5:15). *God's methodology worked!* Look at how Israel responded in Hosea 6:1, "Come, *let us return* to the LORD. For He has torn us, but *He will heal us*; He has wounded us, but *He will bandage us*" (emphasis added).

When the Lord leaves us alone for a time, or rather, when it *feels* as though He has forsaken us, *we need not default to fear, grumbling, self-pity, bitterness, or hard thoughts of God.* God is faithful in His love and kindness to His children. He always accomplishes good in all He does. When He leaves us alone to test our hearts, He wants us to still think well of Him, which means to apply faith in His Word and not to trust in our feelings. Though we *may be tested* to the very depths of our being, and *feel very forsaken and alone,* the reality is that He never leaves us. We know this to be true for He tells us over and over again in His Word (Pss. 73:28; 145:18; Heb. 13:5–6). Times of testing reveal to us whether we believe God enough to draw near to Him, even when our feelings tempt us to withdraw.

We can trust God as Job did when he declared: "But He knows the way I take; when He has tried me, I shall come forth as gold" (23:10). As the psalmist reviewed his life, he rejoiced in the means God used to cause him to grow in sanctification. He said, "For You have tried us, O God; You have refined us as silver is refined. You brought us into the net; You laid an oppressive burden upon our loins. You made men ride over our heads; we went through fire and through water, yet You brought us out into a place of abundance" (Ps. 66:10–12).

Remember that our heavenly Father never tests us to harm us. The trials of unmet expectations prepare our souls to meet further testings—all designed to scour away our sin and produce in us a clean heart (Ps. 51:10). Take courage, fellow tested believer. Your path is the way of all true believers. No one comes through this life without afflictions (Acts 14:22). Trials are necessary for our growth in grace so we can give God greater glory. Heaven will be sweeter because of the difficulties we've endured along the way.

> And I will wait for the LORD who is hiding His face from the house of Jacob; I will even look eagerly for Him (Isa. 8:17).

QUESTIONS for REFLECTION

Chapter 15: Lessons from the Waiting Room

"For you, O God, tested us; you refined us like silver" (Ps. 66:10, NIV).

"Lord, if my life is to be a vessel used to purify a love of God amid a burning heat, so be it, but dear Christ, sit at the furnace mouth to watch the ore that no good from You is lost."[120]
From The Valley of Vision, "Purification"

"But He knows the way I take; When He has tried me, I shall come forth as gold" (Job 23:10).

1. Read David's lament in Psalm 22:1–5. What troubles David the most in the opening verses of this psalm?

2. What truths help David in his time of sorrow and waiting (vv. 3–5)?

3. Scan the rest of Psalm 22. What do you notice about David's response by the time you get to verses 22–31?

4. How did David strengthen his despairing spirit in Psalm 22? How can you follow his example when you find yourself in despair?

5. Asaph records a parallel circumstance in Psalm 77:7–10. How does the psalmist counsel himself in verses 11–15, while he waits for the Lord's comfort?

6. How can you apply the truths from Psalm 77:11–15, when you find yourself in similar circumstances?

7. How have you seen your patience, hope, faith, and endurance strengthened because the Lord allowed you to experience unmet expectations?

---

120   *The Valley of Vision*, 81.

"Behold, I have refined you, but not as silver; I have tested you in the furnace of affliction." Isaiah 48:10

The gold is put into the furnace because it is gold; it would have been of no use to put mere stones and rubbish there. The great Owner of heaven's jewels thinks it worth his while to use a more elaborate and sharp cutting machine upon the most valuable stones: a first-rate diamond is sure to undergo more cutting than an inferior one, because the King desires that it may have many facets, which may throughout eternity, with greater splendour, reflect the light of the glory of his name.

Mayhap, dear brethren, we have thought that Jesus did not care for us because he has not wrought a miracle for our deliverance, and has not interposed in any remarkable way to help us. You are getting gradually poorer and poorer, or you are becoming more and more afflicted in body, and you had hoped that God would have taken some extraordinary method with you, but he has done nothing of the sort. *My dear brother, do you know that sometimes God works a greater wonder when he sustains his people in trouble than he would do if he brought them out of it? For him to let the bush burn on and yet not to be consumed is a grander thing than for him to quench the flame and so save the bush.* God is being glorified in your troubles, and if you realize this you will be ready to say, "Lord, heap on the loads, if it be for thy glory; give me but strength equal to my day, and then pile on the burdens; I shall not be crushed beneath them, but I shall be made to illustrate thy power. My weakness shall glorify thy might."

Possibly the hard suspicion that Jesus does not care for you takes another form. "I do not ask the Lord to work a miracle, but I do ask him to cheer my heart. I want him to apply the promises to my soul. I want his Spirit to visit me, as I know he does for some people, so that my pain may be forgotten in the delight of the Lord's presence. I want to feel such a full assurance of the Saviour's presence that the present trial shall, as it were, be swallowed up in a far more exceeding weight of joy. But, alas, the Lord hides his face from me, and this makes my trial all the heavier." *Beloved, can you not believe in a silent God?* Do you always want tokens from God? Must you be petted like a spoiled child? Is your God of such a character that you must needs mistrust him if his face be veiled? Can you trust him no further than you can *see him?*[121]

---

121 C. H. Spurgeon, "Christ Asleep in the Vessel," *The Metropolitan Tabernacle Pulpit Sermons,* vol. 19 (London: Passmore & Alabaster, 1873), 389–90.

16

God's Handiwork in Thwarted Plans

God in wisdom conceals the comforts He intends to give you at the various stages of your life, so that He may encourage your heart to full dependence upon His faithful promises now.
William Gurnall[122]

The providence of God often goes beyond our imagination, often crosses our desires and designs to our great advantage. He does not give what we fancy, but what His infinite wisdom judges best and most beneficial. It often happens that probabilities are dashed, and things remote and utterly improbable are brought about in very strange and unaccountable methods of providence. Give God the glory for all the providential works that yield comfort to you. You can see His wise, governing providence has ordered all things beyond your own designs.
John Flavel[123]

Surely what is best for you is what providence has appointed, and one day you will agree yourself that it is so.
John Flavel[124]

---

122 William Gurnall, *The Christian in Complete Armour*, I:96-97 quoted in *Voices from the Past*, vol. 1, 43.
123 Ibid., John Flavel, *Works*, IV:392-398, 341.
124 Ibid.

Most people are familiar with at least parts of Joseph's story as it is recorded in the book of Genesis. You may remember he's the guy with the coat of many colors, a bunch of brothers, and some wild dreams, who somehow ends up becoming the second most powerful man in Egypt by devising a plan to save everyone from the famine. What a remarkable life! Joseph was also the "golden child" of his father, Jacob, because Joseph's mother was Jacob's most-loved wife, Rachel. However, this favored beginning didn't protect Joseph from the twists, turns, and trials God was preparing for him. Joseph may have been born with a silver spoon in his mouth, but it was soon to be filled with cod liver oil.

Meet *The* Poster *Child for Unmet Expectations*

It's interesting to consider how life turns out sometimes. Joseph's life started well. But soon God-ordained setbacks, roadblocks, and detours determined the course of his life. Beginning with his birth, it's easy to assume *things might have gone well for Joseph,* if only he hadn't been the long-anticipated son of his father's most-loved wife, Rachel (Gen. 30). As it was, his favored status caused discord and jealousy among his brothers. He might have been able to recover from that handicap and *things might have gone well for Joseph,* except that his mother died while giving birth to his younger brother, Benjamin. Yet, even after these difficult circumstances, *things might have gone well for Joseph* as a young man of seventeen, except that his father, Jacob, sent Joseph out to check on his older brothers. Regrettably for them—and for Joseph—he had to give a bad report about them to his father (Gen. 37:1–2).

Nevertheless, things might have gone well for Joseph, except for an unfortunate event recorded in Genesis 37:3–4: "Now Israel loved Joseph more than all his sons, because he was the son of his old age; and he made him a varicolored tunic. His brothers saw that their father loved him more than all his brothers; and so they hated him and could not speak to him on friendly terms."

Yet, even then, things might have gone well for Joseph, except for the dreams God gave him. Genesis 37:5–11 recounts the details of Joseph's first dream, which he told to his brothers. Joseph dreamed that his brothers were bowing down to him. However, rather than impressing them, it only increased their hatred for him. That episode might have been forgiven and forgotten, except that *Joseph had a second dream* in which his father, mother, and brothers were bowing down before him. None too pleased, Jacob rebuked Joseph for being proud. But his brothers hated him even more. Although Joseph's dreams were given to him by God, the dreams led to his family resenting him.

We can guess that things weren't going to improve for Joseph when shortly after receiving the two dreams, Jacob sent him to check up on the brothers. As he searched for his brothers, we can anticipate that *it wasn't going to go well* for Joseph when he did finally catch up to them because of their abiding contempt toward him. By that time in Joseph's life, his brothers had grown so hateful toward him that they wanted to kill him (Gen. 37:18–24).

At this point, it's possible things might have gone well for Joseph, if it hadn't been for the untimely arrival of some Ishmaelite traders (Gen. 37:25–28). *It did not go well for Joseph* because his brothers sold him as a slave to the traders. The Ishmaelites embarked on, at the very least, a fifteen-day journey on foot through the hot desert with Joseph in tow. *Things were not going well for Joseph.* His descent from being the most-loved son to being a slave to be sold in Egypt could only result in misery upon misery in his heart, mind, and body. *It might have been somewhat easier for Joseph,* if he had any hope that his family might come looking for him. Yet, having experienced his brothers' rage and bitterness, he knew all hope was lost. It's easy to imagine the depth of Joseph's despair at this point in his young life.

In Genesis 39, we read that, once in Egypt, Joseph was bought by Potiphar, who was the captain of Pharaoh's bodyguard. All was not lost, however, for the Lord blessed Joseph so much that, his master, Potiphar, prospered. As time went on, Potiphar entrusted more and more of his household details to Joseph's care. It's quite possible that *things might have gone well for Joseph*, if he had been rather homely and awkward looking. But Potiphar's wife was "lookin' for love in all the wrong places; lookin' for love in too many faces"[125] and she set her sights on Joseph. And though Joseph refused to have an affair with Potiphar's wife, she persisted in her efforts to seduce him day after long and weary day.

Now you might think things would have gone well for a man of such integrity, except for the fury of a woman scorned. One day, while all the other men were "conveniently" absent from the house, Potiphar's wife endeavored to seduce Joseph. When he fled from her advances, she grabbed his outer garment, and loudly insisted that Joseph had tried to rape her. As you can well imagine, Joseph soon found himself in prison on trumped-up charges leveled at him by Potiphar's lying wife. *For all intents and purposes, it looked like things were never going to go well for Joseph. His life was over.* It was universally understood that any slave who did anything as wicked as trying to ravish his master's wife would *never* breathe free air again.

Yet, even in prison, the Lord was with Joseph. *Things appeared to go well*

---

125 https://genius.com/Johnny-lee-lookin-for-love-lyrics

for him. The Lord bestowed favor on Joseph through the chief jailer, who gave him some responsibility to care for his fellow prisoners. It was at that time, according to Genesis 40, that Joseph met Pharaoh's cupbearer and baker, who had been thrown in prison for displeasing the king. Both men had disturbing dreams foretelling their future. When Joseph accurately interpreted the men's dreams, there was a sense in which it seemed that *things might turn around* for Joseph. Yet Joseph's circumstances remained unchanged. The dreams came to pass as Joseph predicted. The cupbearer was restored to his office and the baker was put to death. *Now all might have gone well for Joseph,* if the chief cupbearer had kept his promise to Joseph and put in a good word for him to Pharaoh. But the cupbearer forgot all about him, and Joseph remained in prison for two more years!

There's a bit of anticipation that things might finally begin to go well for Joseph, starting in Genesis 41 where Pharaoh had two scary dreams that his wise men couldn't interpret. The cupbearer saw how disturbed the king was by his dreams. This reminded him of the man who had interpreted his dream in prison. Before Joseph even knew what was happening, he had been plucked from prison, cleaned up, and brought before Pharaoh for the sole purpose of listening to and interpreting his dream. Joseph explained that Pharaoh's dream predicted seven years of plenty, followed by seven years of famine. It was at that moment that *things really did begin to go well for Joseph.* On that very day, Joseph was made ruler in Egypt, second only to Pharaoh in power. Joseph's head must have been spinning from the sudden change in his circumstances. Pharaoh commanded all Egypt to bow down to Joseph and obey him. Joseph was given a wife, who would eventually bear him two sons. *Yet, even in his new place of blessing and favor, Joseph remained separated from his family.*

After the seven years of plenty, back in Canaan, Jacob and his sons and their families were experiencing the discomfort of the famine. They discovered, however, that Egypt had grain (Gen. 42), so Jacob sent his ten sons there to buy some. Jacob didn't allow his youngest son, Benjamin, to go, since he was the only remaining son of his beloved Rachel. Joseph recognized his brothers when they arrived in Egypt, though they didn't recognize him. Through a series of events, he contrived to have Benjamin brought to Egypt. It was then that Joseph revealed his true identity to his astonished brothers, as recorded in Genesis 43–45.

Things really begin to go well for Joseph after twenty-two or so long years of painful trials. He was reunited with his brothers and reassured that his father was still living. He was also encouraged to see that his brothers exhibited no animosity toward Benjamin. In Genesis 45:4–8, we read of the moment Joseph revealed himself to his brothers:

Then Joseph said to his brothers, "Please come closer to me." And they came closer. And he said, "I am your brother Joseph, whom you sold into Egypt. Now do not be grieved or angry with yourselves, because you sold me here, *for God sent me before you to preserve life.* For the famine has been in the land these two years, and there are still five years in which there will be neither plowing nor harvesting. *God sent me before you to preserve for you a remnant in the earth, and to keep you alive by a great deliverance.* Now, therefore, *it was not you who sent me here, but God*; and He has made me a father to Pharaoh and lord of all his household and ruler over all the land of Egypt" (emphasis added).

Three times Joseph proclaimed to his brothers that it was *the Lord's* will to send him to Egypt. In that moment, all the tangled threads of Joseph's life came together, gained purpose, and came into focus. For the first time, he realized that he had been raised up as ruler to provide for his family, ensuring that they would thrive and grow, and become a great nation, as God had promised.

Later, after Jacob died, Joseph's brothers grew afraid that he would punish them for all the mean things they had done to him in the past. To the contrary, Joseph reassured his brothers with these words: "Do not be afraid, for am I in God's place? As for you, you meant evil against me, but God meant it for good in order to bring about this present result, to preserve many people alive" (Gen. 50:19–20). Joseph got it. He recognized God's handiwork in all his thwarted plans, betrayals, loneliness, and sorrows.

As a teenager, Joseph probably expected to live a somewhat "normal" life, but that's not what God intended for him. Yet all those "I never thought that this would happen" expectations were gathered together and given meaning when Joseph realized that God had taken him to Egypt to provide for his family. In a single, crystallized moment, every trial and difficulty, sorrow, and fear was replaced with gratitude, trust, and hope. *"You meant evil against me, but God meant it for good."*

God's Patience in Putting His Plans into Place

One thing that stands out to us as we look at Joseph's life is the patience of God in putting all the pieces in place. In just the right time, in just the right place, with just the right person, God's plan was revealed. We read in Romans 5:6: "For while we were still helpless, *at the right time* Christ died for the ungodly" (emphasis added). In Galatians 4:4 we see: *"But when the fullness of the time came,* God sent forth His Son, born of a woman, born under the Law" (emphasis added). In Titus 1:3 we read that God "*at the proper time manifested, even His word,* in the proclamation with which I was entrusted according to the commandment of God our Savior" (emphasis added). And finally, we read in 1 Peter 5:6: "Therefore humble yourselves under the mighty hand of God, that He may exalt you *at the proper time*" (emphasis added). What do we learn about God's character from these verses? We learn that He is never rushed and always accomplishes His plans perfectly.

When God Plans It, Nothing Can Change It

Job came to understand that when God plans something, nothing can change it. He declared, "I know that You can do all things, and that no purpose of Yours can be thwarted" (42:2). It's so helpful to understand and recall this truth to mind. There have been a few times in my life when it has been as if God lit up Job's declaration with neon lights in my soul. In those moments, I knew with absolute certainty that there was nothing anyone could do to stop God's plan from unfolding. Not surprisingly, those insights of utter clarity about God's sovereign and perfect plan came while facing unmet expectations and trials. Imagine that!

But Do You See Me, Lord?

And while we may understand the Lord's complete sovereignty over every event in the universe, we may sometimes wonder if we somehow got lost in the shuffle. Proverbs 5:21 comforts our fears, telling us, "For the ways of a man are before the eyes of the LORD, and He watches all his paths." Meditating on God's omniscient care brings such comfort when our lives feel small, insignificant, and full of trouble.

God is Kind

The Lord seemed to deal roughly with Joseph at times. His life certainly wasn't easy. However, as Psalm 25:10 attests: "All the paths of the LORD are lovingkindness and truth to those who keep His covenant and His testimonies." Martha Peace addressed this disparity between our circumstances and God's intentions when she noted, "Some of God's ways seem kind; some do not; but, ultimately, all are kind."[126] Psalm 25:10 compels us

---

126 My personal notes from a talk given by Martha Peace called, "The Providence of God" at the Women Discipling Women Conference 2011.

to see that *every path* we travel is paved with God's kindnesses—even when we don't recognize it.

The Lord provided many tangible expressions of love and comfort for Joseph, even during the long years His plans were coming to fruition. We see the Lord's kindness manifested to Joseph in that his father, Jacob, truly loved him. Some kids never know the love of a father. Joseph did. Joseph's brother, Reuben, tried to rescue him from the murderous intentions of his other brothers. At least, Reuben showed some tenderness and concern for him. God allowed Joseph to win Potiphar's favor and enjoy the benefits of being a trusted member of his household. Joseph also won the jailer's favor and again enjoyed the benefits of being a trusted prison employee. We learn in Genesis 39:21 that the Lord instigated these kindnesses: "But the LORD was with Joseph and extended kindness to him, and gave him favor in the sight of the chief jailer." This would have been such a balm to poor Joseph, especially after being falsely accused, thrown into prison, and having all hope of a "normal" life taken away from him.

God's kindness to Joseph didn't end there for we see that He gave Joseph the ability to interpret dreams, which the Lord used for great good. After interpreting Pharaoh's dreams, Joseph was showered with honor. This was after many years of being humbled. However, the years of humbling protected Joseph from growing proud in his new, exalted position. *This too was a kindness from the Lord.* Joseph was reunited with his family and was blessed to see his aged father again. Joseph also had a hand in saving his family from extinction because of the famine. And to this day, Joseph is an example of godliness in the midst of adversity.

Psalm 31:19 joyfully proclaims: "How great is Your goodness, which You have stored up for those who fear You, which You have wrought for those who take refuge in You, before the sons of men!" Joseph stored grain, but God stores up goodness for those who trust in Him.

One of the greatest kindnesses we receive from the Lord is put on display in Romans 2:4: "Or do you think lightly of the riches of His kindness and tolerance and patience, not knowing that the kindness of God leads you to repentance?" God patiently puts up with guilty sinners, like you and me, for the purpose of softening our hearts and bringing us to repentance and faith in Jesus. Titus 3:4–5 tell us that God showed immense mercy and kindness toward us in sending Christ to die on the cross for our sins.

Look at how God describes Himself in Psalm 86:15: "But You, O Lord, are a God merciful and gracious, slow to anger and abundant in lovingkindness and truth." The Lord so wants us to see His kindness that

He provides this glorious description of Himself in at least eight other references in the Scriptures.

Joseph's story reminds us that God's sovereignty and kindness are perfectly mixed. And while it can be comfortable to think about that mixture for Joseph, it's equally important to consider that *God's sovereignty and kindness are poured out in equal measure in our lives too.* Understanding God's kindness in our circumstances makes a difference when we're viewing our own life story without the blessing of hindsight. In his lovely hymn "God Moves in a Mysterious Way" William Cowper wrote, "Behind a frowning providence He hides a smiling face."[127] Like Cowper and Joseph, we need to become experts at peeking behind our "less than wonderful" circumstances so we can see the kind God who has orchestrated them all.

When Your Life Story Parallels Joseph's

Are you in a maze of unmet expectations right now? Do you feel exhausted at trying to make sense of what's happening in your life? Do you constantly work at guarding your heart against the painful "surprises" piling up? Even when you think you've reconciled yourself to the new normal or when you think you've adjusted to the next new set of circumstances, do you find your heart out of balance all over again? Though you hope that the unexpected events of your life might turn out well in the end, you haven't seen the "good" they are supposed to produce.

The problem is related to time. Right now, you're still in the middle of everything. God's work isn't finished, and you're not at the end of your life, or even on the other side of your trial. When you're in the middle, it's difficult to see the good that God will bring from your unmet expectations because you're missing the comfort of perspective. You don't have the luxury of seeing your story all written out, with all the important parts emphasized like you do with the Bible's recounting of Joseph's life.

Yet it's helpful to remember that Joseph didn't get to see his story all written out either. He slogged through times of discouragement, dismay, and times of plain, old "what is happening here," just as we do. If we're going to gain anything from Joseph's story, it's helpful to consider *how* Joseph persevered for twenty-two or more years when his life seemed to get worse and worse.

Joseph coped with his persistent and long-term trials by entrusting himself to the Lord. There is no big secret here. The game changer is that he *kept on* entrusting himself to the Lord. That's the secret to persevering in hard

127   William Cowper, "God Moves in a Mysterious Way," https://library.timelesstruths.org/music/God_Moves_in_a_Mysterious_Way/

times! It takes faith, courage, and grit to keep hoping in the Lord day after day *after day* without seeing any change in the circumstances, when the trials are increasing, or when it seems God isn't answering our prayers. With dogged determination, Joseph *continued* to put his trust in the Lord. And while he was doing that, the Lord was perfectly and sovereignly unfolding His will. The same God who oversaw every detail of Joseph's life, such that Joseph was born at the right time, in the right place, and experienced all the right trials, so he could be made ruler in Egypt in order to preserve the fledging nation of Israel, so that someday the Messiah, Jesus, would be born, and we, by faith in Jesus, could be saved. *That same God* is at work in your life today.

Joseph's God is our God and He has not changed (Mal. 3:6). God's *nature*, *attributes*, and *eternal love* are fixed purposes. We can gain courage and strength from observing God's dealings with Joseph, knowing He is still the same. God was kind to Joseph, and He is kind to us today. God oversaw every detail of Joseph's life, and He oversees every detail of our lives as well. Even the seemingly bad things of Joseph's life served to further God's ultimate plans for his life, just as our trials further His good plans for us.

Joseph had no assurance that the Lord would eventually bring him into a place of blessing. He had no inkling of when his trials would come to an end. He was separated from his family for twenty-two or more years. Those were twenty-two years of waiting, twenty-two years of praying, twenty-two years of persevering in faith, twenty-two years of enduring in difficulty, of trusting the Lord, of not losing heart, of not growing weary. And for those twenty-two years, God's grace enabled Joseph to survive. Not only did he survive, he *thrived* because God was working everything for Joseph's good and for His glory.

> *When through fiery trials thy pathways shall lie,*
> *my grace, all-sufficient, shall be thy supply;*
> *the flame shall not hurt thee; I only design*
> *thy dross to consume, and thy gold to refine.*[128]

You may have no idea why God is doing what He is with your life. But it helps to remember that the Lord employs these teaching methods to make us run to His Word. *"It is good for me that I was afflicted, that I may learn Your statutes"* (Ps. 119:71). It's good for us to learn more about God and His ways from the Scriptures.

When trials, difficulties, and unmet expectations come into our lives and drive us to the Lord and His Word, we will gain wisdom, insight, and

128 "How Firm a Foundation," *Hymns for the Family of God*, (Nashville, TN: Paragon Associates, 1979), 32.

comfort. When we take refuge in the Lord, then the words of Psalm 73:25–28 become the song and sigh of our hearts: "Whom have I in heaven but You? And besides You, I desire nothing on earth. My flesh and my heart may fail, but God is the strength of my heart and my portion forever. For, behold, those who are far from You will perish; You have destroyed all those who are unfaithful to You. But as for me, the nearness of God is my good; I have made the Lord GOD my refuge, that I may tell of all Your works."

Truths to Tell Yourself When You're in the Middle of Your Story

Things can look so black and gloomy when you are in the middle of your story. What you need *in the middle* are the nuts and bolts of how to think rightly, so you can press on "toward the goal for the prize of the upward call of God in Christ Jesus" (Phil. 3:14).

It Won't Last Forever

When you're in the middle of your journey, you need to know that it won't last forever. There will be a conclusion to your time of uncertainty, gloom, sorrow, angst, or whatever it is that you're facing. Second Corinthians 4:16–18 reminds us: "Therefore we do not lose heart, but though our outer man is decaying, yet our inner man is being renewed day by day. For *momentary*, light affliction is producing for us an eternal weight of glory far beyond all comparison, while we look not at the things which are seen, but at the things which are not seen; for the things which are seen are *temporal*, but the things which are not seen are eternal" (emphasis added).

God's Sovereignty Reigns Over Every Event in Your Life

When you're in the middle of your trek, it's so encouraging to know that what God purposes always comes to pass. Jerry Bridges, in his book *Trusting God*, writes, "Your promotion, or lack of it, is in the hand of God....You can trust God in all areas of your life where you are dependent upon the favor or frown of another person. God will move in that person's heart to carry out His will for you."[129] The Lord works in and through men, but no one can thwart God's design. Proverbs 21:1 says, "The king's heart is like channels of water in the hand of the LORD; He turns it wherever He wishes." And just like Joseph, our story reveals God's design, direction, and purpose to do good for us and bring glory to Himself. Bridges writes,

---

129 Bridges, *Trusting God*, 67.

"God will never allow any action against you that is not in accord with His will for you. And His will is always directed to our good."[130]

God Intends Joseph's Story to Encourage You

God preserved the details of Joseph's story in His Word to provide nourishment for *your* soul. This should encourage you to pore over his story while you live your own adventure. Romans 15:4 explains one of the purposes of Joseph's story: "For whatever was written in earlier times was written for our instruction, so that through perseverance and the encouragement of the Scriptures we might have hope." Joseph's tale instructs *and* gives us hope.

Joseph wasn't acquainted with Romans 8:28 because it hadn't yet been written. But today we know "God causes all things to work together for good to those who love God, to those who are called according to His purpose." Joseph was a living, breathing example of Romans 8:28. We see his version of Romans 8:28 at the end of his recorded story: "As for you, you meant evil against me, but God meant it for good in order to bring about this present result, to preserve many people alive" (Gen. 50:20). And like Joseph, when we get to the end of the twists and turns of our life's journey, we too will see the good He has planned for us.

God Will Help You to Live by Faith

If you're not at the place where you can see the good God intends by your present unmet expectations, then cling in *faith* to Romans 8:28 and the precious and magnificent promises of His Word (2 Peter 1:3). Chapter 11 of Hebrews catalogs the "by faith" champions of the past. Some of them saw God's promises fulfilled, but others did not. In fact, Hebrews 11:39 tells us, "And all these, having gained approval through their faith, did not receive what was promised." They died still living by faith, still believing God, *continuing to live with unmet expectations and unchanged circumstances*. They put Hebrews 11:6 into practice, knowing that "without faith it is impossible to please [God], for he who comes to God must believe that He is and that He is a rewarder of those who seek Him."

Charles Spurgeon knew all about pressing on in unchanged or difficult circumstances. He wrote, "Between here and heaven, we have no guarantee that the road will be easy or the sea smooth. We have no promise that we will be kept like flowers in a house, safe from the breath of frost or veiled from the heat of the sun. The voice of wisdom says, 'Be

130 Ibid., 71.

patient, be patient, be patient, for you may need a triple measure of it to be ready for the trial.'"[131] Even if you find yourself a "poster child" for a life of unmet expectations, you're in good company. The Lord is at work, so entrust yourself to Him. Be assured that the unmet expectations in your life have a purpose. Though, at times, they may sting and crush you, God uses them like goads to drive you to Him.

> You have dealt well with Your servant, O Lord, according to Your word.
> Teach me good discernment and knowledge, for I believe in Your commandments.
> Before I was afflicted I went astray, but now I keep Your word.
> You are good and do good; teach me Your statutes.
> The arrogant have forged a lie against me; with all my heart I will observe Your precepts.
> Their heart is covered with fat, but I delight in Your law.
> It is good for me that I was afflicted, that I may learn Your statutes.
> The law of Your mouth is better to me than thousands of gold and silver pieces.
> (Ps. 119:65–72)

---

131 Spurgeon, *Beside Still Waters*, 333.

QUESTIONS for REFLECTION

Chapter 16: God's Handiwork in Thwarted Plans

"Why should I start at the plough of my Lord, that maketh deep furrows on my soul? I know He is no idle husbandman, He purposeth a crop."
Samuel Rutherford[132]

As for you, you meant evil against me, but God meant it for good in order to bring about this present result, to preserve many people alive (Gen. 50:20).

And we know that God causes all things to work together for good to those who love God, to those who are called according to His purpose (Rom. 8:28).

1. Like Joseph, Jeremiah is a fellow poster boy for unmet expectations. Read Lamentations 3:1–18 and briefly list how Jeremiah reacted to his circumstances.

2. The NIV Bible does a great job of translating Lamentations 3:19–20, so we gain a better sense of what Jeremiah is communicating. We read, *"I remember my affliction and my wandering, the bitterness and the gall. I well remember them, and my soul is downcast within me."* Why would we, along with Jeremiah, struggle emotionally and spiritually if verses 19–20 were the constant theme of our thoughts?

3. Lamentations 3:21–22 is the prescription we need to bring healing to our downcast souls. What is the medicine we need to take according to these verses?

4. Read Lamentations 3:22–23. What observations can you make about the Lord's lovingkindness from these verses? How do these truths give you hope, especially when you feel that your life is like Joseph's or Jeremiah's?

5. What truth encourages Jeremiah in Lamentations 3:24? Explain what it means to have the Lord as your *portion* (parcel, inheritance, blessing), once you have read the following verses: Psalms 16:5; 73:26; 142:5. How can that truth strengthen your heart today?

---

132 Samuel Rutherford, *The Loveliness of Christ,* ed. Ellen Lister (Edinburgh: The Banner of Truth Trust, 2008), 8.

6.   After thinking on the Lord's lovingkindnesses and having the Lord as his own inheritance, what truths does Jeremiah consider about the Lord in verse 25? What promises do we have when we *wait* and *seek*? See Psalms 9:10; 86:5; Nahum 1:7; Hebrews 11:6.

7.   How have you applied the principle of focusing your thoughts on the Lord when you find yourself discouraged and hopeless?

8.   For further encouragement read Lamentations 3:37–40. How could these truths strengthen your heart the next time you face unmet expectations?

But whether we see beneficial results in this life or not, we are still called upon to trust God that in His love He will do what is best for us and in His wisdom He knows how to bring it about.
Jerry Bridges[133]

Truly all are safe who are in God's keeping; and nothing can befall them, except that which is for their real good and the glory of their Lord.
John G. Paton, Missionary to the New Hebrides[134]

Charles Spurgeon's Four Comforts When You Face a Severe Trial

There is no curse in your cross.
Your trials are assigned by divine wisdom and love.
When you bear the cross, God gives special comforts that He never gives the healthy.
Trials bring you nearer to God.[135]

---

133   Bridges, *Trusting God*, 123.
134   John G. Paton, *John G. Paton, Missionary to the New Hebrides* (Edinburgh: The Banner of Truth Trust, 2007), 190.
135   Spurgeon, *Beside Still Waters*, 308.

By the time the pioneers reached Oregon, they had been on the trail for months. Yet, before reaching their final destination, the pioneers needed to traverse the perilous Blue Mountains in Oregon. Though weary and more than ready to be at their journey's end, they needed to persevere. When living with continual unmet expectations, it can be tempting to give up toward the end of our journey. Yet, like the pioneers, we must press on faithfully until we arrive home in heaven.

• • • • • • • • • • • • • • •

17

Marathon Meditations

Affliction teaches us to prize and long for heaven.[136]
Thomas Case

*In discipline God takes our hearts away from this present world by degrees,
and makes us look homeward.*[137]
Thomas Case

*Affliction reveals the glory of heaven. To the weary, it is rest; to the banished,
home; to the scorned, glory; to the captive, liberty; to the warrior, conquest;
to the conqueror, a crown of life; to the hungry, hidden manna; to the thirsty,
a fountain of life, and rivers of pleasure; to the grieved, fullness of joy; and
to the mourner it is pleasures for evermore. Heaven is precious and the soul
desires to be with Christ, which is best of all.*[138]
Thomas Case

---

136   Thomas Case, *Selected Works, A Treatise of Afflictions*, pp. 75-78 quoted in *Voices from the Past*, vol. 1, 189.
137   Ibid.
138   Ibid.

In previous chapters, we've looked backward, inward, and outward at the effect our unmet expectations have upon us and our responses to them. We have also looked at how to think biblically when not getting what we want. In this last chapter, we're setting our sights upward, heavenward, and Godward. *When unmet expectations become long-term guests, a heavenly focus keeps our hearts right while we live on earth.*

For some of us, living with unmet expectations has become the norm. Though we have pleaded, waited, and prayed earnestly, they have remained. Because our requests have been denied, we know God's perfect wisdom and love have decreed something better for us. It may be God's will that circumstances continue as they are, at least for the near future, and quite possibly, for the rest of our earthly lives. *As it is with anything that is long term, how we think determines how we will succeed, survive, persevere, and give God glory.* Talk to any long-distance runner, any woman who has endured an exceedingly lengthy labor, any cancer survivor, and they will all tell you their ability to cope with the ongoing trial came down to how they chose to think.

Hope is essential. Maurice Roberts writes, "To have God in his mind and thought is the believer's constant source of strength. The martyr languishes in the flames, but his mind flies upward to God his Savior and looks forward blissfully to the glory that awaits him even as his body sinks to ashes. The imprisoned Christian forgets the harsh regime of the camp, the daily grind and grueling labor, as his mind soars upward on the wings of hope to remember God."[139]

Yet we wonder, "How can we maintain hope and think rightly about our circumstances when life grows impossibly hard?" Maurice Roberts explains, "It remains a principle of universal application that we can cope with our afflictions just so long as 'we look at not the things which are seen, but at the things which are not seen' [2 Cor. 4:18]."[140] Ah, there it is. Coping with life, especially a life filled with unmet hopes, dreams, and prayers, means that we must become experts at looking at the unseen. *Our upward look enables us to press on.*

Don't Lose Heart; Your Spirit is Being Made New

There have been times in my life when the trials have been so enduring and painful that I have been tempted to lose heart. But Paul, in speaking about his many struggles and trials, says, "we do not lose heart. . ." (2 Cor. 4:16). But *why* are Christians encouraged to press on, not to lose heart? To

---

139   Roberts, *The Thought of God*, 4.
140   Ibid., 5.

lose heart means to faint, to be weary and without spirit, to be worn out, exhausted, and lacking courage. When the world sees us, as believers, losing heart and giving up before we reach our journey's end, what does it say to them about our faith and our God?

When we lose heart, we are essentially saying, "My circumstances are greater than my Savior and His grace." *When we lose heart,* it's as if we are saying, "It feels like my Savior doesn't care about my circumstances, that He isn't in control of them." *When we lose heart,* we are saying that the resources of the Holy Spirit aren't enough, the Word of God isn't enough, and the fellowship we have with Jesus Christ isn't enough.

Isaiah understood the danger of giving up and losing heart, which is why he so eloquently reminds us of how God comes to our aid when we are tuckered out and want to sit down and cry:

> Do you not know? Have you not heard? The Everlasting God, the LORD, the Creator of the ends of the earth does not become weary or tired. His understanding is inscrutable. He gives strength to the weary, and to him who lacks might He increases power. Though youths grow weary and tired, and vigorous young men stumble badly, yet those who wait for the LORD will gain new strength; they will mount up with wings like eagles, they will run and not get tired, they will walk and not become weary.
> (Isa. 40:28–31)

The Lord Desires to Strengthen You

The Lord cares about how you are doing. As He does His refining work, He also desires to bolster your faith in the midst of His working in you, which is why He again and again reminds you not to lose heart. Here are a few of the Lord's encouragements:

- *Don't lose heart in prayer, especially long-term prayer.* Luke 18:1 says, "Now He was telling them a parable to show that at all times they ought to pray and not to lose heart." After that statement, Jesus recounted the parable of the widow, who kept going to the judge for help, until finally she wore him out and he helped her. Jesus reminded the people in Luke 18:7 that God will "bring about justice for His elect who cry to Him day and night, and will He delay long over them?" Jesus teaches us that we shouldn't stop bringing our needs to Him. He wants us to understand that, if an unrighteous judge will finally relent to give in to the request of a persistent widow, then surely, our loving Father will answer the prayers of the children He loves.

- *Don't lose heart in doing good.* Galatians 6:9 encourages us, "Let us not lose heart in doing good, for in due time we will reap if we do not grow weary." When are you most tempted to lose heart in doing good? For me, it's when I'm not seeing results or when my efforts don't seem to make a difference. But the Lord reminds us not to lose heart in *continuing* to do good, for God is watching and sees our labors done to honor Him. Amy Carmichael said, "God never wastes His servant's toil."[141] Nothing we do is wasted, if done for the Lord. So then, let us not lose heart.

- *Don't lose heart when others are under trial.* In Ephesians 3:13 Paul said, "Therefore I ask you not to lose heart at my tribulations on your behalf, for they are your glory." Sometimes we grow fainthearted when we view the trials of others, especially loved ones. Paul knew this, which is why he counseled the Ephesians to persevere in faith, even as they observed his many difficulties. The same is true for us. We must press on in faith, with hope, coming alongside our brothers and sisters who are beset with trials. If we turn into a puddle at their distresses, then we miss the opportunity to strengthen their hearts in the Lord.

- *Don't cause others to lose heart.* Colossians 3:21 says, "Fathers, do not exasperate your children, so that they will not lose heart." Though this command is addressed to fathers, there's an underlying principle we can all apply. Sinful attitudes, dismissive responses, or exasperating words or actions can cause others to lose heart. Thankfully, the converse is true too. When we are in less-than-ideal circumstances, our submissive and trusting response to the Lord can strengthen and encourage the saints. That's reason enough for us to respond well when unmet expectations weigh upon our hearts.

- *Remember Jesus died so that you would not lose heart.* The author of Hebrews writes, "For consider Him who has endured such hostility by sinners against Himself, so that you will not grow weary and lose heart" (12:3). Don't let the significance of this verse pass you by. You're urged to think on and remember that Jesus endured pain and suffering for you, so you would not grow weary and lose heart *today*! Jesus' sufferings on your behalf were intended to strengthen your heart in your *present* circumstances. That is fascinating. The Lord Jesus Christ doesn't want you to lose heart in your trials, and desires that you remember that He endured pain, abuse, and sorrow too.

---

141 Amy Carmichael, quoted by Elizabeth R. Skoglund, *Amma: The Life and Words of Amy Carmichael* (Eugene, OR: Wipf and Stock Publishers, 1994), 140.

- *And we're not to lose heart because God's power is best seen in our weakness.* Second Corinthians 4:1 begins a section where Paul explains: "Therefore, since we have this ministry, as we received mercy, we do not lose heart." Paul recognizes God's hand at work in his ministry and life, which helps him to remain hopeful in the midst of many trials. He writes, "But we have this treasure in earthen vessels, so that the surpassing greatness of the power will be of God and not from ourselves" (2 Cor. 4:7). Paul acknowledges his weakness and his dependence upon the Lord's enabling grace. In the next verses, he lists many of the trials he was experiencing—all given for the purpose of putting God's power on display. Paul says he was afflicted, perplexed, persecuted, and struck down. Yet because he chose not to lose heart, he was not crushed, he was not despairing, he didn't feel forsaken, nor was he destroyed by his trials (2 Cor. 4:8–9). God will strengthen you when you are weak but trusting Him, so you can press on until the end.

Maintaining a Renewed Spirit in Spite of "Reality"

And finally, we come to 2 Corinthians 4:16, where we see in even greater detail how not to lose heart, no matter what our circumstances. Paul tells us, "Therefore, we do not lose heart . . . though our outer man is decaying." He could have been tempted to lose heart because his body was wearing away, falling apart, and continuing to experience the erosion of sin and the curse. His outer man was decaying.

It can be so discouraging not being able to do the things we used to do, not being able to hear, see, or remember things the way we once did. If you've been injured in an accident, you may be tempted to lose heart because your body will never be the way it was before the accident. If you've experienced some kind of long-term or chronic condition, you may be tempted to lose heart at the sheer duration of the sickness and its ever-increasing health issues. Paul experienced his body's decline without losing hope.

What did Paul focus on to enable him to progress through his trials and difficulties well? He focused on what was true—according to the Bible. Paul didn't rely on his feelings or the assessments of others. He looked to the Scriptures to view his circumstances properly. Maurice Roberts states it precisely when he writes, "There is a difference between things as they are and things as we perceive them."[142] That's certainly true when it comes to learning how not to lose heart as we cope with our decaying outer man.

142 Roberts, *The Thought of God*, 5.

The Way Things Are

If we listen to our feelings or believe the world's evaluation about aging and our bodies breaking down, we may be utterly discouraged and tempted to give up. Allow me to repeat Roberts here: "There is a difference between things as they are and things as we perceive them."[143] If Paul had focused on his aches, pains, and the limitations of a decaying outer man, he would have lost heart. Instead, he focused on God's perspective, on what is true according to His Word.

We're reminded in 2 Corinthians 4:16: "Therefore we do not lose heart, but though our outer man is decaying, yet *our inner man is being renewed day by day*" (emphasis added). Paul knew his body was growing weaker, suffering the effects of sin and the fall; yet he also knew *the reality* of his inner man being renewed day by day. He was getting older and more frail but, according to God, he was growing stronger spiritually. The same is true for all who know Jesus Christ as their Lord and Savior.

Paul didn't lose heart because he understood that, though our earthly bodies may fail, our eternal spirits will be made new. This is the paradox of God's kingdom. The great sculptor Michelangelo once said, "The more the marble wastes, the more the statue grows."[144] Aptly said! For when God allows the effects of sin to whittle away at our earthly bodies, He simultaneously makes us more like Christ. Physical weakness is used by the Lord to drive us to Him, producing spiritual strength.

The psalmist reiterates this divine whittling and renewing principle in Psalm 73:26: "My flesh and my heart may fail, but God is the strength of my heart and my portion forever." *Our spirit is being renewed day by day!* Our spirit will never get too tired, worn-out, and unable to function well. Our spirit will get better than ever because it is being renewed *day after day*, not once a year (2 Cor. 4:16). There's progress and change that won't be finished until we are made perfect in heaven. *Ahhhh.* Our *bodies* are failing; our spirits aren't. So, don't lose heart. The trial of our failing bodies weans us from world and causes us to long for heaven.

The Last Day It Was Quiet in My Head

One of the things I loved about living in Idaho throughout my childhood and into our marriage was the lovely stillness that would come with a nighttime snowfall as drifting flakes would soothe and hush a noisy world, while wrapping it in a blanket of white. When our kids were in

143 Ibid.
144 Wikiquote contributors, "Michelangelo," *Wikiquote*, , https://en.wikiquote.org/w/index.php?title=-Michelangelo&oldid=2553480 (accessed April 13, 2019).

elementary school, we left Idaho for Southern California when Jack was called to minister in a church there. Living amidst the hustle and bustle of a city, I confess that I longed for quiet. There were days when the city sounds were muted, such as when the fog rolled in during the night, and reduced the morning traffic rumblings to a whisper. Oh, how thankful I was for those foggy days! Then one day, inexplicably, my ears started ringing. To this day, there is a constant, high-pitched hum in my head. The audiologist told me it was due to aging. Since it hadn't affected my hearing, there wasn't any way to treat it! *My flesh and my heart may fail. . .* Though a relatively minor trial, the intrusive, unceasing noise was difficult to bear at first. Even now, hope helps me not to lose heart for, someday—oh, that blessed someday—the ringing in my ears will be replaced with the holy silence of heaven and the rejoicing songs of the saints. Until then, the Lord uses the ringing in my ears to keep my eyes trained on Him. Whatever you may be suffering as a mortal with a decaying body, be encouraged that your physical weakness weans you from the world and teaches you to fasten your eyes on heaven.

Don't Lose Heart; Your Trials are Producing Eternal Glory

God renews our spirits through *affliction*. "Nothing new there," you might say. "I already knew that." Though we may "know" that God uses the fires of trial, pressures, and unmet expectations to make us more Christlike, we seem to forget it when we are suddenly cast into the furnace of affliction. God reminds us in 2 Corinthians 4:17 of the means He uses to make us like Christ. The Scripture says, "*For* momentary, light affliction is producing for us an eternal weight of glory far beyond all comparison" (emphasis added). Whenever we see words like "therefore" or "for," we know that whatever follows is connected to what was previously stated. In this case, it is as follows: there's no reason to lose heart, even though our bodies are failing. *Why?* Because our inner man is being renewed every day. *How?* By using the fires of trial, God removes our dross and produces eternal glory in us.

The word *affliction* means to crush, press, squeeze, burden, and weigh down the spirit. I would expect that you understand this definition because you've lived it. You may have unmet expectations squeezing your heart right now. You may have unanswered prayers burdening you this very moment, pressing you down under their weight. When we read in 2 Corinthians 4:17 that God uses affliction to renew our inner man, we get it.

In verse 17, the Holy Spirit inspired Paul to view his sustained and varied afflictions as *momentary* and *light*. You might be thinking, "Yeah right. You have no idea what's going on in my life. You're telling me that I'm experiencing *light* afflictions? I'd hate to see heavy ones!" It's true. Yes, they are light *and,* yes, I have no idea what you might be going through or some of the hurts and sorrows you might have to bear. But there is Someone who does know about your life—and *He is telling you through the Apostle Paul that your trials are momentary and light.* Wow. Talk about reframing our understanding of reality.

God also reminds us of the temporary nature of trials. He says they are merely momentary and of short duration—in light of eternity. Peter echoes these truths in 1 Peter 1:6–7: "In this you greatly rejoice, even though now *for a little while,* if necessary, you have been distressed by various trials, so that the proof of your faith, being more precious than gold which is perishable, even though tested by fire, may be found to result in praise and glory and honor at the revelation of Jesus Christ" (emphasis added).

Second Corinthians 4:16–17 challenges us to look at our *momentary, little while, light, not worthy-to-be-compared* afflictions in view of the glory of heaven awaiting us. Seeing our afflictions as momentary and light challenges us to align our earthbound thoughts with God's heavenly and eternal perspective. Will we choose to see our hard circumstances with heaven in view or will we live as those who have no hope?

Samuel Rutherford understood the role that trials and unmet expectations play in our lives. He wrote in a letter, "When we shall come home and enter to the possession of our Brother's fair kingdom, and when our head shall find the weight of the eternal crown of glory, and when we shall look back to the pains and sufferings; then shall we see life and sorrow to be less than one step or stride from a prison to glory; and that our little inch of time-suffering is not worthy of our first night's welcome home to heaven."[145]

Truths to Remember When Burdened by Unmet Expectations

I've found the following three principles essential to remember in helping me cope with unmet expectations and trials that are especially burdensome:

Remember 2 Corinthians 12:9–10, literally. Don't forget these verses. Memorize them. Meditate on them. Keep them in your head and heart. Why? Because, in this section of Paul's letter to the Corinthians, he tells

---

145 Samuel Rutherford, *The Loveliness of Christ,* ed. Ellen S. Lister (Edinburgh: The Banner of Truth Trust, reprinted 2008), 16.

of a time when he asked God to deliver him from a painful trial, which he described as his "thorn in the flesh" and a "messenger of Satan" (v. 7). Paul's thorn was so painful and trying that he repeatedly asked the Lord to remove it. The Lord said no three times! Paul recounts, "And He has said to me, 'My grace is sufficient for you, for power is perfected in weakness'" (v. 9).

Upon receiving God's answer, Paul proceeded to embrace God's plan for him: "Most gladly, therefore, I will rather boast about my weaknesses, so that the power of Christ may dwell in me. Therefore I am well content with weaknesses, with insults, with distresses, with persecutions, with difficulties, for Christ's sake; for when I am weak, then I am strong" (v. 10). Priceless nuggets of soul-enriching truths lie hidden in these verses for the one willing to mine their depths. We learn that God's grace is sufficient *for us this very moment*, and the next, and the next, until our life's journey is through. By God's grace, contentment can be found, even in weakness. We can learn to submit to God's will for us, and in doing so, God is put on display. I'm not overreaching when I say that God often gets more glory out of our weakness than He does from our strength.

Remember the trial won't last forever. Consider Psalm 34:19: "Many are the afflictions of the righteous, but the LORD delivers him out of them all." Though God's children encounter many trials and difficulties in this life, the Lord always rescues them. This verse doesn't tell us *how* or *when* God will deliver, but only that *He will*. Eventually, we will be rescued from every pressure and trying situation, including our unmet expectations. No trial will last forever.

Charles Spurgeon tells of a visit to a sweet saint from his congregation, who was dying of consumption. Though death was near for her, Spurgeon said she was happy. She told him, "I am so much closer to the better land. I have fewer of these hard breaths to fetch and fewer of these hard pains to bear. I shall soon be where Jesus is."[146] The closer we are to heaven, the shorter the time we will have to bear up under our present burdens. *Each day brings us nearer to Jesus.*

Eventually lifelong trials will end, and pain, sorrow, and difficulty will cease. Yet we can be assured that their sanctifying effects on earth will go with us into heaven. "There will no longer be any curse; and the throne of God and of the Lamb will be in it, and His bond-servants will serve Him; they will see His face, and His name will be on their foreheads" (Rev. 22:3–4). No more sorrow from deferred hopes, no more suffering, sin, or pain, for on the day we leave our earthly shell, we will be transformed.

---

146 Spurgeon, *Beside Still Waters*, 66.

And then, we will see Jesus, our dear Savior.

> *"Blessèd hope now brightly beaming,*
> *On our God we soon shall gaze;*
> *And in light celestial gleaming,*
> *We shall see our Savior's face."*[147]

Remember the God of the Universe bears our burdens. Let the wondrous words of Psalm 68:19 warm your soul: "Blessed be the Lord, who daily bears our burden. The God who is our salvation." Each day the Lord comes to the aid of His children. He doesn't stand back indifferent to the burdens that may crush us. Are you feeling weak, overwhelmed, fearful? God will come to your aid, walking with you, even when the road leads you through the valley of the shadow of death (Ps. 23:4). Isaiah reminds us of God's never-failing commitment to help His children: "Do not fear, for I am with you; do not anxiously look about you, for I am your God. I will strengthen you, surely I will help you, surely I will uphold you with My righteous right hand" (Isa. 41:10).

Your Unmet Expectations Have Good Purposes

God knows what is best for us. And we need to trust Him as He orchestrates the events of our lives—even when we don't understand why He's doing certain things. The second half of 2 Corinthians 4:17 reveals that our momentary, light afflictions actually have great purpose. We're told that they are producing for us an "eternal weight of glory far beyond all comparison." All the heart-squeezing, faith-challenging unmet expectations have a purpose—enduring glory, which helps us to persevere and not lose heart.

When Paul says in 2 Corinthians 4:17 "For momentary, light affliction is producing for us an eternal weight of glory far beyond all comparison," he contrasts what is *now* with what is *then*. The "momentary" *now* is compared with the "eternal" *then*. The "featherweight" *now* can't even contend with the "heavyweight" *then*, and the "affliction" of *today* will be swallowed up in the "glory" of *eternity*. A. W. Pink said, "Afflictions are light when compared with what we really deserve. They are light when compared with the sufferings of the Lord Jesus. But perhaps their real lightness is best seen by comparing them with the weight of glory which is awaiting

147 Daniel W. Whittle, "Beloved, Now We Are." Hymntime. http://www.hymntime.com/tch/htm/b/n/o/ bnowarwe.htm (accessed March 10, 2019).

us."[148] No earthly cross even comes close in weight to eternal, heavenly glory. In our finite, limited *now*, we can't fathom what eternal glory will be like. *But whatever eternal glory will be like, it's produced through our momentary and light trials.*

You Won't Lose Heart When You Live by Faith

Paul knew the value of seeing things properly. If we gain a correct perspective of our ongoing unmet expectations, we won't lose heart because, rather than looking at the "things which are seen," we're going to look at "the things which are not seen; for the things which are seen are temporal, but the things which are not seen are eternal" (2 Cor. 4:18). This process is simply living by faith. Keeping our eyes firmly fixed on God's ways, God's wisdom, and on God Himself protects us from losing heart while living in the middle of unmet expectations and troubles.

Faith knows that the earthly things that we "see" are temporal, which is why faith won't focus on them (2 Cor. 4:18). Temporal things only last a short time and then they're gone. The sorrows, discouragement, and difficulties that come from unmet expectations only last for a while. Instead, faith looks past the earthly to eternity. Matthew Henry insightfully points out: "Faith enables us to make this right judgment of things."[149] That's exactly what Paul is talking about in 2 Corinthians 4:16–18—to live as seeing the unseen, to live with a view of the eternal—and when we do, we won't lose heart. Faith helps us look at our circumstances and judge them rightly—from God's perspective.

When Faith Perseveres

What does all this talk of persevering and not losing heart have to do with us and the unmet expectations in our lives? *Everything.* What does it say about us when we *persist* in trusting God when life is far different than we had hoped or dreamed? It says that we live with our eyes on that unseen realm, rather than on this temporal one; that we trust our heavenly Father as wise and good; that we take comfort in His perfect sovereignty over every detail of our lives.

Elisabeth Prentiss wrote, "God never places us in any position in which we cannot grow. We may fancy He does. We may fear we are so impeded by fretting, petty cares that we are gaining nothing; but when we are not sending any branches upward, we may be sending roots downward.

148 A. W. Pink, *Comfort for Christians* (Lafayette, IN: Sovereign Grace Publishers, 2007), 71.
149 Matthew Henry, *Matthew Henry's Commentary on the Whole Bible: Complete and Unabridged in One Volume* (Peabody: Hendrickson, 1994), 2283.

Perhaps in the time of our humiliation, when everything seems a failure, we are making the best kind of progress. God delights to try our faith by the conditions in which He places us. A plant set in the shade shows where its heart is by turning towards the sun, even when unable to reach it."[150]

So, *don't lose heart,* even though your life may be littered with unmet expectations. Remember that your spirit is being renewed day by day. *Don't lose heart,* though your life looks different than you had hoped. Remember that your trials are producing spiritual fruit and eternal glory for you. Though you experience dashed hopes and thwarted plans, *don't lose heart,* for God is training you to live by faith, not by sight.

William Dyer, minister of the gospel at Chesham, England wrote:

> O poor soul! This is all the hell that you shall ever have, therefore be of good cheer. Here you have your bad things—your good things are yet to come! Here you have your bitter things—but your sweet things are yet to come! Here you have your prison—but your palace is yet to come!
>
> Here you have your rags—your royal robes are yet to come! Here you have your sorrow—your joy is yet to come! Here you have your hell—your heaven is yet to come! After the cup of affliction—comes the cup of salvation; the sweetness of the crown which shall be enjoyed will make amends for the bitterness of the cross which was endured.
>
> Oh, sirs, under the greatest troubles—lie your greatest treasures! Patience for sorrow. . .shall reap a golden crop of joy in heaven! Those who sow holiness in the seed-time of their lives—shall reap happiness in the harvest of eternity! Oh! sirs, never think to have an end of your sorrow—until there is an end of your sin!
>
> The apostle tells us, "Our light affliction, which is for a moment— works for us a far more exceeding and eternal weight of glory!" A grain of affliction—works a weight of glory! O what a short moment of pain—works to an eternity of pleasures!
>
> Therefore saints, be of good cheer! Here is comfort for you—your best days are yet to come! You are subjects who are beloved entirely, cordially, infinitely, with an undying love![151]

---

150 Sharon James, *Elizabeth Prentiss: More Love to Thee* (Edinburgh: The Banner of Truth Trust, 2006), 205.

151 William Dyer, *The Believer's Golden Chain* (Wheeling, VA: S. S. Henderson, 1849), 55.

QUESTIONS for REFLECTION

Chapter 17: Marathon Meditations

Through Christ's satisfaction for sin, the very nature of affliction is changed with regard to believers. As death, which was, at first, the wages of sin, is now become a bed of rest (Is. 57:2); so afflictions are not the rod of God's anger, but the gentle medicine of a tender father.
Tobias Crisp[152]

God does not lead His children around hardship, but leads them straight through hardship. But He leads! And amidst the hardship, He is nearer to them than ever before.
Otto Dibelius[153]

1.   What does it mean to lose heart?

2.   What are some ways *you've* been tempted to lose heart in the past? What do you think contributed to feeling so weary and fainthearted?

3.   What is the key to not losing heart according to 2 Corinthians 4:16–18?

4.   How are you to view your struggles, unmet expectations, and trials according to 2 Corinthians 4:17? What are some challenges you might face in learning to think the "2 Corinthians 4:17" way about your trials and difficulties?

5.   What is God's purpose in the unmet expectations and continued struggles of your life, according to 2 Corinthians 4:17? How does this help you persevere?

6.   How does 2 Corinthians 4:18 show us what we need to do and how we need to think so that we will not lose heart?

7.   What are some practical ways you can *look at the things which are not seen*? See Romans 8:24–25; 2 Corinthians 5:7; Hebrews 11:1, 13.

8.   As you think over all we've discussed about unmet expectations, what things stand out to you as the way to find hope and help when life turns out far differently than you planned?

---

152   Tobias Crisp, *The New Encyclopedia of Christian Quotations,* ed. Mark Water (Grand Rapids, MI: Baker Books, 2000), 23.

153   Otto Dibelius, *The New Encyclopedia of Christian Quotations*, ed. Mark Water (Grand Rapids, MI: Baker Books, 2000), 23.

Be still, my soul, Jehovah loveth thee;
Fret not nor murmur at thy weary lot;
Though dark and lone thy journey seems to be,
Be sure that thou art never by Him forgot.
He ever loves: then trust Him, trust Him still;
Let all thy care be this,—the doing of His will.

Thy hand in His, like fondest happiest child,
Place thou, nor draw it for a moment thence;
Walk thou with Him, a Father reconciled,
Till in His own good time He calls thee hence.
Walk with Him now,—so shall thy way be bright,
And all thy soul be filled with His most glorious light.

Take courage: faint not, tho' the foe be strong;
Christ is thy strength! He fighteth on thy side:
Swift be thy race; remember 'tis not long,—
The goal is near; the prize He will provide;
And then from earthly toil thou restest ever;
Never again to toil, or fight, or fear:—oh, never!

He comes with His reward; 'tis just at hand:
He comes in glory to His promised throne!
My soul, rejoice; ere long thy feet shall stand
Within the city of the Blesséd One,—
Thy perils past, thy heritage secure,
Thy tears all wiped away, thy joy forever sure![154]

154 Horatius Bonar, "Be Still, My Soul, Jehovah Loveth Thee," https://chicagobible.org/htdbv5/r1004c.htm.

Final Thoughts:
From *If Only* to *Only Him*

It is the Lord*; let Him do what seems good to Him.*
(1 Sam. 3:18)

W e learned in chapter 1 that it's the nature of the human heart to de- sire *more*. Proverbs 13:25 says, "The righteous has enough to satisfy his appetite." The righteous person—that's you if the Lord Jesus is your Savior—understands that craving the "if only" things won't satisfy. But, when "if only" is replaced with "only Him," our soul's restless longing is quieted. Living with unmet expectations doesn't have to be a white-knuck- led and grit-your-teeth kind of experience. *The Lord has promised to help us.*

In the book of First Samuel, the young boy, Samuel, was living in the house of the Lord as a helper to Eli, the priest. The Lord revealed to Samuel that severe judgment was soon to come upon Eli and his sons for their sins and unfaithfulness toward God. Upon hearing God's decree for him, Eli responded with these words, "It is the LORD; let Him do what seems good to Him" (3:18). Eli had many faults but, in this case, he responded with exemplary submission to God's will. No doubt God's declaration of judgment terrified Eli. Certainly, it wasn't what he wanted for himself or for his sons, but he humbly submitted to it. He bowed his heart low before the wisdom and sovereignty of God.

What if we responded with those same words to every circumstance of our lives? *"It is the LORD; let Him do what seems good to Him."* Consider the implications of living out Eli's words when unmet expectations dog our heels. We affirm who is at work—*it is the Lord*. We acknowledge His absolute sovereignty—*let Him do*. We remember His gracious intentions toward us—*He does what seems best*. With the words "to Him," we remind ourselves of His sovereign wisdom—*He does what seems good to Him*. The language of all true heart worship is summed up in 1 Samuel 3:18. And this faith-filled response is what God longs to hear from every one of His children. Our lives bring Him glory when we learn to say, "'It is the LORD; let Him do what seems good to Him.'"

No matter how long it takes, no matter whether our circumstances remain the same or whether they are difficult, if God has given us these unmet expectations, they are for our good and for His glory. Trusting the Lord in the midst of ever-changing circumstances lifts our focus from ourselves and changes our expectation for satisfaction. Instead, we look with expectant hope to the Lord as our "if only" desires are transformed into "only Him" praises.

God uses unmet expectations and their faithful and effective siblings— trials, suffering, difficulty, and distresses—to reveal wrong thinking in our hearts, so He can heal us, transform us, and make us more like Jesus. Along the way, we come to know Him better, learning that nothing else can satisfy our hearts like He can. The journey kindles our desire for Him. So, don't take your bonnet off yet, my fellow pioneer girl. The trail still stretches on before us. The plains of endurance, hills of disappointment, rivers of sorrow, and mountains of difficulty are yet to be crossed. But, one day *soon,* we will arrive at our heavenly destination, where the thirsting of our souls will be fully satisfied *in Him.*

We have learned that God uses the *unmet* part of our expectations to lead us to true heart fulfillment. With each unmet expectation, He strips away worldly ambitions, selfish inclinations, and distracted desires, so that we will look to Him alone. Let my paraphrase of James 1:2–5 encourage you: "Consider it all joy, my bonneted, pioneer girl, when you encounter various unmet expectations, knowing that they test your faith and produce endurance in you. Let the time of your endurance-producing trials do their work in you, so that you may be perfect and complete, lacking in nothing. As you encounter the rocky terrain of life and feel unsure as to how to proceed, ask God for wisdom. He will generously supply you with what you need to make it to your journey's end." May your "if only" expectations bring God glory as you fill your heart with "only Him."

About Shepherd Press Publications

They are gospel driven.
They are heart focused.
They are life changing.

Our Invitation to You

We passionately believe that what we are publishing can be of benefit to you, your family, your friends, and your work colleagues. So we are inviting you to join our online mailing list so that we may reach out to you with news about our latest and forthcoming publications, and with special offers.

Visit:

www.shepherdpress.com/newsletter

and provide your name and email address.